LUCY CALKINS ✦ CORY GILLETTE

BREATHING LIFE INTO ESSAYS

This book is dedicated to Kathleen Tolan.

FirstHand
An imprint of Heinemann
A division of Reed Elsevier Inc.
361 Hanover Street
Portsmouth, NH 03801-3912
www.heinemann.com

Offices and agents throughout the world

Photography: Peter Cunningham

Library of Congress Cataloging-in-Publication Data

CIP data on file with the Library of Congress.
ISBN: 0-325-00866-3
ISBN-13: 978-0-325-00866-0

Printed in the United States of America on acid-free paper
10 09 08 07 ML 3 4 5 6 7

ACKNOWLEDGEMENTS

This book is dedicated to Kathleen Tolan, the Deputy Director for Reading at the Teachers College Reading and Writing Project. Kathleen functions as the Project's master teacher. She adopts schools in deep need of support and develops close partnerships with the leaders and teachers at those schools, helping these people to transform their schools into lab sites that demonstrate the best of what's possible in urban literacy education. In the process of doing this, Kathleen challenges, deepens, and models the Project's best thinking about methods of staff development and methods of teaching of reading and writing. She especially helps the organization adjust our methods to provide the special support that children and teachers in high-need schools deserve. It was Kathleen's close work with the teachers at PS 28 in upper Manhattan and PS 18 in the Bronx which allowed me to develop, pilot, revise, and re-think the ideas in this book. I am grateful to Kathleen for her spectacular teaching, her generosity with her ideas, her extraordinary work ethic, and for her unremitting belief in all children as readers and writers.

I am grateful also to Cory Gillette for her input as contributing author of this book. As a Project staff developer, Cory helped me bring these ideas to the schools throughout New York City. Once we had developed the beginning plan for this unit and piloted it at PS 18, Cory brought it to a study group of teachers, and joined them in learning from their children's efforts to write essays. Cory channeled ideas to me and contributed to the Tailoring your Teachings, as well as to some other sections of the book. Readers will appreciate Cory's commitment to straight-talk and her grounding in the very real world of classroom teaching. I know I do.

This book has relied tremendously on input from Julia Mooney, a writer-in-residence at the Project. Julia helped me fill in gaps in the book—an italics here, some bolds there, a missing mid-workshop teaching point, a tailoring your teaching . . . She is an astute student of literature and of writing, and helped me also to see where my prose bogged down, where my meanings became obscure. Julia Mooney wrote many of the 'Tailoring Your Teachings' for this book, as did Grace Enriquez, a doctoral student at Teachers College and a staff developer and Kathy Collins, co-author of the CD.

This book has benefited also from input from a few teachers in particular. As I mentioned earlier, I developed many of the ideas for the book while learning from the teachers at PS 18 in the Bronx, especially Sue Ottomanelli, and I thank them for opening their classes to me. As I rewrote the book one final time, Mary Chiarella and I were in a study group together; Mary piloted the book's final iteration with her fourth graders, and I thank her for this. Medea McEvoy brought these ideas to life in her fifth-grade classroom, and her children's work is important in this book. Laura Schiller and Linda Demstadt added their knowledge on this topic, and I thank them.

It is impossible to end one of these acknowledgements without giving an extra nod to the contribution made by Kate Montgomery, my editor. Kate is a passionate advocate for the richest possible literacy education, and the fact that she believed this book, on this subject, could be written without compromising all that she and I believe gave me the courage to try.

BREATHING LIFE INTO ESSAYS

Welcome to Unit 3

WELCOME TO THE UNIT

BREATHING LIFE INTO ESSAYS

About the Unit

This unit of study is designed to help students with the difficult and exhilarating work of learning to write well within an expository structure. At the start of this unit, we point out to writers that they could conceivably write about a topic—say a visit to Grandma's—as a narrative, retelling it chronologically, or as a non-narrative, or essay, in which case they'd need to advance a certain idea ("Visits to Grandma's farm feel like time travel," for example). For some students, the fact that they can write about personal topics in a genre other than a personal narrative will be a new realization. The terms *narrative* and *non-narrative* or *essay* refer to structure and genre, not to content. In this unit, each child will write a personal essay in which she advances a theme of personal significance, arguing, for example, "It's hard being an only child," or claiming, "My dog is my best friend."

A Rationale for Teaching Traditional Essay Structure

Before describing the sequence of this unit, I want to share my rationale for teaching students to write fairly traditional thesis-driven essays. I know that some of the nation's writing process advocates will feel as if this unit of study doesn't follow the tenets of that school of thought. I can hear these critics say, "Why would we ask students to write thesis-driven essays when essayists approach essays as journeys of thought, as wandering ruminations? Why would we teach kids to do a kind of writing that *we* don't do and that writers in the world don't do?" I've posed similar challenges in my day, and so I respect these questions.

These are my reasons for teaching children to write traditional thesis-driven essays. First, although I *do* want children to write like writers all over the world write, this does not mean that everything I ask a child to try will be something that Wadsworth or E.B. White or Thoreau would have done. If we simply show children rich, complex

finished publications and say, "Have at it! Write like this!" I agree that some children will progress with remarkable success through a series of approximations. But because I try to truly hold myself accountable to being sure that *all* children truly do make palpable, dramatic progress in their abilities to write well, I think it is important to admit that some children profit from more scaffolding and support. I believe that it is the teacher's job to reduce some of the complexity of finished essays, to highlight the most essential moves an essayist must make, and to show all children that these moves are within their reach. We ask beginning readers to point underneath words as they read, and we later tell them that actually, pointing under the words is not necessary or even forever helpful. In the same way, I think we can teach children to write explicit thesis statements and topic sentences and later tell them that actually, essayists often write towards main ideas that are implied but not explicitly stated, and that essayists often advance one idea for a time, then turn a corner and advance a second idea, creating a text that takes readers on a journey of thought. Although this book teaches children to write within a traditional thesis-driven essay structure, the final book in the series shows children that the structure they learn in this unit is not the only way to structure an essay and that they can, in the end, use this structure in flexible ways.

Another reason for teaching children to write traditional thesis-driven essays is that in fact, I do think this is a structure that real-world writers rely upon often. Most of the chapters in my professional books pose an idea, and then elaborate upon that idea in parallel categories, each introduced by a sub-head. Many of my speeches, grant applications, persuasive letters, and editorials all rely upon this fundamental structure. Then, too, I teach this to children because I think the unit can help teachers as well. Classroom charts and staff development workshops, too, often rely upon structure. Some educators have never been explicitly taught that in a strong presentation, information is organized within parallel categories—a classroom chart entitled, say, Revision Strategies should not include materials or qualities of good writing. Then, too, I think that when children learn that they can, if they so choose, think and write according to what I refer to as a "boxes and bullets" format, this helps them construct a mental model comprised of main ideas and support information as they read expository texts and as they take notes on books and class lectures. Finally, I know that in middle school and high school and on standardized tests, this is the form of writing that children will rely upon most. They will need to write in this form with speed and finesse while also carrying a heavy cargo of disciplinary ideas and information. In most secondary schools, students receive very little introduction in this challenging kind of writing before they are assigned to write an expository essay on books they can barely read. Secondary school teachers, often responsible for well over a hundred students, assign and grade this work but rarely teach it.

Lastly, the reason that I include a unit on the thesis-driven essay (and a subsequent one on writing literary essays) is that I believe children benefit from teachers working together to create a shared curriculum that spirals through the grades, and I am convinced that the only way to take staff development to scale is to adopt a curriculum that incorporates aspects of teaching writing that are priorities to a variety of educators who approach the teaching of writing from a variety of perspectives.

An Overview of the Unit

A teacher could choose to hurry kids through this unit, showing them how to whip up modest yet well-structured and competent little essays. However, I argue that there are many reasons to take one's time instead, harvesting all the learning opportunities found along the way. If we help children write rough drafts and do lots of revision with the goal of learning as much as possible about logical thought, this unit can have enormous payoffs. Then, after helping kids spend a month writing one essay, we can show students that they also have the option of churning out a quick essay in a day—or even in fifteen minutes! This, of course, becomes a form of test preparation.

As with any unit of study in a writing workshop, it is important to begin by helping children develop a repertoire of strategies for collecting entries—this time, entries that can grow into essays. It's important to teach students that their lives are provocative. Writers observe things in the world, recording what we see, and then we shift and write, "The thought I have about this is . . . " or "This makes me realize . . . ." When teaching children to grow essays out of everyday observations, we are really teaching them to free write, and the goal is to help them realize the value of writing

at length without a preconceived content, trusting that ideas will surface as they go along. Children also learn the power of imagining themselves in an evocative place and generating ideas in response to what they "see."

During this early phase of the unit, I also teach children that they can reread entries they collected earlier in the year during narrative units of study and then use those entries as starting points, perhaps again beginning, "The idea I have about this is . . . " or "The thing that surprises me about this is . . . ." A child might jot down a topic, hobby, or issue that he cares about, then collect ideas about that big subject and write at length about one of those ideas. Children should become accustomed to selecting the strategy that works best for them on any given occasion. That is, the strategy the teacher introduces in a minilesson on a particular day is not merely that day's assignment but is one of many in a growing repertoire of strategies that writers draw on as needed.

Essayists need tools to push past their first thoughts, and many find it helps to use thought-prompts to prime the pump of their thoughts. "The surprising thing about this is . . . " an essayist might write in her notebook before spinning out a brand-new thought in letters that scrawl down the page. That is, once a child records an idea, the child will benefit from having strategies to elaborate upon that idea. Using prompts such as, "to add on . . . ," "furthermore . . . ," "this makes me realize . . . ," "the surprising thing about this is . . . ," "on the other hand . . . " allows children to extend their first ideas and to use writing as a way of thinking. They find that new ideas, ideas they never even knew they had, come out of their pencils.

After collecting possible seed ideas, drawing on what they already know about rereading notebooks looking for seeds, young essayists select one idea. In the earlier narrative units of study, they selected a seed *story*; this time they will select a seed *idea*. Writers then revise that idea until they've made a provocative, clear, compelling claim—or thesis statement.

Once students have selected and articulated an idea ("The Dominican Republic feels like home to me," for example), we teach them to elaborate on that idea by generating subordinate ideas ("The Dominican Republic feels like home because my childhood memories are there," and "The Dominican Republic feels like home because my extended family is there," and so forth). The easiest way to support most claims is to provide a few parallel *reasons* for that claim; writers can restate the claim each time and add the transitional word *because* followed by a reason. There are other ways to support a claim (or thesis), and a teacher may or may not teach those alternatives.

Usually children write support ideas through a series of parallel statements. The child elaborated on the thesis, "It's hard being an only child" by saying, "Your parents shower you with too much attention; your parents have too many of their hopes attached to you; and you can be very lonely."

During this planning stage, students can explore their subordinate ideas and decide what they really want to say. In the end, we hope each child has a main idea (a claim or a thesis) and several parallel supporting ideas. I sometimes refer to the main idea and supporting statements as "boxes and bullets." I have found it helps if children take their thesis and record it on the outside of one folder, then make internal folders for each of their bullets (these become topic sentences for their body paragraphs).

When it is time for children to collect materials to support their topic sentences, we teach them that they can first collect stories that illustrate their ideas. It is also important to teach children to angle these stories so they support the idea the writer wants to advance, and for them to learn to "unpack" those stories, just as a teacher debriefs after a demonstration in a minilesson.

Writers can also collect lists to support their topic sentences. We show children how statistics, observations, citations, quotations, and so forth can enrich their work. These bits are collected not in a writer's notebook but on separate bits of paper, and are filed in the appropriate topic-sentence folder.

It is important to help writers select *compelling* evidence from the material they collect in these folders, and to help them ensure that the evidence closely supports their claim. We teach them to look carefully from the claim to the evidence and back again, because often the two aren't as congruent as they appear at first glance. Eventually we teach writers to sort through the materials in each folder, writing well-structured paragraphs.

Once writers have selected the most powerful and pertinent support material for each of their topic sentences, they staple or tape or recopy this information into a paragraph or two that supports each topic sentence, and in this manner construct the rough draft of an essay. Special lessons on transitions, introductions, and conclusions are important here.

The Plan for the Unit

The major "bends in the road" for this unit are as follows:

- Children learn a variety of strategies for living like essayists. They learn to observe the grit of their lives, pushing themselves to develop thoughts in response to what they see. They learn to travel in their minds' eyes to provocative spots, again shifting between describing and ruminating.

- Children learn to generate lists of people, places, issues, or passions and then select any one item and generate ideas about it, selecting one idea to develop in a notebook entry. Similarly, children can reread old entries and grow thoughts in response to them.

- Children learn that one way to elaborate on their ideas is to use the conversational prompts they have used to grow ideas in book talks, phrases such as *in addition . . . another example is . . .* and *the important thing is . . .* to think and write more about their first ideas.

- Children reread their entries and select a seed idea. They tighten and revise this until it is a clear, straightforward thesis statement such as, "It is hard being an only child." Children freewrite to consider if this is really what they want to say.

- Children generate a plan for an essay by considering ways to elaborate on their thesis. Most children add the transitional phrase *because* to their thesis statement: "It is hard being an only child *because . . . ,*" and then generate several reasons. These support ideas (or topic sentences) are each written on the outside of a folder, and children begin collecting material within each folder. We teach them that writers collect stories angled to support the idea, as well as lists, observations, interviews, and so forth, filing everything in the appropriate topic sentence folder. Children revise some of this material as it is collected.

- Children construct one portion of the essay at a time. For each topic sentence, children lay out all the possible support material, select the most convincing material, and design a sequence for it. Then they staple component sections together, rewriting this later to strengthen it with transitional phrases and key words from the thesis.

- Children learn to write introductory and concluding paragraphs.

COLLECTING IDEAS AS ESSAYISTS

When you launch children into a new kind of writing, it is important to teach them the strategies writers use to generate this new kind of writing. In order to teach this first session, you need to think, "Where do ideas for essays come from?" "What is the life work of being an essayist?"

This question is dear to my heart because the keynote speeches and book chapters I write are essays of a sort. So for me, the question is a very personal one. How do I grow the ideas that eventually become themes in my own nonfiction writing?

For me, the challenge is to develop ideas that feel new and significant. I find that the ideas that matter to my listeners, that take them on significant journeys of thought, are those that dawn on me as I pursue the process of writing. The best way I know to grow new ideas (rather than simply restating old, clichéd ideas) is to start with data. I start by putting myself into the hubbub of real life—for me, into classrooms—and I try to observe keenly. I record, and then I push myself to have a thought about what I observe.

My research on writing tells me this is how many writers grow ideas. Malcolm Cowley edited a series, Writers at Work, in which he interviewed dozens of our most famous writers. At the end of that experience, he was asked what he learned about the processes writers use. He answered that above all, he learned that every writer is idiosyncratic, that there is no one shared process all writers experience. But then he added that most writers begin with a precious particle—an observation, an image, a phrase, a bit of data—and grow their writing from that particle.

When I teach children to write essays, I first teach them to pay attention. I teach them to collect bits of life—and then I teach them to take a leap of faith, declaring those bits to be precious, and then surrounding them with the thoughts and responses that make them significant.

IN THIS SESSION, YOU WILL TEACH CHILDREN HOW TO COLLECT WRITING THAT CAN BE DEVELOPED INTO ESSAYS, AND INVITE THEM TO BECOME ESSAY WRITERS. YOU'LL SHOW THEM THAT WRITERS OBSERVE THE WORLD WITH EXTRA CARE AND ALERTNESS AND THEN THINK HARD ABOUT THEIR OBSERVATIONS, RECORDING THEM IN WRITING.

GETTING READY

- Non-narrative notebook entries from students that demonstrate observations, questions, musings, ideas
- Sample essay entries from students, past and current, or from you and your colleagues
- Strategies for Generating Personal Narrative Writing chart (from Units 1 and 2)
- See CD-ROM for resources

MINILESSON

Collecting Ideas as Essayists

CONNECTION

Support your children's identities as writers by exclaiming over their stories and rallying them to write essays.

"Writers, when I heard your personal narratives yesterday, I felt as if I was right there with you, experiencing the small moments of your lives! Congratulations. I think you are ready to graduate."

"The entries you've collected and the stories you've developed are wonderful—but writers don't just write Small Moment stories. We write lots of things—songs and speeches and picture books and essays—and we write in lots of ways. Today we are going to begin writing in a radically different way. Instead of writing *stories*, we will write *essays*. Instead of writing about *small moments*, we will write about *big ideas*."

Name the teaching point. In this case, tell children that essayists observe and then grow ideas about those observations.

"Today, what I want to teach you is this: When writers want to grow ideas, we don't just gaze up in the sky and wait for thoughts to descend. Instead, as writers, we live especially wide-awake lives, giving thoughtful attention to the stuff, the grit, that others might walk past. We listen to the purr of our cat, we notice how each person in our family reads the newspaper differently, we study the stuff that accumulates in desk drawers, we overhear arguments—and we let all this sink into our minds and our notebooks. Then we write, 'This makes me think . . .' or 'I'm realizing that . . . .'"

TEACHING

Tell children the story of a writer who first observed, then pushed herself to develop insights, and then recorded those insights.

"Let me tell you about two writers who've grown ideas by paying attention to the stuff, the grit, of their lives. You'll notice that they first notice, observe, and then they push themselves to think of a new idea, right there on the page."

"You all know Katherine Paterson, author of *Bridge to Terabithia*? Well, when she was asked, 'What is essential to writing?' she told of standing with her son, watching a cicada bug shed its skin. Katherine wrote about how she and David first saw a tiny slit in the bug's back. It grew larger, as if the bug had a waist-length zipper, and then they saw a hint of color as the

You'll find your own ways to talk about the work your children did in the preceding unit and the effect their published writing had on you and others. Recall times in your own life when your hard work was recognized, and remember the way in which this recognition spurred you to work harder. Your children will work harder for you if you can help them feel that their efforts are recognized.

I like beginning a unit by conveying a sense that we're entering a new chapter in children's writing lives. And I do believe that essays are fundamentally different from stories.

Although essays are fundamentally different from narratives, the process of writing is remarkably similar. Whether we are writing stories or essays, we begin by living writerly lives, collecting bits that we grow into developed texts. The bits we collect are structured differently depending on whether we're planning a narrative or an expository text, but the topics can be the same. Keep in mind that people can follow an expository structure while writing about very personal topics— and that's the plan for this unit.

One of the challenges in this unit of study is that I don't have published examples of essays that resemble those I'll ask children to write. The essays by authors like E. B. White and John McPhee are far more complex than those that children can write, and children's bookshelves don't contain anthologies of essays written specifically for youngsters.

wings emerged, first crumpled ribbons and then stretched out. As they stood there, the cicada bug swung like an acrobat onto the twig and flew away, 'oblivious,' Katherine said,' to the wake of wonder that it left behind.'"

"I hope you realize that Katherine *could* have just let the cicada bug's wake of wonder wash over her; but because she was gathering entries for a speech, an essay, she not only put her observations onto the page, she also went one step further. She pushed herself to have a thought about watching that cicada bug with her son. She wrote this passage."

> As I let that wake of wonder wash over me, I realized this was the real gift I want to give my children because what good are straight teeth and trumpet lessons to a child who cannot see the grandeur that the world is charged with. (1981, p. 20)

"And that is a big idea! That cicada bug helped Katherine Paterson realize that it is more important to watch a bug shed its skin with your child than it is to rush your child to trumpet lessons and orthodontist appointments."

"Today I want to teach you that, like Katherine Paterson, you can notice the cicada bugs—the small stuff of your lives—and you can record what you see and hear. Then you can push yourself by saying, as Katherine did, 'This makes me think . . .' or 'I'm realizing that . . . .'"

"Writers do not usually sit and gaze at the sky to grow big ideas. Instead, we live wide-awake lives, noticing the small stuff and letting it provoke big thoughts."

Tell children another example of a writer who first observed, then pushed herself to develop insights, and then recorded those insights.

"Francesca also grew big ideas and did so by first paying close attention to the stuff of her life. Here's what she wrote." *[Fig. I-1]*

> Watching a long tree with a cable like a trap and on the other side, an untrained dog. Watching the dog's sad face lie in the grass. I watch the poor dog lie there. I watch the wind blow in the dog's face and ears.
>
> I think that I could take good care of it and train it and it would run free and be happy forever. It likes me as if I am its owner.
>
> I pet the dog. I see the nice free yard that the dog could be running in now. Too bad I'm only a kid and only a dog lover. But then I remember that the littlest people can change the world. Can I?

On the other hand, there are lots of places where authors use the muscles that we are asking children to use. I use some of those instances as illustrations.

The teaching component of this minilesson is structured in a manner that should be familiar to you. I name what I plan to teach, then teach by showing an example, and soon you'll see that I debrief. In this instance, I'm not teaching by demonstration but instead by referencing a finished product. Because the children need to know how to do likewise, I imagine and describe the process that the author probably used to create the product. It is this process that I am inviting children to adopt.

Of course, writers needn't literally say, "This makes me think . . . " but I find that when I give children the language to get themselves started, I'm giving them a powerful temporary scaffold.

Notice that I shift from describing a published writer to describing a child's writing. I'm hoping to show respect for all children by elevating one child in this way. In this instance, I'm not teaching by demonstration but instead by referencing a finished product.

> Watching a long tree with a cable like a trap and on the other side, an untrained dog. Watching the dog's sad face lie in the grass. I watch the wind blow in the dog's face and ears.
>
> I think that I could take care of it and train it and it would run free and be happy forever. It likes me as if I am it's owner.
>
> I pet the dog. I see the nice free yard that the dog could be running in now. Too bad I'm only a kid and only a dog lover. But then I remember that the littlest people can change the world. Can I?
>
> I walk home sadly. At least when I get my own dogs, I will train it and let it run free and mabey then I could change the world.

Figure I-1 Francesca's notebook entry

I walk home sadly. At least when I get my own dog, I will train it and let it run free and maybe then I can change the world.

"Francesca's entry begins with an observation of a dog, tied to a cable, and ends with her yearning to make a difference in the world. She began by living a wide-awake life, letting what she sees nudge her into big thoughts."

ACTIVE ENGAGEMENT
Ask children to try observing and making a thought about what they observe.

"Let's practice living like essay writers. Look around our classroom or look at something you are wearing, or at some part of you—perhaps at the skin on the inside of your elbow. Partner 1, write in the air (remember, this means to say the exact words you could write) something you observe, and then say, 'This makes me realize . . .' or 'The idea this gives me is . . .' And then push yourself to make a thought." The room erupted into conversation.

Notice that the structure of this teaching component is actually similar to the structure we're trying to hand over to children in this unit of study! I name the idea I will advance, then elaborate on the idea by discussing an example, and finally I summarize the discussion, putting the content into a larger context. That's the structure of a traditional school essay.

When I ask writers to say to a partner the exact words they might write, I call this writing in the air. You'll ask your students to do this often, so it's worth checking to be sure children actually do say the words they could write instead of simply talking about their ideas. If their conversations do not sound to you as if they are dictating the words they could write, stop and clarify the directions. Then hold children to following those directions even if this requires you to stop them midstream yet again.

Debrief. In this case, describe what you heard partners say that could be models for the observation-then-reflection entries you hope children will write.

"I heard Jack noticing that our big clock has the numbers one through twelve, and then Jack said to Tyrone, 'I'm realizing that my watch doesn't have any numbers, only lines, and my watch looks like a wheel with spokes.' Jack, you remind me of Katherine Paterson—the way she looked at the bug's wings and saw they were like crumpled ribbons—you looked at a watch and it reminded you of a wheel!"

"And Alexis said, 'I notice our library corner is surrounded by books and plants. It's the heart of our classroom.' That could definitely become an essay or an editorial in our local or school newspaper."

"Writers, your observations and ideas could make great essay entries, and today you'll be able to start collecting entries in your writer's notebooks."

Obviously you will want to celebrate your own children. In this instance, notice that I select tiny specifics that children said, ones that seem original and provocative, and I help children imagine how these could be developed. You may notice that I rarely come straight out and compliment children's work, preferring to treat the work with such respect that the child feels complimented and yet does not become reliant on an external judge's praise.

LINK

Rename the teaching point. Send children off to begin work in ways they can use now and every day from now on.

"Writers, today we learned that when we want to write essays or other kinds of non-narrative writing (I'll talk later about what I mean by non-narrative), we live like writers—with extra alertness, paying attention to everything we can see, hear, read, notice—and then we can push ourselves to have ideas about what we see. We learned that entries in our writer's notebooks change based on the kind of thing we are writing. Today, you'll start a new section in your writer's notebook, and you'll begin collecting entries that might grow to become essays. You may want to begin your entries with phrases such as *I notice* and then, after you write your observations for a bit, skip a line and switch to phrases such as *I am starting to think that* or *I realize that.*"

I have lots of background information on essays (and non-narrative writing in general) that I could have included in this minilesson, but I decided to save some of this for later so that today I can immediately help children begin to live like essayists. I tend to avoid dumping a lot of information about a genre on kids in minilessons, because I want to teach "how to" do things, not "all about" things.

If you feel as if the content of any one minilesson is repetitive, you are right. During the final moments of a minilesson, I reiterate what I've taught, and I usually show that this new information can be integrated with students' prior knowledge. I also try to send children off with both clear directions (for those who are ready to try the strategy) and an awareness of their choices (for students who are not yet at this stage of the writing process).

WRITING AND CONFERRING

Guiding Small Groups

Although most of your students will by now be very capable of sustaining their work when they write personal narratives, you may find that many of them want encouragement and direction now that they are working in a radically new genre. If lots of kids need you at once, the easiest way to support them all is to go from table to table, providing children with table compliments. That is, draw a chair alongside one table full of kids. Watch what they are doing (or are almost doing) that matches your hopes for today. Then ask for the attention of everyone at the table. "Writers, can I have your attention for a moment?" Wait until you have their full attention. "I need you to know that . . . " You'll need to decide if you want to compliment all of them at once or to spotlight one child. If you decide on the latter, you could say something like, "Nadine is doing something really brilliant. She realized that the things right on her desk are interesting and started to write about her pencil, of all things! She wrote what she sees, using exact words. Listen." After sharing what a child has already done, you could decide what you hope the one child will do next and say something like, "I bet soon Nadine will write about what she thinks. She will probably write something like, 'Looking at this pencil, I realize . . . ' or 'Looking at this pencil makes me wonder . . . ' This is really smart work. She first took something she saw and *described* it, and in a moment I bet she will write what this gets her to think. I bet some of the rest of you will also do this sort of smart work."

Of course, there are lots of things you could notice and compliment. You could notice a child who finished writing one entry and then went on to the next one. The entries will

---

MID-WORKSHOP TEACHING POINT   *Gathering Essay Entries*   "Writers, can I have your eyes and your attention please?" I paused. "When we studied personal narrative writing, we had a chart of strategies for gathering entries that might become true stories, and with the help of those strategies we kept our notebooks brimming with true stories. What I hope you are realizing is that when we write essays (instead of stories), we tailor the strategies we use so that now we come up with material that will lead us toward this new kind of writing."

"Listen to what one of your classmates wrote when she observed the small stuff in her life and then let her observation get her thinking about big ideas. Chloe wrote:

> Sometimes when my three-year-old cousin is watching Teletubbies or Barney, she dances or sways to the music. It's like she is hypnotized! If Barney jumps, so does she. If the Teletubbies are dancing, she does it. It's fun to watch the things kids do when they're comfortable around you because they do silly things.

"Of course, essayists use lots of strategies to collect entries. You have all been observing, you've been paying attention to the small stuff of your lives—but as essayists, you can also gather entries by writing about big issues that matter to you, issues you think about all the time. Essayists sometimes put an issue on the page and then list a few ideas we have about the issue, taking one of those ideas to write about at length. Adam tried this strategy. He decided to write an entry about his illness, and the bigger issue of how children treat people who are different from themselves. He first wrote an entry about how he feels when people stare at his bald head. He circled that idea for a while.

continued on next page

---

probably be short, so writing several entries in a day will be essential. You could notice that a child wrote not just about his or her own life, but also about things that happen in the larger world.

You can predict ways in which your children will need direction. For example, you can be sure that some will continue to write narrative accounts. Plan to tell those children what you see and encourage them to shift from retelling to asking, "What did that make me think?" or "What new idea does this provoke?" This way you'll help children move between recording events and reflecting on ideas. When children write entries in which they first observe and then shift to think about what they've observed, some of them will jot *phrases* instead of writing *sentences*. If a child, for example, wrote just the word *Mom*, nudge that child to add whatever his thought might be: "My mom is one of my best friends." Then, too, some children will write lots and lots of questions. Help these children to entertain those questions.

Above all, your challenge will be to help children see more, think more, feel more. They're apt to want to write one sentence about what they see and one sentence about what they think! Teach them to really look, to take in the world, to be moved by what they see. And then help them understand that they can grow ideas as they write. You'll return to the work of helping writers develop ideas in a later session.

continued from previous page

Then he started a second entry, which I want to read to you. You'll notice that this time he stands back a bit from his own disease and addresses his entry to children who ignore those who are different. Adam generated this entry by recording an issue, then listing the detailed ideas he has about it." *[Fig. I-2]*

> People shouldn't judge people by what they look like. When kids are discriminated by what they look like they are treated very cruelly. It is really mean to do this because you don't really know this person. For example, let's say someone wears a shirt with a stain on it and everybody doesn't want to be your friend because they think you're dirty. The person who did not want to talk to you could have been your future best friend. When I was in kindergarten in this school a lot of people avoided me because I am bald. It took me a long time to make friends. It is harder to go into a new school if you have something different like I do. Before people judge people by what they look like they need to tell themselves, "What would I feel like if I was that kid?" With everybody staring at me and nobody talking to you. Then you look at you and your friends, with everybody admiring you and including you. Then you go over there to the "different kid" and include him and talk to him.

"So remember, you can use the strategies you already know for generating writing—you can start with the small observations and let them lead you to big ideas *or* you can start with big ideas and let them lead you to the details. Okay, go ahead and get back to writing."

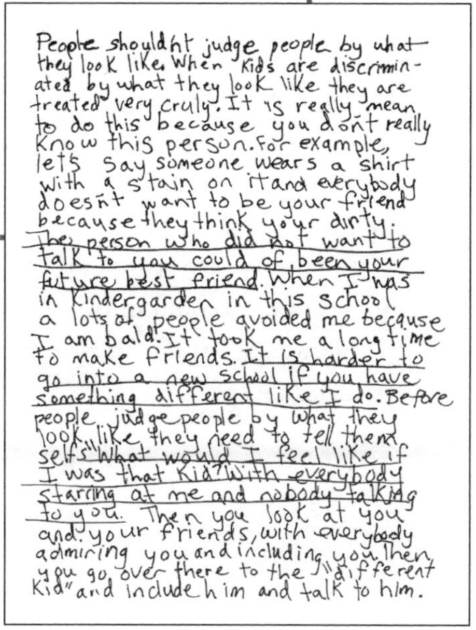

People shouldnt judge people by what they look like. When kids are discriminated by what they look like they are treated very cruly. It is really mean to do this because you dont really know this person. For example, lets say someone wears a shirt with a stain on it and everybody doesnt want to be your friend because they think your dirty. The person who did not want to talk to you could of been your future best friend. When I was in kindergarden in this school a lots of people avoided me because I am bald. It took me a long time to make friends. It is harder to go into a new school if you have something different like I do. Before people judge people by what they look like they need to tell them selfs "What would I feel like if I was that kid? With everybody staring at me and nobody talking to you. Then you look at you and your friends, with everybody admiring you and including you. Then you go over there to the "different kid" and include him and talk to him.

Fig. I-2 Adam's notebook entry

SHARE

Collecting Essay Entries

Rally children to reread and reflect on their essay entries, talking with partners about how these differ from narrative entries.

"The *strategies* for generating entries will be a bit different when we write essays, and the *entries* themselves will also be a bit different. Would you and your partner look back at the entries you collected during our first two units, and then look at the entries you collected today? How are your entries changing?" The children talked with their partners for a few minutes, and I listened in with my clipboard in hand, writing snippets of overheard conversation.

Convene the class and share a few observations.

"Writers, can I have your eyes? I am blown away by your insights. Let me talk about what you said."

"It's true that essay writers are a bit less apt to gather *stories* in our notebooks, and more apt to write observations and ideas."

"It's also true that essay writers sometimes collect tiny entries; some of these entries may not even fill half a page."

"And it's true that essay writers often write with information and facts, as well as with ideas and wonderings. And it is true that essay writers address big topics that exist in the world. The fact is that essayists write with information, with facts, and they also grow ideas about big topics!"

"Today we talked about the differences between personal narrative and essay entries. Another day, we could think and talk about ways in which good writing is the same whether we are writing essays or writing narratives—because the truth is, it's both different and the same."

Because this is the first session in a unit, you should anticipate that it will resemble (and refer back to) Sessions I and II of the previous two units. In this session, as in the first sessions of every other unit, you will again need to teach writers strategies for generating entries. It's important that your students realize this new teaching stands on the shoulders of (and contrasts with) earlier work on generating narrative entries. It is also important for you to see that one unit of study expands upon another.

When we ask children to talk in pairs, then listen in on their conversations and report back some of what we hear, we can word our reports in ways that provide the class with clear guidelines. To report back on a conversation overheard during the turn-and-talk, the teacher is essentially using the same muscles we use when we notice what a child has done and turn that observation into a Mid-Workshop Teaching Point.

Those of you who worried that the first two units produced overly constrained and channeled writing and put undue emphasis on focused, chronological entries will perhaps feel more comfortable now as this unit reclaims the value of entries in which the writer observes, questions, wanders, meanders, backtracks, sidetracks.

HOMEWORK ***Collecting and Thinking About Small Surprises*** Writers, a while ago I spent time with Karla Kuskin, the author of *The Philharmonic Gets Dressed.* I asked her, "What do you do when you sit down to write a picture book?" and she answered, "I don't *sit down* to write." She went on to say, "My writing starts with catching glimpses or snatches." To demonstrate, she told me that on her way to our meeting, she'd seen a big, beautiful truck bearing the name Manhasset Imperial Sewage—and she thought, "I could make something out of that." For her, writing often begins with catching a glimpse of something which lends an idea to dawn on her. She went on to explain that her book about the philharmonic orchestra getting dressed actually began when she was at a child's birthday party. The child was given a doll and the first thing she did was lift up the doll's skirt to check out the underpants. That one observation sparked the idea for a whole book about the layers of clothing the orchestra members don each day.

Tonight, would you try to live an especially wide-awake life? Pay attention to anything surprising. Record what strikes you: a phrase, an observation, a little kid checking out her doll's underpants. You won't write long entries, but I am hoping you will, as Don Murray says, see more, hear more, think more, notice more because you are writing. Describing his notebook as "a great garage sale of life," Don Murray says, "I compost my life, piling up . . . lines overheard in restaurants, scenes caught in the corner of my eyes, pages not yet understood." Do that sort of collecting, that sort of paying attention, tonight. Your writing should fill up at least a page, which may mean you collect several entries. Be sure you observe—*and* have a thought about what you see. Notice that Takuma takes the time to really see the fake butterflies, before letting them spark memories and ideas.

I'm enclosing Takuma's writing to give you an idea for the sort of writing—and living—you might do tonight. *[Figs. I-3 and I-4]*

I couldmy see the fake butterflies hanging down the string. The butterflie shines when a light comes to it as if it was a mirror. Slowly shaking by the wind. Almost as if they were real live butterflies. They are all lined up on one string, all wobbling almost falling. Purple orange, green, light blue, dark blue, all lined up on one single string. It reminds me of my family because there lined up in one house. One wing reminds me of my dad all fall. The others wing would remind me about my mom. And the body would remind me of my sister. Flap flap flap

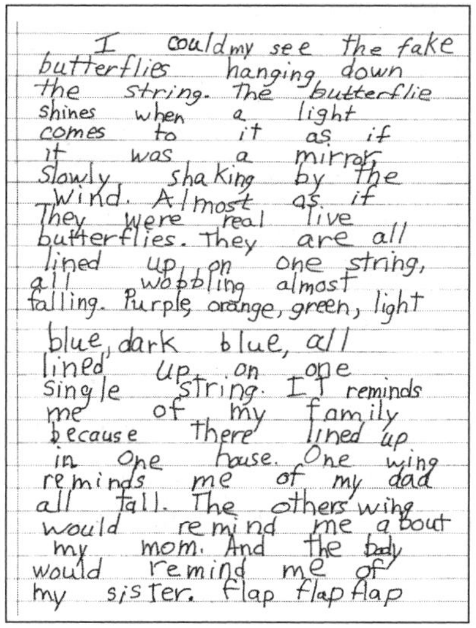

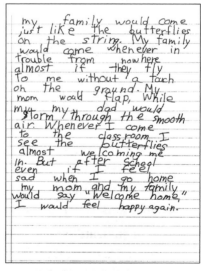

Fig. I-3 Takuma observes and has a thought

my family would come just like the butterflies on the string. My family would come whenever in trouble from nowhere almost if they fly to me without a tuch on the ground. My mom would flap, while my my dad would storm through the smooth air. Whenever I come to the classroom I see the butterflies almost welcoming me in. But after school even if I feel sad when I go home my mom and my family would say "Welcome home," I would feel happy again.

Fig. I-4 Takuma's notebook entry page 2

If your children don't seem to have grasped the concepts of this minilesson . . . don't be surprised. They have just spent two units writing texts that follow an entirely different structure. You have now asked them to shift gears and start moving toward a new way to look at the world as writers. You might decide to move forward even if many of your children are still writing narratives because Session II will provide more strategies for generating non-narrative entries.

If your children have worked through this unit in previous years, and you'd like to vary the minilesson . . . keep in mind that in *Living Between the Lines*, my theme is that writing well is not only desk work but also life work. You'll find the book brims with examples of children who've collected entries that reflect this wide-awakeness and examples, too, of writers who celebrate the importance of wide-awake attentiveness. You can take any of these bits and develop minilessons around them. Take Faulkner's quote, for example, "I have finally found that my little postage stamp of native soil is worth writing about, that I will never live long enough to exhaust it." (Cowley 1958, p.141) Or take this observation referenced in *Living Between the Lines* but made by journalist Roy Peter Clark:

> The ordinary person walks down the street and sees a bar, a wig
> shop, a grocery store, a pharmacy and a shoe store. The journalist
> sees dozens of story ideas behind the facades of those businesses. He
> sees people and issues and asks himself, "Who drinks in that bar at
> 9:00 in the morning?" "What kind of market is there for those huge
> rainbow-colored wigs in the shop window?"(Calkins 1991, p. 226)

If you set a quote such as one of these alongside an excerpt from a familiar read-aloud book (an excerpt in which the author relays a bit of life and then reflects on it), and then add a bit of practical how-to advice for how writers can gather and combine and record in similar ways, you'll soon have a brand-new minilesson.

If your students' observations tend to be characterized by statements of the obvious or by generalities rather than specifics . . . you may want to do a lesson where you help your students slow down and observe not only the object or subject of observation but also the world around it. For example, you might begin a lesson by saying something like, "Over the weekend my friend Diane visited me. She's a painter, and she designs textiles, you know, the designs on wallpaper, sheets, and dishes, and I noticed that she makes observations like an artist. For example, we went out for a walk after the rain, and she told me she loves the shades of green that come alive after the rain. I had never noticed that before, but once she said that, I couldn't help but see all the different greens around us. That got me thinking about observations, how people observe differently. Like my neighbor, who is a nurse. She notices the littlest things about how people look. She once mentioned someone's fingernails! She said that this guy must smoke a lot because his fingernails have the 'smoker's curve' to them. Who knew! I never noticed fingernails before. Anyway, today I want to teach you one thing I think I know about how writers observe . . . when we observe, we try to take in all that we see and then have some sort of thought about it. I tried it. For example, last night I looked at my bed before I got into it. I jotted down my observations and I wrote this: "My pillow, full and fluffy at the head of my bed, seems to be luring me there. It's as if it is smiling its warmest smile at me, inviting me to lie down." You see, I didn't just describe my pillow—'My pillow is fluffy and it's got a yellow pillowcase on it. It's at the head of my bed.' No, I added some thought to the observation."

For the active engagement, you could say, "So right now, let's try it. Let's take our notebooks over to the window. Look outside at something that catches your eye. Then as you're writing, have a thought about what you're observing. We'll share with our partners in three minutes."

COLLABORATING WITH COLLEAGUES

When you and your colleagues meet to learn together about this new work, it is important to begin with the understanding that this unit will be very different from the previous two. In fact, many linguists, philosophers, and literacy scholars have suggested that there are two fundamentally different ways of thinking and of organizing discourse. People use different terms to distinguish between the two different modes: literary and nonliterary (Langar), aesthetic or efferent (Rosenblatt), narrative or paradigmatic (Bruner), spectator or participant (Britton), subjective or objective experience (Langar), and narrative or expository (secondary school teachers).

The important thing to realize is that people can choose how we will relate to, learn from, and think, talk, or write about an experience. Judith Langar, in *Envisioning Literature,* writes about this:

> Say, for example, you are taking piano lessons and want to play well. You might study sight reading and musical theory . . . tape record your own playing in order to critique it. (1995, New York: Teachers College Press, p. 6)

That is, you could study music in a nonliterary, objective fashion in which you strive to gain control of the topics and subtopics, applying ideas to the material. But, Langar points out, there is another option. You could learn about music in a more literary (subjective, participant) way, immersing yourself in a few musicians and their playing:

> You could let their music invade your senses and seduce you by their sounds, as their best playing can do. By internalizing their music, you respond…you put yourself in their places, you can even begin to sense the feel of their (your) fingers on the keys and the sounds in their (your) ears—the same, but different, heard through the filter of your own experience. (p. 6)

To explore the fundamental differences between narrative and expository ways of thinking, you and your colleagues may want to select a shared experience—say, a recent faculty meeting—and try thinking about it in a narrative and then in an expository way, noticing and discussing how those two views feel fundamentally different. You will find you use different language in general, and in particular for transitions (when you are in the narrative mode, you'll rely on chronology to tell the story, whereas in the expository mode, when you analyze what happened, you'll rely on categorization and comparison). You may also notice that the point from which you, as narrator, experience the event seems different. When I'm in a narrative mode I find myself starting at the beginning and walking chronologically through time. When I'm in the expository mode, on the other hand, I feel as if I'm flying overhead, looking at the event from a more removed perspective.

It is crucial for you to become comfortable with the subject you are teaching. In this instance, you and your colleagues may want to recall and discuss television shows that are organized in an expository way versus those that are narrative. News reporters on one channel, for example, may teach the main ideas about say, a big weather-related event, whereas on another channel the same content will be conveyed through a first-hand narrative, as when one person relives his or her experience of the event. The two "texts" will use different organizational frames, different voices, different perspectives, different vocabulary, and different transitional phrases.

IN THIS SESSION, YOU WILL AGAIN TEACH CHILDREN WAYS WRITERS COLLECT WRITING FOR ESSAYS. YOU'LL TEACH THEM ESPECIALLY TO BE MORE THOUGHTFUL ABOUT WHAT THEY SEE, WRITING AT GREATER LENGTH.

GETTING READY

- Non-narrative notebook entries from students that demonstrate observations, questions, musings, ideas
- T-chart written on chart paper, headed "What I Notice" on one side and "What It Makes Me Think" on the other, filled in with an example
- Strategies for Generating Essay Entries chart
- Writing samples by published authors (e.g. *The Lightwell*, by Laurence Yep; *Alone*, by Jean Little), you, or students that demonstrate observation and reflection
- Writing sample with a subject (a person, place, or object), ideas related to that subject, and one developed idea

See CD-ROM for resources

GROWING ESSAY IDEAS IN NOTEBOOKS

I once asked a group of teachers to tell me the one time when professional development most mattered to them. I wondered if they'd choose summer institutes, or cite a particularly brimful course of study. To my surprise, each teacher selected a moment when a literacy staff developer or an administrator came into that teacher's classroom, observed the teaching, and then met with the teacher to say, "This is what I notice about your teaching." For us, as practitioners, few things are more precious than the gift of recognition. By recognition, I do not mean prizes and awards. I mean that it is enormously helpful if someone we respect watches us as we work and then demonstrates that she understands our struggles and notices our successes.

Children, too, want the gift of recognition. If we can, in a minilesson, let children know that we understand the predicaments they encounter and the struggles they face, then they'll trust our teaching. If children first feel seen and heard, they'll draw close when we say, "I have one tip I want to share."

You'll find that although my purpose in this session is to address a predicament I see many students facing (their entries are short), I use the session to repeat everything I said in the first session. I cycle right back to the idea that writers who want to compose personal essays live wide-awake lives, but this time I address problems I notice many children have encountered with that charge. One problem is that their entries are short. A related problem is that many children seem to suffer a crisis of confidence. They write about the loose buttons in their pocket or the homeless man who sells poems in the park, but then they look at these entries with wavering doubt, thinking, "So what?" I help children realize it is okay to have those doubts, and encourage them to take the risk of investing themselves in their little observations, using those observations to prompt big thinking about the details of their lives. If my theories about these children apply to your children as well, borrow them. If not, try to put into words whatever it is you see your children doing.

Later I teach children another strategy for generating essay entries. Under the auspices of teaching this second strategy, I share writing that resembles the writing I hope children will do.

MINILESSON

Growing Essay Ideas in Notebooks

CONNECTION

Support your children's identities as essay writers by exclaiming over the entries they collected at home. Then name the problem your teaching point will address. In this case, children seem to feel their entries are insignificant.

"So, many of you have been living like writers collecting bits and pieces of your lives. Listen to a portion of John's writing": *[Fig. II-1]*

> Imagine you have been looking at the floor and it just comes into your mind tan, red, tan, red. Then all of a sudden it goes red, red, tan. Sometimes I feel like ripping out the tiles and replacing them. When I look at the tiles I start to wonder why is this tile here? Or is this a mistake. HOW CAN THE SMALLEST THING STAND OUT SO MUCH?
>
> "Why does it really matter?" my mom said.
>
> "It just caught my eye," I said. "It's that why are the tiles different? Instead of tan red tan red it went tan, tan, tan. Will it leave my mind? Why do I care?"
>
> "I think that tiles shouldn't matter," my dad said.
>
> As the thought stayed in my mind, I started to change my mind, but something wouldn't let it go away.
>
> The tiles go tan tan red—it doesn't sound like a pattern!

"When I see what you all collected last night, I am reminded of Donald Hall, who says that as a writer, he goes through life collecting 'string too short to be saved.' And I'm reminded of Malcolm Cowley, who says that every writer always begins writing with 'a precious particle.' You all have lots of little strings, lots of precious particles, in your notebooks. You are becoming essay writers!"

"But some of you told me this morning that you aren't sure whether your entries are precious. You told me, 'I just wrote down what I saw.' You aren't sure whether your particles are significant."

COACHING

It is incredibly important to teach children to value the details of their lives. So many children come to school saying, "I don't have anything to write about" and "My life is boring." Just as photographers go through life seeing potential pictures (whether or not they have a camera with them), writers go through life seeing significance in the ordinary fabric of our lives. I can think of few goals more important than that of helping kindle children's interest in the stuff of their lives. Although this is a unit on personal essay writing, some of the instruction addresses goals that don't fit into the confines of a single unit.

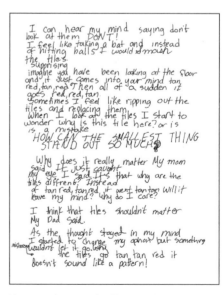

Fig. II-1 John's notebook entry

Name the teaching point. In this case, tell children that essay writers develop systems that help us not only to observe but also to grow ideas.

"Today I want to teach you that when we collect the stuff of our lives in our notebooks, that stuff doesn't come with ideas attached. We just have a bunch of buttons from our inside-out pockets, or the image of a child checking out her doll's underpants, or a yellow truck with the name Manhasset Imperial Sewage. In a way, we don't start with much."

"But if we are going to make something out of the stuff of our lives, we need not only to collect it, we also need to grow ideas around it. To be sure that our entries begin with our observations and end with our thoughts, we can do one of two things: We can push ourselves to shift between observing and saying, 'and the thought I have about this is . . .' Or, we can write in two columns, one for what we see, hear, and notice and the other for what we think."

TEACHING
Name and then demonstrate a system you use to push yourself to develop thoughts from your observations.

"Writers, I am like many of you. I often begin my entries by writing what I see or hear in the world around me. But I know that to get a good seed idea for an essay, it is important for me to shift from seeing (or hearing or noticing or remembering) to thinking. I have two ways to push myself to go from noticing to thinking."

"One thing I do a lot is this: after I put the stuff of my life onto the page, I turn a corner in my writing. I do this by almost forcing myself to write, 'and the idea I have about that is . . .' I don't always use those exact words. I might instead write, 'This makes me realize . . .' or 'This reminds me of . . .' Either way, though, I give myself an assignment to switch gears so that I stop recording what is actually there in life and begin instead to record my thoughts about what I noticed."

"I'm going to try this right now. I'll begin and describe something I notice. After I describe for a few sentences, Emily, will you coach me by saying, 'And the idea I have about this is . . .' Then I'll try to have an idea at that very second, right in front of you."

Shifting into the role of writer, I said, "I'll start," and I took a big breath. "I'm looking at our fish tank. I see that there is some fine, hairy green stuff growing on the pebbles on the tank floor. It's practically invisible, but it waves a bit as fish swim by, and when it does that, you can see it."

When I got married, the writing researcher Don Graves (who'd been my minister when I was a child) conducted the service. He began by describing John and me to the congregation, and said of me, "Lucy, who knows how to live off the land. Who turns sticks and stones into toys for little children." At the time I was taken aback by the description, but over the years I have come to think Graves was paying a beautiful compliment. As a writer, teacher, thinker, person, I so hope that I live off the land. I want to be the kind of person who takes the everyday stuff of life and declares it to be significant. And I believe that significance is made, not found.

The teaching component of our minilessons is designed to teach youngsters 'how to' do something. For this reason, this section of most minilessons will be structured chronologically. We retell the step-by-step procedures we follow to solve a problem or to use a strategy. We do so in a sequenced, chronological way. We sometimes come out and literally say, "First I . . . then I . . . finally I . . . ." The Teaching component of a minilesson is usually a procedural (or how-to) text.

Notice that I observe for a while, lingering to see specifics. When children are asked to take over my role and continue observing, on the other hand, they tend to observe one thing, then move to another, then to something else.

It's not an accident that I observe something that all of us have passed by. I'm hoping to show that our everyday world is waiting to be rediscovered. I am writing in the air, not writing on chart paper. I do this to save time.

When I nodded to remind her to do so, Emily interrupted me and said, "And the idea I have about this is . . ."

"Thank you, Emily. And the idea I have about this is . . . I'm wondering if this green stuff is good for the fish. I know we sprinkle fish food into the tank, but I wonder if fish also eat the stuff that grows in their tanks. How do they know what to eat and what not to eat? It's interesting how animals have ways to take care of themselves."

I try to coach Emily to say this with rising intonation so that her phrase serves to prime my pump, to help me generate ideas. If you think the partner's intervention puts words into writer's mouths, you are right. But I find it also puts words into their minds, and the words become tools for thought.

Debrief, naming what you did in such a way that it is transferable to another day and another topic. Spotlight a child who already used the strategy you just demonstrated in his writing.

Stepping out of the role of writer and back into my role as a teacher, I said, "Did you see how I first observed and then used the phrase, 'And the idea I have about this is . . .' to help me switch gears and have a brand-new thought, sparked by what I'd just observed? "

"Sophie started her entry by recording what she noticed. If she had just stopped there, her entry wouldn't be much. But the great thing is that she pushed her writing to take a turn, and asked herself, 'What does this make me think? What does this remind me of?'" *[Figs. II-2 and II-3]*

Notice that in both Sessions I and II, I incorporate two examples into the Teaching component of the minilesson—one adult example and one child example. You may decide your children need briefer minilessons, in which case you will use only one example. Of course, it is best if you use examples from your own writing and your own students', but if need be, borrow these examples.

When I look at the wind chime, I think about my great-grandmother Evelyne. And how my wind chime has an angel on it, and angels are in heaven. My great-grandmother is in heaven. I think about how strong she was, before she passed away. I think about how she held my hand and she kissed it, and how I thought that she would be all right. When I look at my wind chime, I think about how much time we spent together. I realize how hard it must have been to be her and how she went through all that pain. When I empathize with my great-grandmother, I think about how she laid in bed, and how she could not get up; it'll be too painful. When I empathize with my great-grandmother, I think about how nervous she must have been for her to be passing away. I think about how she might want to live longer. That is how I empathize with my great-grandmother. When I really think about it, I think about all the time we could have spent together, but instead I was doing something else. It's like I didn't even care. When I really think about this deeply, I think we had the time but I wasted it, but then I just close my eyes and talk. We still have the time. All the time we want together, me and her.

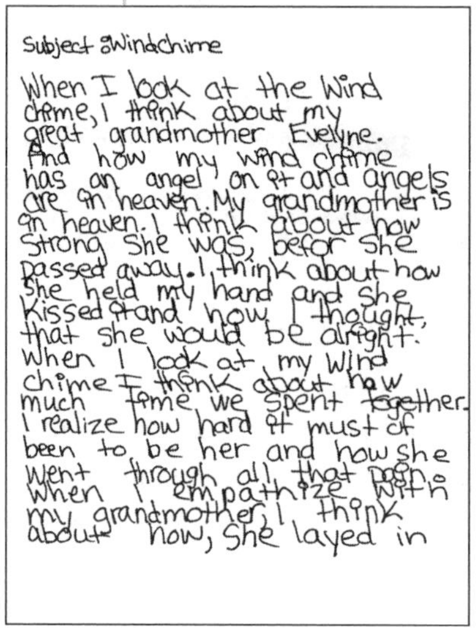
Subject: Wind chime
When I look at the Wind chime, I think about my great grandmother Evelyne. And how my wind chime has an angel on it and angels are in heaven. My grandmother is in heaven. I think about how strong she was, befor she passed away. I think about how she held my hand and she kissed it and how I thought that she would be alright. When I look at my Wind chime I think about how much time we spent together. I realize how hard it must of been to be her and how she went through all that pain. When I empathize with my grandmother, I think about how, she layed in

Fig. II-2 Sophie's notebook entry

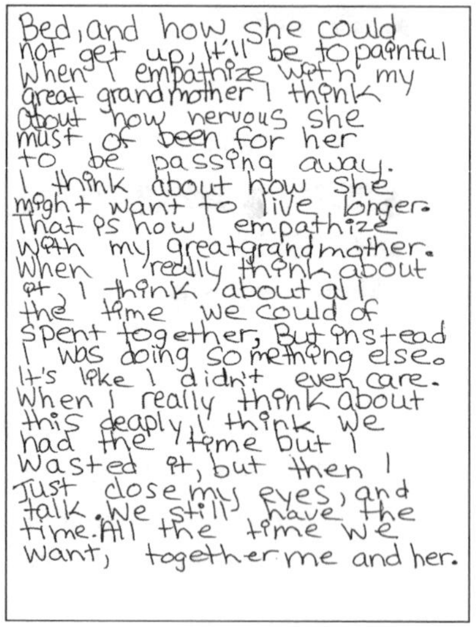
Bed, and how she could not get up, it'll be to painful When I empathize with my great grandmother I think about how nervous she must of been for her to be passing away. I think about how she might want to live longer. That is how I empathize with my great grandmother. When I really think about it, I think about all the time we could of spent together, But instead I was doing something else. It's like I didn't even care. When I really think about this deaply, I think we had the time but then I wasted it, but then I just close my eyes, and talk. We still have the time. All the time we want, together me and her.

Fig. II-3 Sophie's entry page 2

"Do you see how Sophie uses what she sees to spark a thought, and then she keeps herself going? She looks at the chime, then writes what it makes her think, and then looks back at the chime, and thinks more on the same topic. When her new thought subsides, she pushes herself to keep going, 'When I empathize . . .' she writes. 'When I really think about it . . .' and 'When I really think about this deeply.' Study the ways Sophie pushes herself to think more and more deeply. This entry ends up as the source for an essay on her great-grandmother."

Name and then demonstrate a second strategy you use to nudge yourself to shift from observing to growing ideas.

"Another system I sometimes use is that I gather observations and information on the left-hand side of my notebook and then use the right side as a place to think about what I've written. The chart could look something like this."

What I Notice	What It Makes Me Think
Two girls sit together, showing off their lunches to each other.	I used to show off my lunch. Why are kids so competitive? It is not fair to kids whose parents have less money. Or to kids with moms who won't buy sugary foods.

"Now you have two ways to push yourself."

Debrief, reminding writers that they can use either of these systems.

"So writers, yesterday you were collectors, gathering bits and pieces in your writer's notebooks. Today I showed you two ways in which we can give those bits the attention they deserve. It is important not only to collect entries in our notebooks, but also to collect and to think. Writers have strategies for doing both. Sometimes after we put the stuff of our lives onto the page, we then write a phrase like, 'The idea I have about this is . . .' to spark a thought. And sometimes we use the white space on the left-hand side of our notebooks as an invitation to mull, to grow ideas."

It is very important to notice that minilessons are not a vehicle for doling out a daily assignment. Instead of saying, "Today, I'd like you to each make a two-column chart. On the top of the left column, write . . . ," I say, "Another system I sometimes use is . . ." The goal of a minilesson is to add to students' repertoire of skills and strategies, not to dole out that day's assignment.

You may, of course, decide to teach this second strategy for generating entries in a separate minilesson, or you may not teach it at all. One thing to notice is that this strategy involves filling in a chart rather than writing full pages. Decide if you want to encourage listing and charting as ways to generate ideas in a notebook, or if you prefer that children write more expansively, as we saw Sophie doing on the preceding page.

It's probably accurate to say that essayists are collectors. We collect, sort, categorize. Children, of course, are collectors as well. They may collect stickers, sea glass, Barbie dolls, comic books, or bean bag animals, but collecting almost seems to be part of childhood. So build on this! This is an idea that could be made into a Big Idea. It could be the subject of a chapter, a minilesson, a keynote speech. You'll want to become accustomed to noticing big ideas—and mentally starring them. That is, as someone who is teaching essayists, cultivate in yourself the ability to recognize passing comments that could be developed into big theories, because this is part of the mind-set that essayists and nonfiction writers bring to our lives.

ACTIVE ENGAGEMENT

Set children up to try thinking within a mental structure in which they shift between observing for a while, then reflecting for a while.

"So let's try this together. Partner 1, look around the room (or open your desk or your backpack, and look in it). Let your eye fall on something, anything, that you can describe. Thumbs up if you have something. Okay, now you are going to write in the air, saying aloud the exact words you'd write if you had a pen and were writing one paragraph of observations. Partner 1, describe what you see to your partner. Start by saying, 'I see . . .' and keep observing that one thing until I guide you to do something different."

After a minute, I interjected, saying loudly, with rising intonation, "and the thought I have about this is . . ." I tucked in the quick instructions: "Repeat what I just said and keep going." I said this in such a way that the children shifted gears, incorporated the phrase 'and the thought I have about this is . . .,' and continued talking.

Again set children up to observe and then to articulate a thought about that observation, but this time teach them to observe a distant place that they must conjure up in their minds' eyes.

"Let's try it again. Partner 2, this time you are going to see something in your memory. Pretend you are at home. Put yourself in your kitchen, your living room, on the front stoop, or the branch of your climbing tree. Watch something—your cat as she purrs on the couch, the pile of books beside your bed. Thumbs up when you've got something in mind that you are observing. Okay, you'll start by just describing exactly what you see in your mind's eye. Say, 'I see . . .' (and keep going)."

After a minute, I again interjected, saying loudly and in a way that channeled the speakers' remarks "and (repeat after me) the idea I have about this is . . .". The children carried on, talking now about the ideas they generated from their observations.

"Writers, you've come up with great ideas!"

You'll recall that yesterday you also asked children to write essay entries in the air. You'll probably find that it is much easier for children to write narratives in the air (to storytell) than to write essays or expository texts in the air. You may want to encourage children to watch television shows that are designed to teach, like the shows about exotic animals or news features, and listen to the language on these shows. It's important that they become comfortable talking in this genre. Terms such as 'on the other hand,' 'consequently,' 'three factors account for,' or 'notice that' all need to become part of your children's speaking, reading, and eventually writing repertoire. To encourage children to listen to teaching shows on television and acquire some of the lingo, you could videotape such a show and view a bit of it together. If you can, go a step further and encourage children to role-play being professors or news reporters, teaching each other about any subject at all. You could even take the time that once was set aside for children to storytell and now designate it as a time for informal speeches designed to teach or to persuade.

Notice that the strategies I teach become progressively more sophisticated. First children observed what was before their eyes, then they traveled in their minds to another place and observed what they conjured up. When I design units of study, I plan to move children up a gradient of difficulty as we proceed. It is always important to teach so that children can be successful, but we want them to be successful at progressively more demanding work.

The idea of observing in one's mind is an empowering and important twist to this minilesson. If your children can't take it in today, save it for another day, but don't miss the chance to teach children that we can sit at our desks and mentally conjure up distant places and events, writing what we see and what we think about what we see. This technique opens worlds.

Remind children that today and always, when they want to collect entries that can become essays, they can draw on their growing tool chest of strategies.

"I hope that from this day on and for the rest of your lives, you always remember that we not only collect the stuff of our lives, but we also grow ideas about what we collect. In your notebook, you can use any of these strategies to generate more entries. I put them together in a chart—draw on them as needed."

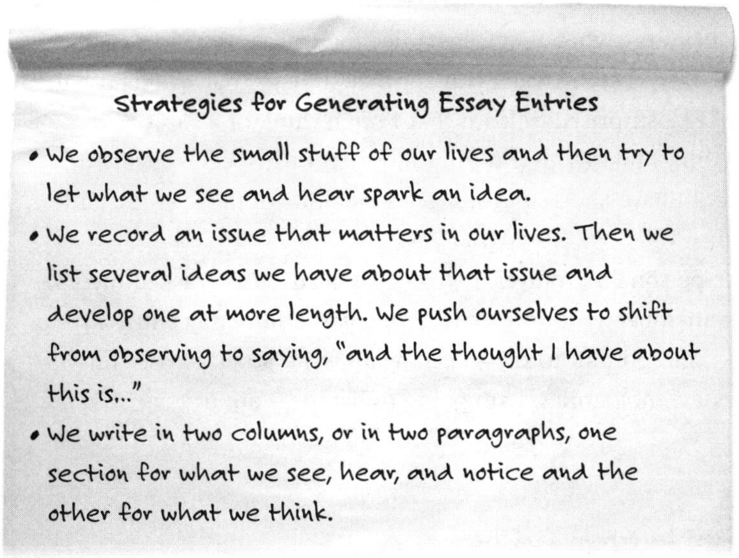

Strategies for Generating Essay Entries

• We observe the small stuff of our lives and then try to let what we see and hear spark an idea.

• We record an issue that matters in our lives. Then we list several ideas we have about that issue and develop one at more length. We push ourselves to shift from observing to saying, "and the thought I have about this is..."

• We write in two columns, or in two paragraphs, one section for what we see, hear, and notice and the other for what we think.

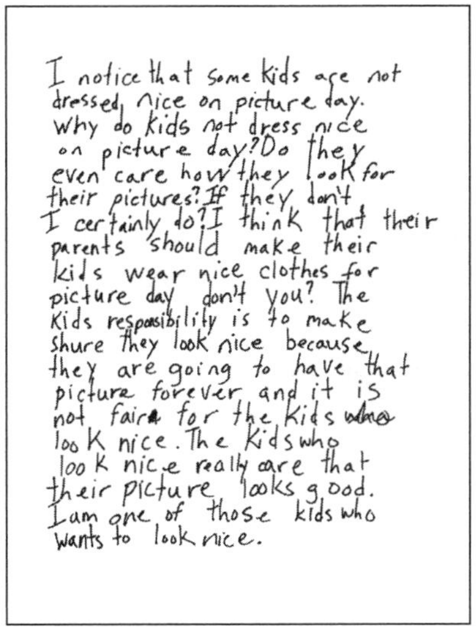

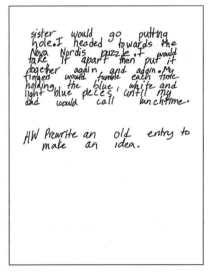

I notice that some kids are not dressed nice on picture day. Why do kids not dress nice on picture day? Do they even care how they look for their pictures? If they don't I certainly do? I think that their parents should make their kids wear nice clothes for picture day don't you? The kids responsibility is to make shure they look nice because they are going to have that picture forever and it is not fair for the kids who look nice. The kids who look nice really care that their picture looks good. I am one of those kids who wants to look nice.

Fig. II-4 Alejandro's notebook entry asking questions as a strategy for developing ideas

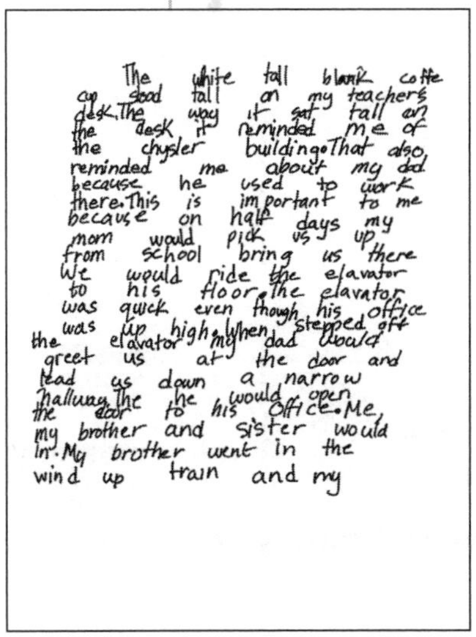

The white tall blank coffe cup stood tall on my teachers desk. The desk, the way it sat tall an the chysler building. That also reminded me about my dad because he used to work there. This is important to me because on half days my mom would pick us up. We would ride the elavator to his floor. The elavator was quick even though his office was up high. When my dad would step off the elavator my dad would greet us at the door and lead us down a narrow hallway. The door to his office would open. Me, my brother and sister would in. My brother went in the wind up train and my

sister would go putting hole. I headed towards the Nova Nordis puzzle. I would take it apart then put it together again and again. My fingers would fumble each time holding the blue, white and light blue pieces, until my dad would call lunchtime.

HW Prewrite an old entry to make an idea.

Fig. II-5 Olivia's notebook entry with brief observations then a well-structured entry

Fig. II-6 Olivia's entry page 2

WRITING AND CONFERRING

Providing Guided Practice

If you notice that several students are having difficulty making the transition from writing stories to writing about ideas, you may want to do a shared writing activity to support these children. Gather them and grab chart paper and a marker. Tell them that as a group they're all going to write one shared entry, and that doing this will help them feel the difference between writing a story—a personal narrative—and writing about an idea—an essay. Point out that one possible first step is to make an observation.

When I did this recently, Sydni offered her observation: "All the kids are running around like crazy at recess."

Then I said, "So if we want to write an entry starting with Sydni's observation, we need to say thoughts about it."

Aidan said, "Recess is when we get to be free."

I guided, "Say more about that—tell a reason or give an example or compare recess to something else." Then I showed children that to get themselves started thinking more, they could reread the one idea Aidan had already shared, letting the thought hang in the air.

Roy did this and then piped up, "There aren't any assignments."

I wrote this and again we reread what we'd written so far and waited. Then I quietly muttered, "We've got to say more," and eyed those who hadn't spoken. "What is your idea about recess and how there aren't any assignments?" I asked Chris, adding, "Remember, we try to think of more to say about the main thought." I reread it again.

Chris dictated, "Kids should have more recess!" and I recorded this at the growing edge of the paragraph.

> **MID-WORKSHOP TEACHING POINT** *Generating More Essay Entries* "Writers, your entries are briefer than they were when you were collecting true stories. So you'll need to write more entries in a day. Let me teach you another strategy that writers use to gather essay entries. You won't be surprised to learn that I often think of a subject (perhaps a person, place, or thing) that matters to me, and then I list specific ideas (this time not stories but ideas) that I have about that subject. I take one of those ideas, and think more about it in an entry."
>
> "Remember when I wrote personal narratives, I wrote, 'My Dad.' Then I asked myself, 'What small moments do I remember about my dad?' When gathering essay entries, I again jot down a subject that is important to me—I can again write 'My Dad,' but this time, because I am writing essays, not stories, I am going to list ideas about my dad. I'll list them on my fingers."
>
> My Dad
> - one of my most important teachers
> - always been a colorful character
> - helped me care about writing
>
> Debriefing, I said, "Did you notice that when generating ideas for essay entries, I again started with a subject—a person, place, or thing—that matters to me, but this time I didn't list small moments; rather, I listed ideas related to the subject? Now I will take one of those ideas (the second one) and begin to write about it."
>
> *continued on next page*

In this manner we continued to write an entry together about recess. The entry consisted of a list of related ideas, each written in a sentence. This wasn't perfect writing, but my goal wasn't perfection! After a few minutes of work, I reviewed what we had done together, asking the children to talk about how it felt to write about ideas instead of writing stories. Then I told them to take that "idea-writing feeling" back to their seats and try writing another idea in their own notebooks—this time on their own topics. "I'll come soon and see how you're doing," I said.

You might find it helpful to notice and name what children are doing when they observe and then write their ideas about observations so that this concept becomes familiar to them. So if one child writes, "I see the green plant. It has one long stem which only has two tiny leaves," I'm apt to say, "I love the way you first named the big picture of what you see—the whole plant—and then instead of moving on to observe something else, you zoomed in and noticed details. You described those details about the plants' leaves with lots of words." I'm apt to end my comment by saying, "Writers do this. We see the big picture of whatever we are observing, but then we don't just move on to look at something else. Instead we linger, we see closely, we elaborate, and we say more."

As you make teaching moves such as this one, notice that you are essentially doing what essayists do all the time. Like writers, you will also shift between a particular example and an overarching generalization. You will make mountains out of molehills! What I can describe now—the teaching move that involves naming what you see a child or an author doing and then making a fuss about what you see—is an essential move that teachers and writers both make all the time. Learning to do this well will lift the level of your teaching from this day forward, for always.

continued from previous page

My dad has always been a colorful character. On Christmas Day, he went to move a log in the fireplace and gouged his head on one of the nails from which the Christmas stockings hung. To stop the ferocious bleeding, he held a bag of frozen peas on the top of his bald head. Guests arrived for our Christmas party and he greeted them with the peas draped over his forehead. The guests weren't surprised to see Dad's odd ice-pack because he's always done what he pleases without much concern for fitting into social norms. It isn't important to him to dress "right." He wears his red plaid hunting cap everywhere. When I was a teenager and he wore that hunting cap to my school events, I was embarrassed by him. But now I'm proud of his values and hope my life demonstrates similar values.

"You may think, 'Isn't that a personal narrative?' and it's true that essayists often illustrate our ideas with stories. The entry does contain a story, but it also contains a discussion of how that story relates to my main idea. You'll notice that the entry definitely advances the idea that my dad is a colorful character."

continued on next page

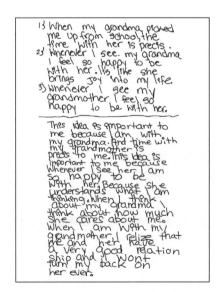

Fig. II-7 Here Sophie selects one idea—her first—and writes about it

Remember that your Mid-Workshop Teaching Point provides you with an opportunity to respond to the specific challenges you see in your classroom. So if it seems that an inordinate number of children are lining up behind you, then you have a forum for reminding them that they can be teachers for each other. If they've forgotten to punctuate now that they are in this new unit, remind them that forgetting to punctuate is as odd as forgetting one's shoes.

I like to tuck management pointers into discussions of what writers often do. You could, for example, say, "I notice that you are talking among yourselves a lot during this unit, more than when you were writing narratives, and my hunch is this is because your entries are getting you excited about ideas. This happens a lot for writers. What I want to suggest, however, is that writers try to write instead of talk; we want to channel our thoughts onto the page rather than into the air."

continued from previous page

"Writers, did you notice how I first took a subject that matters to me, then listed ideas I have about that subject, and then selected one of those ideas to write about? Let's pretend you were gathering entries for this unit and you started by saying, 'What is a subject that matters to me?' Let's say you thought not of a person but of a place, and you wrote 'Our Meeting Area' on your paper. Then you'd need to ask yourself, 'What ideas do I have about our meeting area?' Right now, list several ideas about our meeting area across your fingers. Then take one idea and 'talk long' about it." The children talked to their partners for a moment.

"So writers, remember that writers have a saying: 'When you are done, you've just begun.' After you write one entry, leave a space and write another. To do that, you can use any of these strategies for generating essay entries from our chart," and I added the new strategy to the chart.

Strategies for Generating Essay Entries

- We observe the small stuff of our lives and then try to let what we see and hear spark an idea.
- We record an issue that matters in our lives. Then we list several ideas we have about that issue and develop one at more length. We push ourselves to shift from observing to saying, "and the thought I have about this is..."
- We write in two columns, or in two paragraphs, one section for what we see, hear, and notice and the other for what we think.
- We pick a subject that matters to us, then list ideas about that subject, then select one of those ideas to write about.

SHARE

Generating Even More Essay Entries

Offer students an example of how living like a writer can help generate entries. Let children share their entries with their partners.

"Writers, you've learned a handful of strategies for generating essay entries, and gotten good at shifting between observing and thinking. I know these strategies have helped you collect some interesting material in your notebook. I also hope the writing you've been doing has helped you see that writing can change your life. A writer I know once said, 'Writers notice the things that others pass right by.' I think many of us, in our lives, are so busy running here and there that we don't see what's in front of our noses. Have you ever found yourself at school, hardly able to remember how you got there? Well, writing is one way people stay alert to our own lives. And when someone writes, suddenly parts of life that once seemed mundane become interesting."

"In this entry, notice that Emily is riding the school bus home as a writer, seeing things that she—and many people—never noticed before. Then she pushes herself to name her idea about what she sees."

> When I ride the bus home after school, I notice that things change in different neighborhoods. Like where the school is, the houses look so bad. They are kind of beat up, like crumpled-up paper. And then when the bus goes a few blocks away, the houses have lots of pretty colors, flowers everywhere, and nice yards. Also, by the school there is a lot of trash in the gutters, but in that other neighborhood it looks like somebody sweeps the whole street every day!
>
> Everybody should have nice houses, not just some people. My bus ride home shows me that the world is not very fair.

"The extraordinary thing about Emily is that she not only sees—she also lets what she sees get through to her. Would you give me a thumbs up if you, like Emily, wrote what you saw, and then let what you saw affect you, and wrote your response to what you saw?"

I think of the first sessions in all of these units as a course in living writerly lives and keeping writer's notebooks. As you'll recall, at the start of the year I didn't yet expect children to carry notebooks between home and school. By now, expectations for children to live writerly lives have grown. Later sessions across all the units will combine to form a course on drafting; still later sessions across all the units combine to offer a course on revision and editing.

When I ask children if they've ever found themselves at school, hardly able to remember how they got there, I'm referring to an anecdote Don Graves once shared. He talked once about how many of us sometimes drive to school as if on autopilot. We pull into the parking lot and think, with a start, "How did I get here? Am I dressed?" In my minilesson, I left out the latter question— and didn't feel the need to tell children the source of the anecdote. You can, in a similar way, borrow from every source possible when you teach.

HOMEWORK ***Finding Significance in Ordinary Moments*** In school, you learned how writers gave our attention to a time in the day that most people don't regard as especially provocative—the bus ride home, for example. Tonight, would you take a time in your day that you usually don't think much about, and play the believing game. Say to yourself, "I know for sure that a lot of really interesting ideas occur to me at this time." Say that to yourself even if, frankly, you are not convinced. You might choose to pay attention to moments just after the final bell at the end of school when you go to your locker. You might choose the instant when you walk into your house, into your kitchen perhaps—what happens? What do you think? Notice? What observations can you collect if you pay close attention to that time? What ideas can you gather?

The other evening, a teacher I know shared his writing with me and he'd done just what writers do. He paid attention on his walk home from school, and he recorded what he saw. Then he pushed himself to have a big idea about all that he'd seen. Listen. *[Figs. II-8 and II-9]*

> Observations
>
> Trees with lime green leaves
>
> Trees with lemon yellow leaves
>
> Trees with fire red leaves
>
> People walking to and from
>
> Boys behind the school partaking in drink
>
> Old men talking in their native West Indies accents
>
> People getting haircuts.
>
> The South Bronx is my Home Sweet Home! I love all that it is, and all that it is not. I love the Projects. Yes, I know people talk down the Projects. The Projects for me are opening presents on Christmas morning. They are washing dishes with Grandma when everyone goes home after Thanksgiving dinner. In the Projects, I learned how to ride my first bike. In the Projects, I cried when my training wheels were taken off. In the Projects, this is where I saw all four seasons—winter, spring, summer, and fall. It's where I learned the importance of street smarts, but it's also where I learned the importance of a good education.

You all can learn from this how to shift between observing and having a thought.

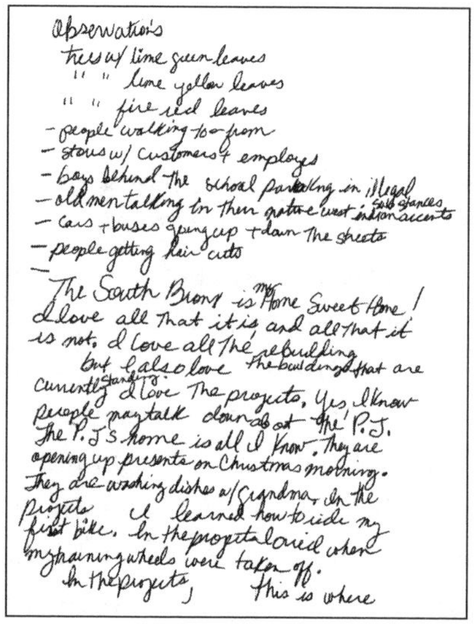
Observations
Trees w/ lime green leaves
" " lime yellow leaves
" " fire red leaves
- people walking to + from
- stores w/ customers + employees
- boys behind the school partaking in illegal ...
- old men talking in their native west indian accents
- cars + buses going up + down the streets
- people getting hair cuts
The South Bronx is my Home Sweet Home! I love all that it is and all that it is not. I love all the rebuilding but I also love the buildings that are currently standing. I love the projects. Yes, I know people may talk down at the P.J. The P.J.'s home is all I know. They are opening up presents on Christmas morning. They are washing dishes w/ Grandma. In the projects I learned how to ride my first bike. In the projects I cried when my training wheels were taken off. In the projects, this is where

Fig. II-8 Dyon's notebook entry

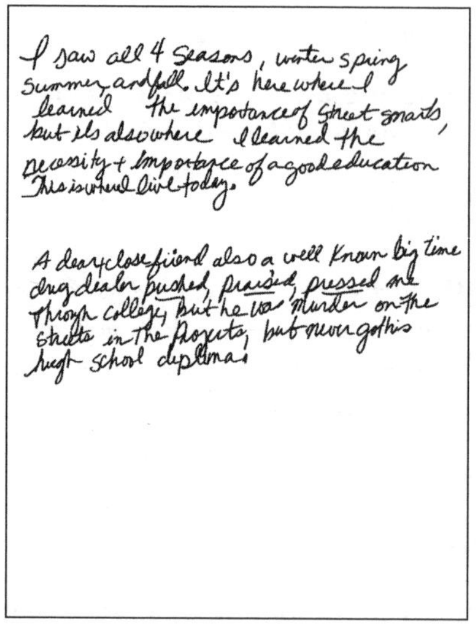
I saw all 4 seasons, winter spring summer and fall. It's here where I learned the importance of street smarts, but its also where I learned the necessity + importance of a good education. This is where I live today.

A dear close friend also a well known big time drug dealer pushed, praised, pressed me through college, but he was murder on the streets in the projects, but never got his high school diploma.

Fig. II-9 Dyon's entry page 2

If your children are looking for unusual things to observe and therefore struggling...
you might teach them that anything can prompt reflection—even a piece of blank paper, as
in this entry, *[Fig. II-10]*

> A paper is a mysterious object. The blank, white coat
> makes it seem to be daring you to write on it. It can
> contain a poem, a story, a document, or a project. It can
> be any one of these, and can't be predicted. A paper
> can be cut, ripped, or crumpled. It can be written on by
> pen, marker, crayon, paint, or a pencil. It can be a
> magical object that can destroy one's hope, or rise one's.
> A paper can be all of those things and more.

If you notice that your students' observation entries tend to be rushed or bland... it
may be helpful to teach them strategies for slowing down an observation so that it is fresh
and detailed. Often, you may find that students name just what they see in this way: "I see
my friend waiting for me. She's standing in front of her door looking at the street." In
essence, they are observing only the "outline" of the scene. You'll want to teach them how
to take the scene in and slow down so they can really capture the details and write the true
words that fit what they see. When a writer does this, an entry can turn into something like:

> "I see my friend waiting for me, her face turned toward the street. I
> don't mean to be late again, so I begin to run. She's wearing her
> light blue down jacket and her white hat is pulled down low. Her
> arms are crossed in front of her chest and her book bag is on the
> ground, which probably means she's cold and has been waiting for a
> little too long . . . "

For the demonstration part of the lesson, you might decide to show two entries that
contrast, such as the observations above. You'll want to read the first one, the surface-level
observation, and respond in a "hmm, so what . . . " sort of way. Then read the second one
aloud followed by a quick accounting of the differences. "Writers," you might say, "did you
notice how in the first entry, the writer just told the very basic stuff? It's like we got a sketch
in our minds. In the second entry, the writer shared more details, so it's like we got a
painting (or a movie) in our minds." You'll want to tell them that in order to write
observations well, writers train themselves to push for the precisely honest words that fit
what they see. For the Active Engagement portion of the lesson, you might cite examples of

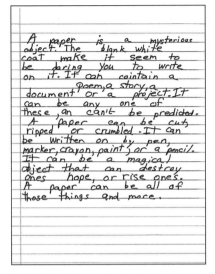

Fig. II-10 Sadie's notebook entry

powerful observations from literature. For example, you could reference *The Lightwell*, by Lawrence Yep. He writes, "the lightwell seems to stretch endlessly upward and downward among the many buildings. At its brightest, it is filled with a kind of tired twilight." After you share the example, you may ask your students to turn to a partner and talk about what the author did to write the observation well. As you listen in to the partner talk, you can gather items for a chart that may be entitled Tricks to Writing Observations.

COLLABORATING WITH COLLEAGUES

The work that you'll ask your children to do in this unit is much more challenging and intriguing than it appears to be on the surface. The best way to appreciate its hidden complexities is to try your hand at it. In even just twenty minutes of writing time, you could use a few of the strategies for generating essay entries that you've invited your students to use. Try it! The added bonus is that you'll have your own entry to use in place of the one about my dad. That entry about my father threads its way through this unit, so I strongly recommend you come up with your own replacement. If this feels a bit scary, stay close to my model at first. Try choosing a person who matters to you and then list some of the ideas you have about that person. Be precisely honest, and you'll find your writing flows from a power source within you. If it's hard for you to generate ideas, try thinking of the person as a character and ask yourself, "So what are his/her character traits?" Be sure you state your idea with crystal clarity—don't equivocate or say too much. Then write an entry in which you elaborate on your claim about this person. You might want to borrow my structure and write a short, angled anecdote that illustrates your point, and then talk briefly about one or two other ways in which the person demonstrates whatever you are trying to say.

Try, also, the strategy of observing a place that matters to you, then writing specifics about it. Write about your mother's kitchen, your front yard, wherever—and as you write, try to capture the details that keep your yard from being just anyone's yard, your mom's kitchen from being anyone's kitchen. Then push yourself to skip a line and start with the phrase, 'The thought I have about this is . . . '

You'll definitely want to use your own writing in an upcoming lesson. To create the text you need for Session IV, put an entry that you wrote in a previous session in front of you. If you haven't yet written one, then select a person or place that matters to you and write one thought about that person or place, extending it with a second or third sentence. Or observe something for even just a few sentences. In any case, put an entry in front of you.

Now ask a colleague or a child to dictate a series of prompts to you, one prompt every three minutes. When that person says the prompt, write down the exact words of that prompt and quickly continue from where the prompt leaves off, writing whatever comes to mind. Try these prompts (or others):

- To add on . . .
- An example of this is . . .
- I'm realizing . . .
- The surprising thing is . . .
- This is important because . . .
- On the other hand . . .

Try, as you do this work, to experience the way in which you can let brand-new thoughts come out of the tip of your pen.

CONTRASTING NARRATIVE AND NON-NARRATIVE STRUCTURES

IN THIS SESSION, YOU WILL ORIENT CHILDREN TO THE GENRE OF ESSAYS BY CONTRASTING ESSAY STRUCTURE WITH THAT OF NARRATIVES. YOU WILL TEACH CHILDREN THAT WRITERS NEED A SENSE OF WHAT THEY ARE AIMING FOR IN ORDER TO COLLECT, ELABORATE ON, AND STRUCTURE THEIR WRITING.

GETTING READY

- List of features of non-narrative writing, written on chart paper
- Your own writing sample that tells the story of a subject and a non-narrative version that discusses ideas about the same subject
- Photocopies of narrative and non-narrative writing examples, one set placed on each desk
- See CD-ROM for resources

Children have a way of cutting to the chase, *of pointing out the elephant in the room that no one wants to admit is there! So when Sophie told me she didn't really 'get' what essays are, I had to face the question. The question is challenging because if you look at the variety of essays published in books, journals, and magazines, you'll see essays come in many types.*

Technically, the term "essay" comes from a Latin root word that means "to wander." Great essayists such as Lewis Thomas, John McPhee, and E.B. White don't write with a single controlling idea and with paragraphs that are tightly linked to that thesis! Yet on College Entrance exams, Advanced Placement exams, and in their coursework, secondary school students are expected to write a school version of the essay and those school essays do require a thesis, elucidated by a series of supporting paragraphs, each beginning with a clear topic sentence related to the thesis.

You will need to come to terms with what you want your children to learn. You may resist teaching the genre of school essays, arguing that it is not an authentic form of writing—a reasonable concern. As the mother of two teenage sons, I feel that as long as secondary schools and standardized assessments require thesis-driven five-paragraph essays, I will argue that upper-elementary-grade children need to be explicitly taught the skills required to write them. It's not fair to withhold teaching when the stakes are high.

Then, too, the writing muscles children develop as they learn to craft thesis-driven essays are valuable. Although I do not write five-paragraph essays, most of the nonfiction texts I do write (speeches, grants, chapters) are structured similarly: I propose an idea; then I develop different parts of the idea.

These, then, are my reasons for teaching Sophie and her classmates to write in a genre that is rarely found in libraries. The next challenge is to explain the genre, and to do so without the benefit of published examples. You'll see, in this session, how I attempt to do this.

MINILESSON

Contrasting Narrative and Non-Narrative Structures

CONNECTION

Establish the reason for today's teaching point: writers need to imagine the kind of text they're writing.

"Writers, yesterday Sophie asked me a really smart question. We were waiting for the buses together, talking about our new unit of study, and she said, 'I'm not totally sure what I am trying to make.' She went on to say, '*Before*, I knew we were writing stories, true stories. But what is an essay?'"

"I wish there was a simple description that I could give to Sophie and to all of you, but the truth is that different people mean different things when they talk about writing essays. And across this year, you will learn about several different ways to write essays. Sophie is so smart to think, 'What kind of thing are we writing?' Writers do need to know what a genre is like in order to write well in that genre."

Contrast the features of narrative and non-narrative writing.

"One thing you need to know for starters is this: Essays are a kind of *non-narrative* writing. You already know a lot about writing *narratives*, or stories. In this unit, we are going to write *non*-narratives. So what does that mean? Well, *non* means 'not.' Nonreturnable purchases mean that you can*not* return the purchases to the store. Nonfat milk means there is *not* fat in the milk. So when I say we will be working on *non*-narrative writing, this means that the writing we do will *not* be the same as the narratives we've been working on."

"Here are some ways to distinguish *non*-narratives from narratives."

- Stories tell what happened first, next, and next. Non-narrative essays don't.

- Stories show a character—in our personal narratives, we are the main character—going through a sequence of events. Non-narratives don't.

- Stories lead the reader through the sequence of events. Non-narratives don't.

COACHING

When I first work with teachers to help them learn to give effective minilessons, I emphasize the architecture of a minilesson, showing the contribution that each component makes to the whole. But after a short while, I think the spotlight needs to shift. Next, I encourage teachers to notice that minilessons are meant to be replicable and memorable. In this minilesson, I open with a tiny, tiny anecdote. I'm trying to win children's attentive interest.

It always helps learners to know the big picture of what we're trying to do before focusing on fitting the small pieces together. It's easier to fit together the pieces of a jigsaw puzzle if we've seen the picture on the box! So it is best to give children a big picture of what they will (and will not) be writing during this unit. This is challenging, however, because the sort of essay I will help them write is a school genre, one that secondary-school students write all the time in literature and history classes, but not a genre that fills the bookshelves of our libraries.

When I list items orally, I try to help listeners grasp that my text is a list. It's also an option to make a quick chart. When listing, I often use the same opening word or phrase for each new item in the list. Especially if the class contains many English Language Learners I'm apt to touch first one and then the next finger while naming items in the list.

I pointed to the first characteristic on the chart and said, "Instead of being organized by time (this happened, then this happened, then finally this happened), non-narratives are organized by ideas. They might go, "I think this one thing, I also think this other thing, and furthermore, I think this third thing." Or, they might go, "This is true because of A, because of B, and, most of all, because of C.""

I pointed to the second characteristic on the chart and said, "Instead of being held together by a character who travels through the whole story, non-narratives are held together by an idea that is developed (or an argument that is advanced) across the whole text."

I pointed to the third characteristic on the chart and said, "Instead of being written so the reader can participate in the event, non-narratives are written so the reader can think about the topic."

"What do non-narratives, essays, contain?" I asked. Then I revealed a chart.

Characteristics of Non-Narratives (and of Essays)

- Non-narratives are organized by ideas. (They might go, "I think this one thing, I also think this other thing, and, furthermore, I think this third thing.")
- Non-narratives are held together by an idea that is developed (or an argument that is advanced) across the whole text.
- Non-narratives are written so the reader can think about the topic.

Name the teaching point. In this case, tell children that writers can usually choose whether to structure a text as a narrative (a story) or a non-narrative (an essay).

"Today and throughout this unit, I will teach you that as a writer you can often choose to write in either genre. Whenever you are writing, it is helpful to have a little voice in the back of your head that asks, 'Wait, am I writing a narrative (which means a story) or am I writing a non-narrative (an essay)?' This is an important question to ask because these two major kinds of writing are usually organized and written in different ways. They are also judged by different criteria."

There are many visual clues I can give to help children grasp what I'm saying. For example, when I talk about the sequence of a narrative, my hands progress along a horizontal line. When I talk about the logical hierarchy in an expository text, my hands create an outline in the air.

Notice that I first listed three characteristics of narratives, and then said non-narratives do not have those three characteristics. Then I returned to the list and said non-narratives do have three alternative characteristics. The two lists follow the same sequence. That is, the first item in both lists addresses contrasting ways to structure texts, and the next item in the lists deals with contrasting ways to unify the text. It is worth noticing that the patterned way in which this minilesson is written illustrates a feature of non-narrative texts! Writers of expository texts often think about the design, shape, and balance of a discussion.

Life is not really this definitive. Many texts have sections that are narratives and sections that are organized in a more expository fashion. Eventually we'll show children that within a single piece they can shift between these two ways to organize texts. The last unit of the year invites children to draw from and integrate both narrative and expository structures. And even this unit will show children that narratives are often embedded into essays.

TEACHING

Demonstrate how you might write about one topic in either a narrative or a non-narrative fashion.

"So watch me as I decide whether I am writing a narrative or a non-narrative piece. Let's see . . . I think I want to write about my visit to the park."

"Hmm . . . is this going to be a narrative or a non-narrative?" I asked, pausing for an extra long time as if mulling over the right answer to the question. Then, leaning in to the group as if to tell them a secret, I said, "Writers, you need to realize that I could write about this topic (or almost any topic) and make my writing be either a narrative or a non-narrative! For example, I could write about my trip to the park yesterday and tell the story of what happened first, next, and next. Or I could write about the same visit as a non-narrative and teach people my ideas about the park."

"Watch how I write in the air about this topic first as a *narrative*. I want to remember what happened and make a movie in my mind." I said, as if writing:

> It was windy yesterday when I got off the subway. First I headed to the park. I held my coat around me and still the wind was cold. When I got to the park, I passed people walking quickly with their coats drawn around them. Soon after that, I got to the dog park. Only one guy was there with his dog. I just stayed a little bit and then I hurried to the pond. No one was there so I left.

"Now watch while I write about this in a *non*-narrative way, and see if you can list across your fingers ways that this writing is different."

"Okay, let me look over the notes I took about how to get an essay started, and think, 'What idea do I have about this?' Oh! I know," I said, as if just realizing how to go about it. I began voicing:

> When I visited the park yesterday, I saw signs of winter everywhere:

To show I was about to articulate my first subordinate thought, I touched one finger.

> People walked differently from how they walked just a few weeks ago. We pulled our coats around us closely, leaned into the wind, and walked with our heads down.

I use the teaching method of demonstration to act out the process and the mind work I go through to write as a narrative; then I provide a contrasting demonstration showing the process and mind work involved in writing an essay. Notice that I'm not displaying two finished texts. I'm instead composing in front of the children. My tone reveals that I'm mulling things over. My tone would be very different if I were simply holding up examples to illustrate that I wrote about one subject in two different ways.

You can decide whether to actually write the entry with a marker on chart paper, or to scrawl it on your clipboard, voicing aloud as you proceed. The latter allows you to move much faster because you can write in shorthand, or not write at all. If you decide on the chart paper alternative, abbreviate the text! Another choice is to write in the air, dictating what you "write" as you move your hand across the chart paper, leaving no visual trace.

When I ask children to list something across their fingers, I'm giving them a graphic organizer and practice at doing something that is fundamental to essay writing: organizing information.

Notice that the text I create begins by advancing a main idea, and then this idea is developed in two parallel sections. Each of those two sections begins with a big idea and then that idea is supported. Obviously essays often are not this symmetrical, but for now I'm putting forth a very clear model. I don't, however, point these features out to children just yet. I'm trying to give them the felt-sense for how narratives and essays contrast with each other.

I raised a second finger to address a second subordinate thought.

> Places that used to be full were empty now. There was only one man and his dog at the dog park. Just two weeks ago, dozens of dogs scampered there. And there were no longer kids lining the edge of the pond.

Because I'm trying to highlight the impact of the decision to write this as a narrative or a non-narrative piece, the only thing that distinguishes the two versions is that one conveys the information through a narrative, the other, through an essay. I try to keep the other variables constant, so the two pieces are otherwise the same.

Debrief. Remind children that writers can decide on the structure with which they will write.

"So you see, as writers you need to decide whether you are going to end up writing a story (a narrative) or an essay (a non-narrative). And if you are writing a non-narrative, your piece will be organized not by a chronological sequence but instead by different reasons or different examples or different categories."

ACTIVE ENGAGEMENT
Set children up to write in the air about a class event, first as a narrative then as a non-narrative.

"You should realize by now that you could write about one topic—maybe about arriving at school this morning—in a *narrative way*. You could retell what happened with phrases like *First we . . . and then we . . .* Try telling a quick narrative to your partner about this morning." The room erupted into talk.

"Can I stop you? Now, what I want you to realize is that you could also write about arriving this morning in a *non-narrative* way. To do this, you need to have an idea you want to convey. So before you can write a non-narrative, an essay, in the air, you need to ask yourself, 'What's my idea about this morning?' Squeeze your mind and see if you can come up with an idea, an opinion, about this morning." I gave children a minute to do so, and then said, "If any of you are having a hard time coming up with something, try thinking to yourself, 'What did I notice or observe this morning?'" I left a little space for silence. "Then, in your mind, say something like, 'The idea I have about this is . . .'."

"Give me a thumbs up if you have an idea about this morning," I said. "Good. If you don't have an idea yet, try this one: 'Mornings in school are chaotic.'"

"Okay, now, because you are writing a non-narrative (or an essay) piece, you will need to teach us about your main idea, and then you'll need to share reasons for it, or make points about it. In your mind, repeat your idea about this morning and then list across your

I ask children to try what I've just demonstrated, using a topic I give them because I hope this will serve as a quick practice exercise. Later, once they disperse, they'll apply what they've learned to their own topics.

Notice that although there is one main Teaching point in a minilesson, this doesn't stop us from tucking lots of subordinate tips into our teaching. Not every student will catch and hold every teaching point, but those who are ready will. This is one way to differentiate our instruction, providing more instruction for students who are ready for it.

I want everyone to have a chance to get aboard this work, so I'll resort to giving a thesis if necessary. Of course, in a few minutes children will disperse to work on their own writing, and they'll find their own topics and ideas about those topics.

fingers a few points you could make about your main idea. You might come up with your points by using the word because." They did this quietly in their minds. "Now partner 1, teach partner 2 your main idea about this morning, making specific points."

Earlier children told stories across their fingers; now they do corresponding work with essays. They again list (and elaborate upon) points by talking across their fingers. The hand is a perfect graphic organizer! Some children will not totally and immediately grasp what you want them to do, but others will, and soon they'll learn from each other.

LINK
Rename the teaching point. Set children up to spend some time reading exemplar texts, dividing them into narratives and non-narratives. Then ask children to study the exemplar non-narrative texts.

"So today, you are going to continue to use all those strategies that we've imagined for growing ideas. And when you pick up your pen to write about a topic—like 'My cousin came over last weekend'—remember, you already know that you can write about that topic as a narrative, telling what happened first and then next. Now you also know you can try writing about it instead as a non-narrative, in ways that state (or claim) an idea and then support that idea."

"Before you get started writing today, I've left a very small stack of narratives and non-narratives in a basket on each of your desks. Would you take some time to read through these, making two piles so that you separate the narratives and non-narratives, the stories and the essays? Then, with your partner, find an essay you like. Talk about what the writer has done that you admire."

You'll want to share a variety of texts with your children, choosing texts which are somewhat within your children's reach. If you'd like a published text, I recommend Judy Blume's The Pain and the Great One, *which rather closely resembles an essay. Depending on your children's writing abilities and interests, you might include a sample essay from the ACT writing test (www.act.org). Remember to include narratives as well as essays so children have a chance to differentiate.*

WRITING AND CONFERRING

Supporting the Minilesson

You will probably want to use some of your conferring time to bring children together in informal small groups to talk about what they notice in the essays you've given them to read. Help children distinguish narratives from non-narratives, and help them see the overall structure in the essays they're studying. You will have chosen essays that follow a very obvious, heavy-handed organizational pattern, so children should be able to spot the fact that near the start of each piece, the writer states his or her big idea (the thesis). Then in subsequent paragraphs, the writer develops this thesis with examples and discussion. Point out that each paragraph addresses one subtopic, starting with an overarching sentence that lays out a main idea.

It is not crucial that children notice all the fine features of the essay genre. They will have plenty of time later in this unit to notice transitional phrases words, to study the job that the final paragraph does in the essay, or to see the variety of evidence that authors use to support their claims. For now, you are simply trying to give kids a general sense of what it is they will be making, while at the same time reminding them that writers take the time to read the sort of thing they aim to write.

> MID-WORKSHOP TEACHING POINT **Studying Essay Structures** "Writers, you all are making incredible discoveries about the essays you are reading. Some of you noticed that essays have sections or parts. Give me a thumbs up if you noticed that essays are often organized into categories, or sections, of information. You should be able to box out the sections, the categories in a text, and write a subheading for each section or each category. Later today, see if you can do that. You can write on the texts I've given you."
>
> "Others of you noticed that often there is a sentence or two toward the start of an essay that lays out the main premise, the main idea, of the essay. There are also main-idea sentences (some people call them topic sentences) at the beginning of many paragraphs. See if you can find the sentences that lay out big ideas in your paragraphs and underline those sentences."
>
> *continued on next page*

Meanwhile, you'll also want to remind writers that they have many choices for how they'll spend their writing time today. Soon you will herd all children through a very set sequence of work, so for now, it is important to emphasize that writers have options. In conferences, encourage children to realize that they are expected to make wise choices. Do they want to write entries in which they observe and then push themselves to think? And if so, do they want to try a double-entry format or to write in paragraphs, shifting at some point between observing and reflecting? On the other hand, perhaps a child wants to take a subject and list ideas related to that subject, then develop one of those ideas. Many writers will spend most of today reading and talking about the sample essays you've distributed, and that, too, is an option.

Teach your writers to think, "What can I do with my time that will help me to write thoughtful, original, significant entries?" Help each child feel that he or she is "the boss" of his or her own writing. Remind children that once they decide on a strategy, they need to make themselves a planning box, as they did in the previous unit, (Raising the Quality of Narrative Writing) in which they recorded the strategy they planned to use.

When a child decides to follow a particular strategy—say, observing and then having a thought—be sure the writer knows that the strategy is not a goal. It's only a means to a goal—and the goal is to write in ways which are provocative, insightful, original, and significant.

continued from previous page

"Let's look together at this one brief essay," [Figs. III-1, III-2, and III-3] I said, and used an overhead to enlarge one of the essays. "I'm going to read it aloud; will you and your partner see if you can help me figure out how to box and label the main chunks, the main categories, of this essay? How could we name each major chunk?" They did this, and two children offered suggestions. "Now will you and your partner see if there is a big-idea sentence that sets up the entire essay and others that set up each separate paragraph?" They did this.

"So writers, I'm hoping that you are beginning to sense the sort of thing that we are making, and that having a sense for this will help you. I know when I put together a jigsaw puzzle, it helps me if I've seen the picture on the cover—and always, when you write in a form or genre that's new to you, it's helpful to spend a bit of time reading pieces that resemble what you want to write."

EFFECTS OF PARENTS FIGHTING
Parents fighting effects kids very much. Two people a kid loves yelling at each other really penetrates a kids mind. It makes kids yell for things, it makes them choose sides between their parents, the most terrible thing abut parents fighting is that it makes the kid start not trusting people.

Parents fighting makes kids yell for things instead of asking nicely. One time my parents fought and I watched. So when I went to school I wanted the glue so I yelled for it because that's how my parents get things from each other. Another time my parents had a fight and I watched and then I went to my cousins house and yelled at them for the controller because it was my turn to play Nintendo. Another time my parents had a fight and I watched and then I was hungry and I yelled at Mom to make

dinner faster. All this was encouraged by my parents fighting.

Parents fighting also makes kids choose sides between their parents. One time my parents were fighting and my Mom said something totally inappropriate and snap I'm on my Dads side. Another time my Dad said something totally inappropriate and snap I'm on my Moms side.

Another time my parents were fighting and my Dad said something totally inappropriate and snap I'm on my Moms side, but then my Mom said something just as bad back so snap . . . I couldn't decide both sides were pushing me and I felt like I was falling apart and that was what it was like during a lot of their fights.

The worst part about parents fighting is that it makes kids not trust people. One time my Mom couldn't trust Dad to get a

carton of milk so when I went to school I couldn't trust my friend to watch my lunch. Another time my Dad couldn't trust my Mom to give him his mail so when I went to my friends house I couldn't trust my friend to look at my cards because I thought he'd steal one. Another time my parents couldn't trust each other to watch me and my sisters so I couldn't trust Dad to stay with me at the Yankee game.

Parents fighting is an ugly thing. It really does penetrate a kid. I know what it's like to choose sides and yell for things and not trust people. It doesn't exactly feel good. Imagine having a war going on insides your head. Well that's what it's like when parents fight.

Fig. III-1 Andy's essay, page 1

Fig. III-2 Andy's essay, page 2

Fig. III-3 Andy's essay, page 3

SHARE

Clarifying "Writing About Ideas"

Share a conversation you had with a student that could be helpful to the whole class. In this case, clarify the meaning of "writing about ideas."

"Writers, I want to tell you about a conversation I had today with Neha. I complimented her on the ideas that she had come up with and asked if she could tell me more about her ideas. She looked at me with an odd expression and said, 'I am confused. I don't understand what you mean when you say you want to hear more about my *ideas*. What *are* my ideas about drama?' Neha and I realized that she wasn't sure which part of what she wrote constituted an idea, and we thought some of you might be unsure, too."

"You have ideas every day. You have ideas about people, school, your family, the texts you read. You have ideas about what your mom said last night, about school lunches, about our president. An idea has two things: a subject and something you think about the subject; a subject and a point you want to make about it."

"But an idea is not quite the same as a fact. It's not usually something you just plain know, like 'My idea is that our benches are made of wood,' because it would be hard to keep thinking about that fact and talking about it in interesting ways. I suppose you could, but it would be difficult. On the other hand, your *thoughts* about our benches are your ideas. If you said that benches help us keep things fair in our discussions, that is an idea that you could say lots and lots about."

"If you said, 'Benches are good things to have,' that would be an idea, but it would not be a focused or specific idea. If, on the other hand, you said, 'Sitting on benches (that'd be your subject) helps kids listen to each other (that would be your point),' then you'd be voicing a specific idea—and we'd all want to hear your reasons for believing this!"

"So listen to just the start of Neha's writing, and I'm sure you'll agree with me that she has lots of ideas."

> Taking drama is hard work.

"That's an idea."

> We usually have little contests in which we have to say certain
> expressions while the rest of the class can laugh at you. Doing drama
> is worth it because it is fun to pretend you are someone else.

"That's an idea, and a specific one. I'm dying to hear her reasons, aren't you?"

Every discipline has its own lingo, and this is as true for those of us who teach writing as it is for a blacksmith, a botanist, or a sculptor. If children are going to become active agents of their own writing development, we need to be able to discern their sources of confusion and to teach as explicitly as possible. When Neha suggested she wasn't clear what I meant when I asked her to write her ideas, I realized she was not alone. Therefore, I used a share session as a teaching opportunity.

Clearly, you will choose a different teaching point if your students are having no problem generating ideas. You could use this time instead to share some of the ideas children have written in their notebooks. This will prime the pump for more ideas to pour forth, just as sharing stories inevitably leads to more stories. Alternatively, you could use any of the extensions as a way to angle this share session.

Ask partners to talk with each other about their writing so far, pointing out each other's ideas or noting starting points for ideas.

"First of all, let's read each other's entries and search for ideas. Then secondly, let's search for ideas that leap off the page, ideas that seem insightful and noteworthy. Put a little check in the margin beside any passage which contains ideas that make you, as the reader, go 'Wow,' or 'Hmm!' and mark places where there is an idea that you could turn into an essay. You can also mark places that are just crying out loud to become longer pieces—bits of writing where you are curious about where the thinking might lead. Okay, go ahead."

I listened as Olivia shared this entry with Rebecca, who wanted to give a stream of check marks alongside the margin of the entire entry. *[Fig. III-4]*

> When I am cranky sometimes I act up and say words I don't mean to say. For example, I started getting cranky one night in Montana to wear a certain pjs, and gave my mom a hard time without even caring.
>
> That made me realize to not give my mom a hard time because she works hard to make me happy, and I didn't care about that. So that shows me it's not okay to only think about yourself.
>
> This event also reminds me moms give good advice and I rejected that and only cared for myself. I really just forgot about my mom as a piece of dust and went on with my life. Then later on I feel like wow, I just rejected one of the most important people in my life.

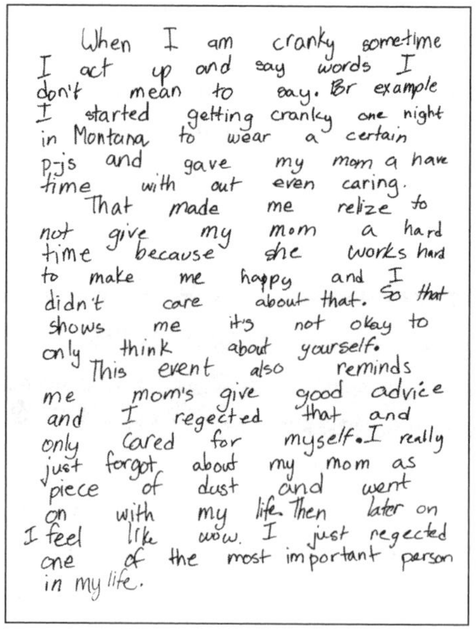
When I am cranky sometime I act up and say words I don't mean to say. Br example I started getting cranky one night in Montana to wear a certain p-js and gave my mom a have time with out even caring.
That made me relize to not give my mom a hard time because she works hard to make me happy and I didn't care about that. So that shows me it's not okay to only think about yourself.
This event also reminds me mom's give good advice and I regected that and only cared for myself. I really just forgot about my mom as piece of dust and went on with my life. Then later on I feel like wow. I just regected one of the most important person in my life.

Fig. III-4 Olivia's entry

HOMEWORK ***Collecting Essay Talk from Life*** Recently, I spoke on the phone with my dad and he told me how much he likes having grown-up children. His reasons were that we can take care of ourselves, we become more like friends, and as we get older he sees more and more of himself in us. As I listened, it seemed like he was writing an essay over the phone, and I could almost picture how his essay could go. I wrote down his idea and his reasons.

> I like having grown-up children.
> - because they can take care of themselves
> - because they become more like friends
> - because I see myself in them as they grow into themselves

You will find that once you get into this unit, you see the world through the lens of essays, finding examples everywhere. Make sure you collect at least some of these examples to share with your students!

Writers, the reason that I shared this story with you this story is that tonight I want you to record a few conversations you overhear in your family into your notebook. Record a conversation in which one person claims a big idea and then supports that idea with reasons. If no one talks like this naturally, then you'll need to prompt people to talk in this way. If you know your father worries about the president's decision, ask him what his reasons are. Have your pen ready! If your friend is angry that her visiting grandmother is sleeping in your friend's bedroom, ask her why this is so inconvenient. Catch what she says in the pages of your notebook. Collect several overheard essays—and be sure that in one of those entries you are transcribing your own talking!

TAILORING YOUR TEACHING

If you'd like to help children glean a big picture of how essays tend to go . . . you may decide to box out sections of one essay, labeling each box and then asking children to do similar work with an unmarked essay. You could, in the first essay, identify these component parts:

- a catchy lead
- a thesis statement that overviews the main idea of the essay
- the first of several body paragraphs
- the topic sentence of this paragraph.
- supporting information—a story angled to support the topic sentence
- a discussion of the story that is cited for evidence
- other evidence supporting the topic sentence
- a second body paragraph
- a second topic sentence
- evidence supporting the second topic sentence
- a conclusion that repeats the thesis and adds a new spin

If children would benefit from seeing more examples of essays and parts of essays . . . you may want to tell children that this form is also very prevalent in their content area textbooks and in some nonfiction books. You might, as an example, show them an excerpt such as this one from Vogel and Goldman's *The Great Yellowstone Fire* (1990).

Yellowstone's patchwork of habitats provides homes for many kinds of animals. Near steaming geysers and hot springs, bison graze in upper meadows. Moose and deer browse on tender shoots of cottonwood and willow. On steep mountainsides, golden eagles build nests on rocky ledges, and bighorn sheep traverse the jagged rocks. The rivers and lakes of the park provide food and resting sites for trumpeter swans, white pelicans, and other water birds. (p.6)

You could steer the children to their social studies or science textbooks to see if they can spot examples of texts which are constructed similarly. Chances are not good that you'll see the entire structure of an academic essay in these texts, but you'll see paragraphs like the one I cited.

If children could benefit from further orientation to the genre . . . you could teach them how to assess essays.

Anne Ruggles Gene and Kelly Sassi's book, *Writing on Demand,* is designed for older students—it's touted as helpful for SAT, ACT, AP, and State Assessment Exams—but the rubric they suggest using for evaluating essays is certainly within reach for fifth graders. You may show children how you to use a rubric to assess an essay, using one of the essays we provided.

If you notice that in their attempts to clearly express ideas your students tend to write in a repetitive, circuitous manner . . . you will need to remind your students in a minilesson, mid-workshop teaching point, or a share session that writers reread their writing for lots of reasons. One of the reasons is that they want to make sure it's crystal clear. You might say something like, "Writers, you know what I've noticed? So many of you have really compelling ideas you're trying to share in your writing, which is great! Sometimes, though, as you try to really help the reader understand the point you're trying to make, you repeat things often. People think that when you repeat things, you make your point stronger. But think about it. If your babysitter tells you fifty times to clean your room before your parents come home, does that make you do it faster? No, I bet it kind of drives you a little crazy and you begin to tune it out. Well the same thing can happen to readers. If a writer repeats something over and over and over, the writer might tune it out or else go crazy!"

"One of the things I've learned from essayists is that they make their points as clearly and as briefly as possible. In other words, they try not to repeat things. When you reread your piece, look for places where you're saying the same thing over and over again, and cross out the repetitive parts. You don't need to say the same thing over and over again!"

If you'd like to use a sample text to illustrate this point but don't want to use a student's writing as a troubled example, you can create your own repetitive text. Here's an example of one.

> Last night when we watched the news the weatherman warned that there would be a huge snowstorm coming over the weekend. Everyone in my family started to complain about it except for the kids. I don't understand why grown-ups complain about it. They didn't have any good to say, just complaining and whining. They complained, but the kids were like, "Yeah! Snow!" My grandma was crabby when she heard about the snowstorm and my dad was swearing about it and my mom was annoyed and like, "They better not call off school!" I couldn't believe that they were complaining so much. I said, "I think it's good news!" I think grown ups should just relax a little and not complain about snowstorms because snowstorms can be good for us.

For an Active Engagement portion of a minilesson, you could ask children to work with their partners to revise this example.

ASSESSMENT

It is always a special treat to collect children's work after the first few days of a new unit of study. When you look over what children have done, you may see that a few of them haven't yet ventured out from the haven of narrative writing. It probably took your kids a while to grasp what it meant to write narratives, so it's not surprising that some will now be reluctant to loosen their hold on that structure! Alternatively, you will find some children who've put aside the confines and structures of narrative writing but who now seem to be writing in an utterly unstructured fashion. Their writing may seem to have gone haywire. Their entries may be stream-of-consciousness, repetitive, general, chaotic, or all of these! For example, look at what Rie wrote. *[Figs. III-5, III-6, and III-7]*

Practice finding something to celebrate, even in the writing that doesn't at first impress you. When children are new at something, it may not be immediately obvious what you want to celebrate, so look closely. In conferences, mid-workshop teaching points, and shares, you need to be able to name what one child has done that you hope they repeat and others emulate. I notice that Rie writes with honesty. She risks putting herself on the page. She also cuts to the quick. Her entries are brief, but each one says something important. And although Rie may not realize it, there is a message that unites her entries. In a sense, this is already shaped as an essay, with one idea being advanced across the pages and with a collage of support materials assembled!

Practice, also, reading your children's writing as if you are seeing it from an airplane, looking down at the whole text. Notice how the text is structured in the same way you might study a landscape from the air—you can see its divisions into fields, roads, and cemeteries. What main parts does a child's entry contain? How long are those main parts? How does the child seem to connect one part with another?

Very often, when I look at children's entries, it will seem as if a sentence about an overarching topic contains a single word that then triggers a

discussion of that word. The writer may, for example, begin by writing about basketball, which leads him to mention his sneakers, and soon he has followed that trajectory and written about shoe stores (something utterly unrelated to the initial topic of basketball). I notice that children often use this train-of-thought system when they first write non-narratives. They don't have an overarching idea that acts as a big tent over the whole text, pulling everything together. Instead, they have one idea at the start of the entry and another idea (often only tangentially related to the first) later.

Fig. III-5 Rie

Fig. III-6 Rie's second entry

Fig. III-7 Rie's third entry

Sometimes a single paragraph, as in Figure III-8, can contain many different, only loosely related ideas.

> This photo reminds me of how my mom would carry a camera everywhere we went and would at any time save that moment forever. But now I hate having pictures taken because I always have to look nice and pose. I think, "My mom is going to frame it and I want to remember a perfect moment." But I love to see my face on a photo and many years later wonder about that moment when you posed, smiled, and said cheese. I think a picture tells a lot about someone. But it doesn't show the "truth" about yourself.

This photo reminds me of how my mom would carry a camera every-where we went and would at any time save that moment for-ever. But now I hate having pictures taken because I always have to look nice and pose. I think my mom going to frame it and I want to remember a perfect moment. But I love to see my face on a photo and many years later wonder about that moment when you posed, smiled, and sold cheese. I think that a picture tells a lot about someone.

Fig. III-8 This single paragraph contains many ideas

At first glance, I noticed that this one entry contained lots of loosely related ideas. But when I took a wider view and looked down on the terrain of this piece, I could see how it could turn into an essay. I could map it like this:

The photo shows my mom carried camera everywhere to capture moments (no example)

I both like and don't like my mom's inclination to take photos

Pros	Cons
• You can keep photo forever	• I worry about posing to make a perfect moment
• I love to see myself in an old photo and ask questions	• It doesn't show the truth about yourself
• I think photos tell about someone	

I think it is very helpful if we, as teachers, can look at some of the entries children write and see nascent expository structure hiding within their texts. How helpful it is when we can see what students are almost doing, instead of seeing only what they can't yet do.

USING CONVERSATIONAL PROMPTS TO SPUR ELABORATION

IN THIS SESSION, YOU'LL TEACH CHILDREN THAT THEY NEED TO STAY WITH THEIR ESSAY TOPICS FOR LONGER STRETCHES OF TIME BY TALKING ABOUT THEIR IDEAS.

GETTING READY

- Transcript of an earlier book talk in which students used prompts to push their thinking, on chart paper
- Idea to build on using prompts
- Pushing Our Thinking list of prompts, written on chart paper
- Idea the class can build on using prompts
- Examples of student entries where thinking is extended, either with prompts or another way
- See CD-ROM for resources

When you invite children to write essays, you are inviting them to have, develop, and share their own ideas. You'll find that many students begin by writing (and perhaps thinking) in what the great writing researcher, Mina Shaughnessey, referred to as "sentences of thought." Your goal will be to push children to write, instead, in passages of thought.

It's easiest to teach children to elaborate on their ideas in writing if they've already done this in conversations. This session depends on your first helping children not only to have ideas about books, but also to grow those ideas through talking about them. If you haven't done so already, read aloud a text and when you pause, ask children to turn and share their ideas about the text with a partner. After a few minutes, ask, "Could someone get us started in a conversation about what we just read?"

Once one child has said something provocative and central to the text, repeat that idea as if it is fascinating to you; let the class see you mulling over the idea. Then say to the group, "Let's all talk and think more about Raffi's idea." You might say, "Would you look back at the text and talk with your partner about ways you agree with what Raffi said and want to add to it, or ways you disagree with his idea and want to talk back to it?" Then convene the class and help them work together for ten minutes to add on and talk back to that one idea. At first, you'll need to provide the conversational prompts. "Raffi said . . . who'd like to add on to that idea? Do the rest of you agree or disagree? Tell Raffi. Tell him why you agree. Give him examples."

"So Marco agrees because . . . Let's look at that part of the text, and think whether the rest of you want to add on, or whether we see another example of this, or whether you see this differently." Children can very quickly learn that once an idea is "on the floor," they need to elaborate upon it and talk back to it. And once children can do this sort of accountable talk in their whole-class conversations, they'll be ready for this session.

Minilesson

Using Conversational Prompts to Spur Elaboration

Connection

Celebrate that children are writing provocative ideas and point out that they could be saying even more.

"Writers, I brought your notebooks home last night. I made myself a cup of tea, wrapped myself in a blanket, and put the pile of notebooks beside me. You know what happened? I would read a few sentences in one of your notebooks, and then your writing would get me thinking. I'd look further on the page to learn what *you* thought next about the topic, and then I'd find that you had jumped onto a whole new topic! That happened over and over with so many notebooks. I wanted to phone you guys. I wanted to say, 'If this is true, then …?' or 'What's an example of this?'"

Name the teaching point. In this case, tell children that essayists talk back to our own ideas.

"I think we've turned a corner in this unit of study. You have gotten really great at coming up with entries that spark all kinds of thoughts. Today I want to teach you that *you need to hold on to those thoughts for longer stretches of time*—right on the page. Specifically, I want to teach you that after you've written a provocative idea, stay with it. Our ideas can get bigger when we talk back to them, just like I talked back to your ideas when I read them at home last night. When we write, we have a discussion with ourselves about our own ideas."

Teaching

Tell children that the phrases they use to grow ideas during whole-class book talks can also be used to grow ideas in their entries. Use a transcript of a book talk as evidence.

"You already know how to grow ideas by talking back to them, because you've been doing this a lot during our book talks. This is a transcript of a book talk you had earlier this year about *Because of Winn-Dixie*." I projected a typed transcript onto the wall using an overhead projector. "Notice how you used a bunch of phrases to talk back to—to grow—Rashid's idea, his claim."

COACHING

When children are learning to write expository texts, they need to learn elaboration. This was an important quality of good expository writing even before The New York Times reported that Les Perelman, director of writing at MIT, found a stunning correlation between longer SAT essays and higher scores. "I have never found a quantifiable predictor in twenty-five years of grading that was anywhere near as strong as this one," he said (The New York Times, 2005).

I'm hoping children will understand the need for elaboration if I situate this within the context of an interested reader who's dying to get into a grand conversation over their ideas.

When I say, "I think we've turned a corner in this unit," I mean that quite literally. When I plan units of study, I think of bends in the road. Usually children will work at one kind of thing for a few sessions; then I'll try to raise the level of their work or redirect the course of their journey—hence the image of turning a corner.

It is crucial to teach children to talk back to each other's ideas. The single most common limitation in children's writing is that ideas are underdeveloped. By teaching children to talk back to each other's ideas, you also teach them to talk back to (and extend) their own ideas.

As I read each line of the transcript aloud, I underlined the phrases that children had used that could help them in writing essays.

Rashid: I think Opal is lonely <u>because</u> she's new in the town, so she hasn't yet made many friends. That's why she wants Winn–Dixie, the dog.

Jason: <u>To add on</u> I think she is lonely also <u>because</u> her father never talks to her. He is too busy being a preacher.

Joline: <u>For example,</u> the book says he is too busy with suffering souls to go to the grocery store, so she goes alone. <u>This is important because</u> she doesn't have a mother either, so she feels like an orphan.

Rashid: <u>This gives me the idea</u> that the reason Opal talks so much to the dog is that she doesn't have friends and she can't talk with her father. <u>This connects with</u> how I sometimes tell my cat things I don't tell anyone else.

Leo: <u>The thing that surprises me</u> is that this stray dog has the power to change Opal.

Roy: <u>I am getting an idea that</u> the book might be all about how a dog changes a person and that is why it is called *Because of Winn-Dixie*.

"Did you notice the phrases we used in this book talk helped us say more and grow our ideas?"

Demonstrate that conversational prompts help a person grow ideas.

"Writers, you and I can use these same phrases to push ourselves to say more when we write essays. I'll read you a very short entry that I wrote."

> Lots of teachers ask kids to line up in two lines, one for boys and one for girls.

"Rebecca, would you choose from the list of prompts," I said, signaling to a list I had prepared on chart paper. "Coach me by saying a prompt you want me to use, and I'll use that prompt to think more about my claim. I won't actually write my further thoughts; instead I'll say them aloud." I began by repeating the entry.

Rebecca interjected, "In addition ..." I repeated my claim and the prompt, paused in thought, and then completed that sentence.

> Lots of teachers ask kids to line up in two lines, one for boys and one for girls. In addition, boys and girls sometimes only play with each other on the playground.

Remember that our goals always extend beyond the reading and writing workshop. It is important to teach writing in part because writing is a powerful tool for thought. This session goes a long way towards helping children use writing as a tool for growing ideas on the page. We're explicitly teaching children to say more and think more, to extend their first thoughts, and to know what it is to see new ideas emerge from the tips of their pens. This is important!

When children begin to bring these phrases into their writing, you'll notice a child may write a phrase such as "This makes me realize . . . " without being aware of the meaning in that phrase. If you see a writer write that phrase, point to the words and say, "Oh! This tells me you are having a brand-new idea right now. I can't wait to see it!" If the writer writes, "This is important because . . . " exclaim, "I can't wait to see what you figure the real significance of this is! I can't wait to see your decision." In this fashion, you can induct children into a culture that values words, and you can teach children what these hard-to-pin-down words mean.

As I said earlier, this minilesson presumes that you've taught your children to build on and develop each other's ideas within book talks. I describe this instruction in The Art of Teaching Reading.

You'll recall that earlier I taught children to use prompts to turn the corner from simply observing to having a thought about what they observed: "The idea I have about this is . . . ". In this minilesson, you use a wider array of prompts to promote thoughtfulness.

Then Rebecca said, "For example . . ." Reiterating her prompt, I smiled in thanks and said:

> For example, yesterday, I saw a large group of boys playing kickball outside during recess, and a large group of girls playing on the swings.

Rebecca inserted, "This is important because . . ." I again repeated her prompt and said:

> This is important because I know both boys and girls like to play kickball and play on the swings, so I don't understand why they wouldn't be playing together most of the time.

In a similar fashion I proceeded to add:

> "The thing that surprises me is that boys and girls play together so much in this classroom, and then interactions change when kids leave the classroom. I now realize that the forces that make boys and girls divide are stronger than anything I've so far built in this classroom, and I need to try harder."

As I do this, I try to demonstrate that a writer can use one of these prompts even without having a clue what she'll say next. We write (or say) a thought and then write (or say) one of these conversational prompts, such as "This is important because . . ." As we articulate those words, our mind leaps ahead, thinking, "Why is it important?" In this fashion, then, I'm hoping to demonstrate that writing can be a tool to grow brand-new thoughts. Children already know that we write to record well-fashioned ideas that we've decided to present to the world; now I'm helping them learn that we also write to muse, speculate, meander—to go out on a limb and risk having new insights.

ACTIVE ENGAGEMENT
Set children up to practice using conversational prompts to extend an idea you give them.

"Now it's your turn to try this, and this time let's try it through writing, not talking. Let's all start with a shared, whole-class idea, just as a place to practice. I'm going to show you how to use the prompts to push yourselves. Let's start with this idea."

> I learn new things during lunch time.

"Write that down and listen for a prompt that I'll say. When I say the prompt, even if you aren't finished with what you are writing, write the prompt and use it to push yourself to say more." Pausing to make certain every child had his or her pen poised, I said, "Okay, I'll first reread our claim. Then I'll add a prompt." I did so, saying first, "I learn new things during lunch time. For example, today . . ." I left time for children to record the prompt and then use it to generate more. When it seemed that they'd finished writing a sentence or two, I inserted a second prompt: "Another example is . . ." Before long, I said, "To add on . . ." I prefaced my next prompt with a parenthetical aside, "Here's a hard one," and then dictated, "This makes me realize . . ." Again I said in an aside, "One last hard one," and then I said, "This is important because . . ."

You'll notice that I'm upping the ante. I demonstrated by talking (or by writing in the air), and now I'm suggesting that children can do similar work on paper.

This may seem a bit crazy to you, but it is astonishingly successful. Just don't let kids slow you down. Teach them to write whatever they can and to keep going.

Ask children to reflect on what it feels like to use conversational prompts to extend thoughts.

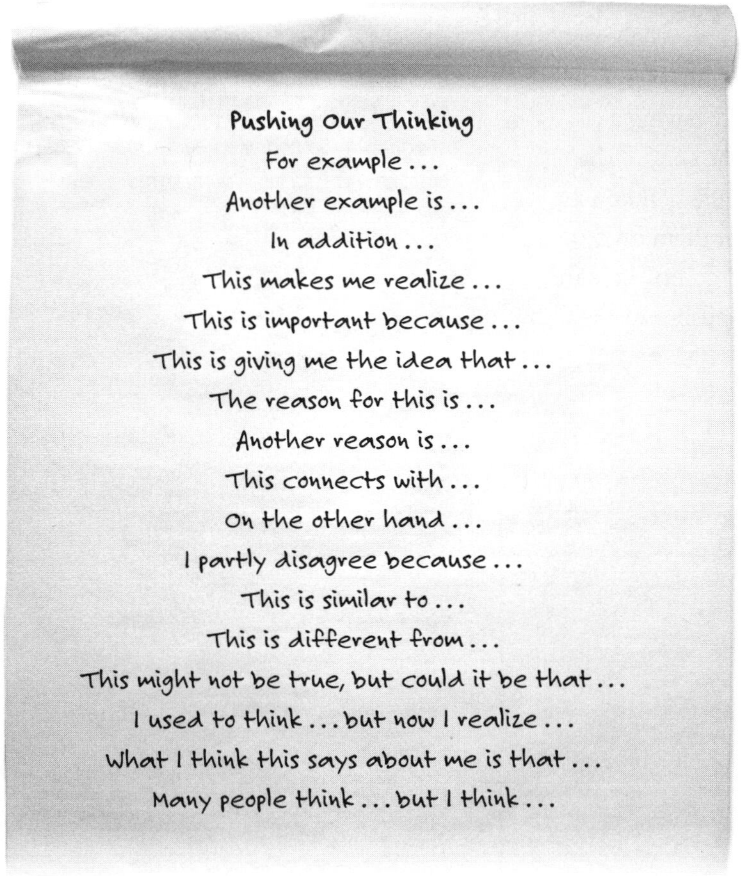

Pushing Our Thinking

For example . . .

Another example is . . .

In addition . . .

This makes me realize . . .

This is important because . . .

This is giving me the idea that . . .

The reason for this is . . .

Another reason is . . .

This connects with . . .

On the other hand . . .

I partly disagree because . . .

This is similar to . . .

This is different from . . .

This might not be true, but could it be that . . .

I used to think . . . but now I realize . . .

What I think this says about me is that . . .

Many people think . . . but I think . . .

"Okay writers, let's stop. How was that?"

Jonathan said, "My hand and my brain are tired."

"Your brain should be tired, because you were really focused! Now take a minute to read over what you have written." After a minute, I said, "Would you read what you've written to your partner and talk about how it felt using these conversational prompts to get yourself writing new ideas?"

Try this work yourself. It's almost magically powerful. The children become tickled by seeing their ideas emerge on the paper, and you will as well.

One interesting thing to realize is that different prompts channel children toward different kinds and even different levels of thinking. A prompt such as "For example . . . " or "Another example is . . . " or "To add on . . . " can lead children to provide examples and then to add on, to think associatively. My hunch is that prompts such as "This makes me realize . . . " or "This is giving me the idea that . . . " can lead them to progress from one thought to another thought, probably in a free-association fashion. "On the other hand . . . " and "But" and "I partly disagree because . . . " can lead a child to question. The prompts "This is similar to . . . " and "This is different from . . . " can lead to comparison.

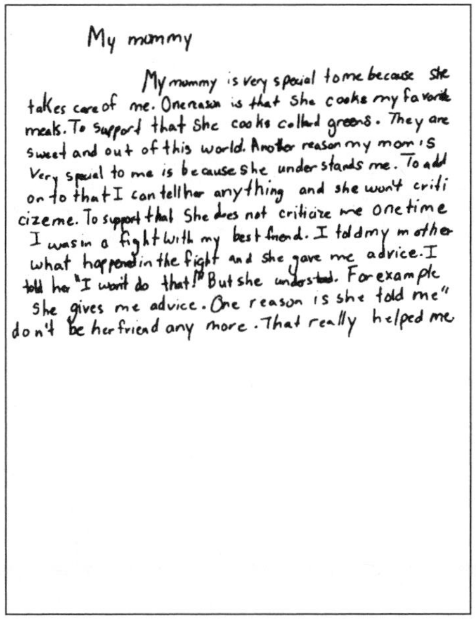

My mommy

My mommy is very special to me because she takes care of me. One reason is that she cooks my favorite meals. To support that she cooks collard greens. They are sweet and out of this world. Another reason my mom is very special to me is because she understands me. To add on to that I can tell her anything and she won't criticize me. To support that she does not criticize me one time I was in a fight with my best friend. I told my mother what happened in the fight and she gave me advice. I told her "I won't do that." But she understood. For example she gives me advice. One reason is she told me "don't be her friend any more. That really helped me

Fig. IV-1 LaKeya has used conversational prompts to extend her first thought

LINK
Rename the teaching point. Rally writers to use prompts as scaffolds to help them extend their own ideas as they write.

"What I am suggesting, writers, is that our writing needs to get us thinking. When we hope to develop essays, our writing needs to get us into a conversation with ourselves that will yield wonderful ideas, like our book talks do. Only when we write we are having a conversation on the paper, and we carry it on with ourselves." I pointed to the chart. "The conversational prompts that helped us talk back to each other in our book talks can now be prompts that help us talk back to (and think with) our own ideas as we meet them on our pages in our writing. Of course, we can use all the prompts in the world and go nowhere in our thinking, so keep in mind as we use these prompts the whole idea is to push ourselves to grow insightful, surprising, provocative ideas."

Notice the journey of thought I try to scaffold in this little speech. I make a point, and then push off from that point to a higher-level point. This journey-of-thought work is at the heart of what, in the end, we need to teach essayists to do. If you practice this yourself, you may more readily see it in your children's papers.

WRITING AND CONFERRING

Noting Qualities of Good Essay Writing in Children's Work

When you confer with children, try to let their entries teach you (and your students) ways to talk and think about essay writing. Notice entries that children have written that for some reason work especially well, and then join children in trying to put into words why those particular entries work. Be very specific and ask children to be specific, too. For example, ask "What do you mean when you say, 'It's detailed?' Point to the details you used."

Notice problems that you see in children's essays as well, and again join children in trying to put those problems into words. We all need to develop a vocabulary for talking about our goals as we teach writing.

I suspect you'll notice that we always have the option of writing about an idea at a greater or lesser level of abstraction. For example, earlier I jotted ideas I had about my dad. One idea was that he has been one of my most important teachers. That is a fairly general idea, high on a ladder of abstraction. Think of it as Roman numeral I in an outline. I could move down a notch in level of generalization and write, "My dad has taught me to fail with grace." Think of that as the A in the outline. Or I could move toward an even more specific/less abstract idea (the number 1 in the outline) and say, "When my dad was fired, he taught my brothers and sisters and me the truth of the saying, 'When one door closes, another opens.'" My feeling is that essay writing works best when there is only a little bit of writing at the highest level of abstraction, and much more writing at the lowest level. But all of the writing at the lower levels of abstraction needs to fit under the reach of the writing at the higher levels of abstraction. It is important for children to learn to shift between greater and lower levels of abstraction, and for our teaching to support that flexibility.

MID-WORKSHOP
TEACHING POINT   *Sharing an Example* "Writers, I want to compliment you. You are making important choices and gathering intriguing entries. I want to share with you another example of an entry that is poised to be an essay, so that you get more and more of a sense of how this kind of writing can start." *[Figs. IV-2 and IV-3]*

> I've been thinking about civilization. Civilization is a big word. When I hear it I conjure up images of the beginning of nations and empires. I think of Rome with its seven hills and I think of its future of beauty. It makes me think.
>
> What does it really mean? I think it describes the essence of our race, it is our culture, our technology, and our cities all combined. It is the computer program Civilization II that made me really think. Evan and I always call it . . .

continued on next page

Fig. IV-2 Miles' civilization notebook entry   Fig. IV-3 Miles' notebook entry page 2

You'll probably also notice that some of your children's entries feel fresh and others feel clichéd. Try to discern what makes some writing feel brand new, alive, unique; and why other writing feels prepackaged. I suspect you will find that when writing feels fresh, it is characterized by honesty. The writer may not use fancy words, but he or she reaches to put into words something that defies language, and the effort to pin down the truth gives those words power.

Look, for example, at Emily's entry about how she once referred to one color of crayon as dinosaur skin. *[Fig. IV-4]*

> When I was little I called crayons dinosaur skin. Nobody knows for sure what color dinosaurs really were. For years I looked at pictures of them, trusting that whomever was in charge of coloring them was doing it based on a scientific fact, but the truth is they were guessing.
>
> If it was up to me to put a wrapper around a crayon and name its color, I would call it dinosaur skin. I used to think I knew what color that was, I believed when I was little that dinosaurs are neon pink.

I think you will find that texts also work when they are cohesive, and one important way to make a text cohesive is through the use of repetition and parallelism. You may notice that in some essay entries, a key phrase or word (perhaps from the opening line) recurs, almost like a refrain. As the text unfolds, bits of the text harken back to earlier passages. This creates resonance, and it is often what takes my breath away in an essay. When children do this it is usually a lucky accident. Find these accidents and let the young author (and his or her classmates) know the effect on you!

---

continued from previous page

> . . . Civ II. I wondered why. I now think it is because Civilization is such a massive word to describe this game, Civilization II is a big and complex . . . but it might not be big enough. I think that to make an ultimate civilization, the closest to true civilization, you would need to be able to make a theater and be able to walk in and watch a play that would be affected by your culture so it tells you something about your nation. You would need to be able to say a speech and have it affect your population.
>
> On <u>that</u> game's box, the creators could say that the game was worthy of the title "civilization."
>
> Maybe Civ II might be worthy, but I have not felt perfection yet. I might never.

"I know many of you have entries that muse like this, and it's a great way to begin the process of writing an essay. You can carry the flavor of this thinking with you as you go back to your own writing."

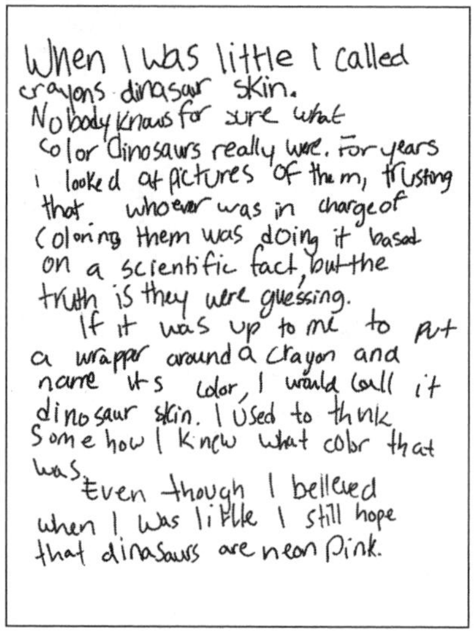

When I was little I called crayons dinasaur skin. Nobody knows for sure what color dinosaurs really were. For years I looked at pictures of them, trusting that whoever was in charge of coloring them was doing it based on a scientific fact, but the truth is they were guessing.

If it was up to me to put a wrapper around a crayon and name its color, I would call it dinosaur skin. I used to think somehow I knew what color that was. Even though I believed when I was little I still hope that dinosaurs are neon pink.

Fig. IV-4 Emily's notebook entry

SHARE

Celebrating Extended Thinking

Ask partners to talk over the development of the thinking in their notebooks—with or without prompts.

"Would you get with your partner and share an entry in which you really pushed yourself to talk back to your ideas, or to follow a journey of ideas? After you've read the entry, talk together, sharing your observations about whether the writer used any of the prompts on our class list, or tried another way to grow ideas."

Share examples by students who used prompts to extend their thinking.

"Listen to these examples from your classmates! See how their thinking grows and grows?" You'll notice that Ellie definitely uses thought prompts, and she uses more and more sophisticated ones as her entry progresses along. First she uses 'for example', but soon she's nudging her thinking with 'I realize . . .' and 'What surprises me is . . .'."

> I hate it when I am doing something important and then I get interrupted.
>
> For example, when I'm reading a book and my mom calls, "Ellie, it's time to go to sleep" but I really want to finish the book because that's what I am into. I realize that this happens a lot to me, like when I'm watching TV or having fun with my friends. What surprises me is I always have a lot of time and no one interrupts me when I am doing things I don't like, like homework or practicing my oboe or other things.

"Listen to Max's writing. You'll see he also goes on a journey of thought, only he does not use thought prompts. Listen for the way Max grows an umbrella idea towards the end of his entry. Later you'll have a chance to tell your partner about a strategy Max has used that you think you could use as well."[*Figs. IV-5 and IV-6*]

> We got a dog when Mom came from Africa because she said we could when she left. We all thought she would not keep her word, but I should have known better because she did, the weekend she came back.

> We got a dog when mom came from Africa because she said we could when she left. We all thought she would not keep her word, but I should have known better because she did, the weekend she came back. Mom was also the first person who the dog, Monty, really loved. Both Monty and I really have a lot of emotion for mommy. Mom takes care of me, cooks for me, and makes me feel happy.
>
> I love her so much. I also love my dad so much because he is the nicest guy I know, he works five days a week – just so he can support my family and me. Sometimes he even goes to work on the days you usually have off. And he does our house, our food, our clothes. And I am glad to have a father like that. But sometimes I don't think I

Fig. IV-5 Max's entry represents a journey of thought

Mom was also the first person who the dog, Monty, really loved. Both Monty and I really have a lot of emotion for Mommy. Mom takes care of me, cooks for me, and makes me feel happy. I love her so much.

I also love my dad so much because he is the nicest guy I know, he works five days a week—just so he can support my family and me. Sometimes he even goes to work on the weekends! You have to really have a good reason to work on the days you usually have off. And he does. Our house, our food, our clothes. And I am glad to have a father like that.

But sometimes I don't think I appreciate him enough, even though I should.

There are a lot of people/things that I think we should appreciate more. There should be a holiday called "National Appreciation Day" when we take time to appreciate the things that we usually forget to. There are many people in the past that invented things for us, our troops who give their lives for us, teachers.

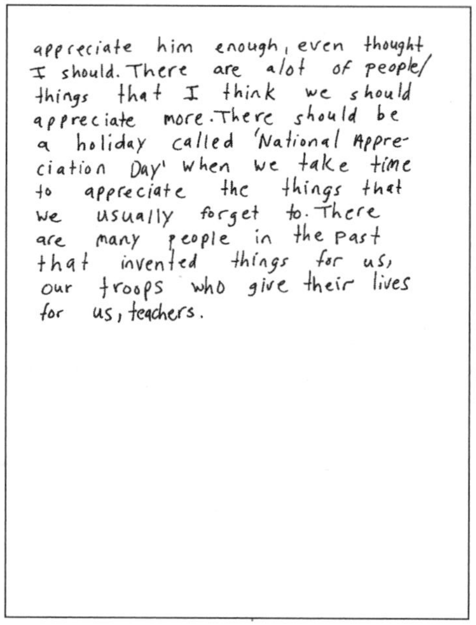

"Turn to your partner and talk about what these two writers have done that you'd like to try."

appreciate him enough, even thought I should. There are a lot of people/ things that I think we should appreciate more. There should be a holiday called 'National Appreciation Day' when we take time to appreciate the things that we usually forget to. There are many people in the past that invented things for us, our troops who give their lives for us, teachers.

Fig. IV-6 Max's notebook entry page 2

I'm enthralled by Max's writing and his mind, and haven't yet figured out just what it is he is able to do. You'll come to know him well in the last two books of the series.

⊙ [HOMEWORK] **Elaborating on First Thoughts** Tonight, practice using some of the thought prompts at home. Have a little conversation with yourself while you are walking down the street, or brushing your teeth, or looking out the window. For example, you can walk down the street and pick a prompt out of the air. Say to yourself "I'm learning that . . . " Fill in the sentence in a way that surprises you. Then add on. Say another prompt "For example . . . " Or try more complicated prompts (they're the later ones on your list), like "I used to think that . . . but now I think that . . . " "What surprises me about this is . . . " or "Many people think . . . but I think . . . "

When you do this work, try to make sure that you don't only say these phrases but that you use them. Use the phrases to make your initial idea become richer, more complex, and more original. Suppose I say, "I like dogs" and add, "This is important because . . . " but then I simply say, "it just is" and add, "Furthermore, I like cats too." I wouldn't be using these terms as tools for thought. What a difference there would be if instead my thought train went like this:

> I like dogs. This is important to me because my mother's dogs
> sometimes seem to matter as much to her as we, her children, do. I
> find myself growing up to be like her. Furthermore, now that my
> oldest son is going off to college, I've been thinking of getting myself
> a new puppy.

Most of your homework tonight won't be written, it will instead be thought, said, or lived. But also, in your writer's notebook, re-create and extend one train of thought, one that leads you into especially provocative areas.

TAILORING YOUR TEACHING

If your students are skilled at using conversational prompts for extending their thinking . . . you may want to try a more sophisticated variation on this lesson where you teach students that these prompts can be categorized and used for particular kinds of elaboration. You can show them that by selecting particular prompts they can channel themselves into a kind of elaboration. For example, if a writer wants to think of more examples of something, he could use transitional words such as *for instance, for example, most importantly, in addition,* and so on.

If a writer is trying to provide examples, you could suggest that instead of piling them up, one after the other, careful essayists think about a hierarchy of importance when offering examples. Some transitional words they might use are *of course, more important, equally important is, most importantly,* and so on. Another way a writer might sort examples is temporally, by using phrases like *in the beginning, later; next, in the end, finally,* etc. If a writer is trying to think of reasons behind the points she is trying to make, she could use other transitions, such as *because, this is caused by, one reason for this is, another reason is,* and so on. If the writer wanted to imagine counterarguments (which, by the way, is a lesson worth saving for another day), he might use phrases such as on the other hand, however, yet, still, but, another way to look at this is, etc.

ASSESSMENT

One of the most important things to keep an eye on as you work with kids is their level of energy. Ask yourself, "Is this unit tapping into my children's motivations to write?" Take some time to watch during the writing workshop and also to read through the entries your students have written. Look at their products as windows onto student engagement, because few things matter more. If your students are invested in this work, anything's possible. But if they are proceeding in a perfunctory, passive fashion, it'll be hard to achieve any successes until you rally their enthusiasm. If your children haven't yet become invested in essay writing, it will be important to address this.

Guard against trying to hook kids into their writing by throwing compliments around fast and loose. You can inadvertently create compliment addicts. Then, too, if you offer too many compliments, the positive things you say will no longer carry real weight. Try instead to build student energy by showing respectful attention to kids' writing and to their subjects. This works!

One sure way to generate energy is to allow the children's work to bowl you over. You may not love their writing (often, in fact, it'll seem like their writing is dramatically worse once kids leave the safe haven of narrative). But if you look more closely and with forgiving eyes, you'll probably see that amid all the bad writing, some kids have recorded quirky, funny, provocative, or fresh ideas. Pay attention to those ideas and let the less-than-great stuff float away. Repeat the powerful fresh bits to yourself as

if you were letting the idea the child has articulated dawn on you for the first time. Take the idea in. Let it matter. Be intrigued or surprised by bits of your children's thinking. Then, tomorrow, be ready to convene your class and share with all your children some of the ideas that their classmates have written. If your children see that their words matter to *you*, this will help them listen to their own and each other's words with new attentiveness.

I recently visited a class of special-needs students. My intention had been to just stick my head into their classroom and say a few words to their teacher. But then I saw that their classroom was a converted bathroom. The room was so despicable that I couldn't leave without somehow trying to bring sunlight to the children. So I simply asked if I could read their writing. As all the children listened, I turned through the stack of work, reading aloud the start of one story and then another, and another. I read as if the stories radiated beauty. I did nothing but read parts of each text aloud—but the children's mouths were open in astonishment at what they'd written. To tell you the truth, a fair portion of this was due not to what they had written but to the way I read their words. Try it. You can read "I once had a dog" like those are Shakespeare's words. If you read your students' essay entries as if they sizzle with insight, your children's deep freeze will thaw and they'll begin to care about this new unit of study.

Be sure to channel students' energy toward more writing. Say to one, "You've *got* to add on to this!" Whisper to the next child, "I can't wait to read what you write next!"

GETTING READY

- Student entry showing how writing extended the level of thinking
- One of your personal narrative entries from last unit of study to revisit
- Questions Writers Ask of Earlier Entries, on chart paper
- Strategies for Generating Essay Entries chart
- Student entry where a previous entry inspired ideas
- See CD-ROM for resources

GENERATING ESSAY WRITING FROM NARRATIVE WRITING

Katherine Paterson, author of Bridge to Terabithia, says, "Writing is something like a seed that grows in the dark . . . or a grain of sand that keeps rubbing at your vitals until you find you are building a coating around it. The growth of a book takes time . . . I talk, I look, I listen, I hate, I fear, I love, I weep, and somehow all of my life gets wrapped around the grain" (Paterson 1981).

This quote exactly matches my understanding of how writers build depth and intensity in a piece of writing. For example, I might jot down an anecdote. When I reread it, something stirs inside me. I find myself layering the anecdote with an insight. I drive in my car, thinking of my writing, and pass something by the side of the road that somehow fits with the original anecdote and its accompanying insight. By now my mental seed idea takes on extra skins, like one of those surprise balls given as favors at a child's birthday party, the kind with layers of crepe paper hiding all sorts of embedded treasures. I write, I reread, I remember, I listen, and all of this gets wrapped around the initial idea.

One way to teach children to layer their ideas and memories is to teach them to reread entries—especially narrative entries—and to catch the thoughts they have as they do this rereading. For example, I might reread my story about my father with his improvised ice pack, and suddenly I'm thinking of how there are never enough classroom supplies, so teachers, too, are always jerry-rigging things together to make do. I've sometimes defined creativity as a willingness to live off the land, to improvise in a resourceful fashion. Now I think, "This is no longer about my dad, this is a bigger idea, an idea about creativity—what it is and where it comes from. Where do I want to go with this trail of thought?"

In this session, we teach children to reread, rethink, and to layer their experiences with insights. We teach them to reread entries and ask themselves questions: "Why did I write this? What surprises me here?"

This session is about finding meaning and messages in the stories and lessons of our lives, and I hope it can bring you and your children to the heart of writing.

MINILESSON

Generating Essay Writing from Narrative Writing

CONNECTION

Celebrate that your children are extending their initial ideas.

"Writers, yesterday I watched many of you slow yourselves down so that instead of writing one new idea after another and another, you wrote an idea and then extended that one idea using a prompt that got you to think more."

"This is really smart work because you are writing an idea and then having more thoughts about it. A lot of people believe that the most important reason to write is that when we write, we fasten our first thoughts onto the page so we can think about our thinking."

"When you write something like 'It is important to have a best friend' and then reread what you have written and push yourself to write and think more, this is powerful work! Your ideas become more complex. Listen to what Tyrone wrote."

> It is important to have one best friend. This is important because having one best friend is like having a home in the world. Some people think that it's best to have lots of friends and to think of them all as equal, but I find it comforting to know that Amy will always be there for me no matter what.

"Do you see how this writer started with a rather simple, straightforward thought— 'It is important to have a best friend'—and he actually used writing to ratchet up the level of his thinking?"

Name your teaching point. In this case, explain that writers can become inspired by rereading and reflecting on their own previous entries.

"Today I am going to teach you that as writers we push ourselves to write not only from what we've just written but also from ideas and moments we recorded days, weeks, and months earlier. I often reread my old writing, find an entry I care about, and write *another* entry in which I reflect on and think about the first one. This is a way for writing to grow like the rings of a tree, with layers of insight and thoughtfulness."

COACHING

You'll recall that at the start of this unit of study, I told children that when writers want to write about big ideas, most of us don't sit in an armchair and squeeze our brains, hoping to produce an insight. Instead, we head into the fray of life, and do so with an extra effectiveness. That session nudged children to observe and to grow ideas from those observations. But it could have instead nudged children to reread their notebooks, attending to the particles of life collected in those pages, trusting that those bits of life could evoke big ideas. Don't miss teaching this lesson. It's one that has unbelievable potential!

You plan for your students to write in paragraphs of thought, not sentences of thought. Over time, watch whether their initial ideas always fit into the confines of one sentence. As writers become more sophisticated, they'll use the whole paragraphs not so much to elaborate upon a one-sentence idea, but to lay out the idea in the first place. If you wanted to do so, you could explicitly teach this.

Notice the reference to ideas growing like rings of a tree. You'll recall that Sandra Cisneros used this metaphor in "Eleven." It's great when your teaching can contain echoes from another day's teaching. This gives a new layer of meaning to your earlier instruction, just as you are asking children to give new layers of meaning to their earlier words.

TEACHING
Demonstrate returning to a personal narrative entry and using it to inspire a new entry.

Earlier this year I wrote a narrative entry about my father picking me up at a basketball game. I want you to watch how I now reread part of that entry and reflect on what I had written. First let me reread the end of the entry to get myself started."

> When the [basketball] game was almost over, I glanced toward the doorway and saw my father striding across the gym floor toward me, his red plaid hunting cap perched on his head, his rubber galoshes flapping. Why couldn't he wait in the car like all the other dads, I thought. Then, in a voice that boomed through the room, my dad called, "Lukers!" and began to climb the bleachers toward me and the other kids. I wanted the floor to open up and swallow me.

"I've read this over, and now I'm going to try asking myself some questions. Pay attention to the questions I ask myself, because they might work for you as well." I read from the list I had prepared on chart paper.

Questions Writers Ask of Earlier Entries

- Why is this important to me?
- What is the important thing about this?
- Why am I remembering this? How does it connect to who I am or to important issues in my life?
- What other entries does this connect with?
- What does this show about me? About life? What does this make me realize?
- Why did I write this?
- What do I want readers to know about this?
- What surprises me about this?

"I'll try the first question. I'm not sure of the answer, but I'll try to let some ideas come out of my pen."

> Why is this story about the basketball game important to me? I think I wrote about being embarrassed by my father because when I was young, it bothered me that my dad didn't act like other fathers.

"I could leave it at that, but I'll try to push myself to say more. Let's see . . . I'll reread and then just tell myself, 'Keep going.'"

> Why is this story about the basketball game important to me? I think when I was young, it bothered me that my father didn't act like other fathers.
>
> For example, he didn't wait in the car like other fathers, but instead, tromped right into our basketball games. He didn't know parents were expected to stay in the background. He'd go up to my friends, introduce himself, and soon he'd be deep in conversations with them. My cheeks would burn because he didn't stay inside the traditional father role.
>
> That was long ago, however, and I've since come to see the beauty in my father's arrival at that basketball game . . .

Debrief, naming what you've done in a way that is transferable to other days and other topics.

"Did you see how I reread an entry I had already written, and then asked myself just one or two questions? In that way I explored the meaning of the first entry. Writers do this often."

ACTIVE ENGAGEMENT
Set up partners to practice what you demonstrate.

"Right now, partner 1, please open your notebook and turn to a narrative entry from our first or second unit. Read the entry you select aloud to partner 2, and then try to have some thoughts about what you have written. Partner 2, you may want to ask one of the questions from our chart," I said, gesturing to the Questions Writers Ask of Earlier Entries chart.

"After you have said a thought and talked about it until you feel talked out, partner 2 can interject prompts from our list," I gestured to the Pushing Our Thinking list, "one that might work to keep you thinking more. For example, partner 2 might insert, 'This is important because . . . ,' 'To add on . . . ,' or 'This connects with . . . '. The goal is for partner 1 to write in the air what he or she could conceivably write in an entry."

Notice that these minilessons contain echoes of each other. In prior lessons children have already written in the air, inserted prompts to nudge each other's thinking, and used language to elicit new ideas. Therefore, this should all be accessible for them. This teaching wouldn't have made a lot of sense, however, had prior sessions not taught these strategies.

LINK
Ask children to list and share ways they can live like essayists during today's workshop and their lives.

"Writers, today you have forty-five minutes of writing time left. You should have lots of options in mind for productive ways in which you could spend your time today. Would you look over our charts, think over your writing, and work with your partner to come up with four possible things that writers in this room could be doing today?" Each child turned knee to knee with his or her partner and the room buzzed with talk.

You'll see that this link has a different spin to it than most. I ask children to list four options, instead of doing so myself. If you feel your kids need to be more active in more sections of your minilessons, you could do this sort of thing often.

"I heard you say that you could use our Strategies for Generating Essay Entries chart, which now has a new item on it."

Strategies for Generating Essay Entries

- We observe the small stuff of our lives and then try to let what we see and hear spark an insight or an idea.
- We record an issue that matters in our lives. Then we list several ideas we have about that issue and choose one of those ideas to develop at more length. We push ourselves to shift from observing to saying, "and the thought I have about this is . . . "
- We write in two columns, or in two sections, one section for what we see, hear, and notice and the other for what we think.
- We take a subject (a person, place, or object) that matters to us, and list ideas related to that subject. Then we take one of those ideas and write about it.
- We reread our earlier writing, and we have new thoughts about it. We sometimes ask questions of those earlier entries.

"I also heard you say that you could try to have discussions on paper in which you grow your first ideas, using the same thought prompts that we use in book talks. Some of you will try free writing. And some of you didn't get a chance to look at the non-narrative examples we brought in, so you'll be doing that today. I can't wait to admire the work you do!"

WRITING AND CONFERRING

Encouraging Children to Make Choices

The good thing is that this unit of study allows you to teach your students many things that will be new for them. The bad thing is that this unit is more directive than the others and does less to strengthen children's ability to make choices and work independently. That is, because this unit brings children to a new and challenging kind of writing, you'll often need to ask them to spend the workshop doing whatever you taught that day, instead of adding the day's strategy to a repertoire to be called on at will.

You have a little window of time now, before the complexity heightens, in which you can encourage children to make choices, so I suggest you make a special point of doing this. Begin your conferences by researching what it is they've chosen to do. Ask, "What are you working on as a writer?" and expect from their response not only a topic but also a strategy—one they've chosen for particular reasons to meet particular goals. Be aware that children will quickly learn the words to use to impress you; nudge and probe to be sure they mean what they say. Ask, "Where exactly did you do that?"

Once you know what a writer is trying to do and the strategies he or she has used, you'll want to learn more. Ask that writer how the strategy is working and if he needs any help with it. Wait for the child to articulate an answer, so that the child feels responsibility for what to write and for how his choices are working. Try to help the child judge whether a strategy is working well by encouraging him to notice whether he is learning during writing. Ask, "What did you learn by writing this entry?" and "What new idea did you form as you wrote?" Your questions show that writers can expect to learn new things as they write, and can choose ways to make sure that happens.

> **MID-WORKSHOP TEACHING POINT**
>
> ***Generating Essay Writing from Literature*** "I want to congratulate you on the decisions you are making about how to use your time. And I want to point out that you can not only choose from all the strategies on our chart—you can also invent your own strategies for generating essay entries. You already have! Marcus just told me that instead of writing from his earlier entries, he has been writing off of *Because of Winn-Dixie,* our read-aloud book. He went back to reread parts and now he has an entry about fathers and kids, and one about how dogs can be company—and both entries were sparked by that one book! Listen to what Marcus wrote about fathers and kids."
>
> > When I reread the part in the beginning of <u>Winn Dixie</u> where Opal was trying to get her dad's attention, it made me think about my relationship with my dad. My dad works at home and it seems like he is always working. I try to talk to him, but he says, "Can't you see that I'm in the middle of something?" Opal's dad was like that too. He was always working on his sermons so he didn't spend time with her or tell her about her mom. That's what she wanted to know. I just want to spend time with him. I wish he was like other dads.
>
> "Some of you may want to borrow Marcus' strategy (I'll add it to our list) and some of you may want to invent other strategies that you'll teach to the rest of us."
>
> *continued on next page*

Remember that after learning what a child is already doing, you'll want to find something to compliment. Then tell the writer that you could, if she is game, offer a tip, a pointer. Say, "Can I teach you one thing that'll make what you are doing even more effective?" After this, your conference will resemble a mini-minilesson.

If you feel unsure of what to teach during the teaching component of the conference, keep in mind that the class charts can be a resource for you as well as for young writers. If the child is unsure of what to write and a chart is posted titled Strategies for Generating Essay Entries, then you'll want to remind the writer that when he is stuck he can reach for a strategy from his mental toolbox. Another resource which you and the child can draw on are the final drafts of previous year's student essays that children brought home to study earlier. For example, if a child says that her problem is she doesn't know what to write after she's recorded a big idea (or if she hasn't paused for a moment, instead blithely moving from one idea to a totally disconnected idea) then you can say, "Well, let's look at what some of our mentor authors have done that you could try—that's what I often do when I'm stuck." Then a glance at the mentor text might suggest that one way a writer can say more is to shift from the level of generality to that of specificity, using a phrase such as, "For example, one day . . ." to help.

Remember as you confer with children that they are still writing entries, and are not writing formal essays. The authors haven't intended to write these entries in an essay shape, with a topic sentence and then support, and there is no reason that their entries need to follow this pattern. The goal has been thoughtfulness and insight.

Strategies for Generating Essay Entries

- We observe the small stuff of our lives and then try to let what we see and hear spark an insight or an idea.
- We record an issue that matters in our lives. Then we list several ideas we have about that issue and choose one of those ideas to develop at more length. We push ourselves to shift from observing to saying, "and the thought I have about this is . . ."
- We write in two columns, or in two sections, one section for what we see, hear, and notice and the other for what we think.
- We take a subject (a person, place, or object) that matters to us, and list ideas related to that subject. Then we take one of those ideas and write about it.
- We reread our earlier writing, and we have new thoughts about it. We sometimes ask questions of those earlier entries.
- We write off of the books we read.

SHARE

Hearing Essays Based on Narratives

Share an example of idea-based writing generated by narrative writing.

"Writers, I want to share with you what Francesca did. She went back to a personal narrative story she wrote earlier this year about how, when she was sledding, she accidentally bumped into a child and the father yelled at her so harshly that she felt like a little kid again. And Francesca wrote a couple of pages of thoughts about that one entry! Listen." [Figs. V-1, V-2, and V-3 on next page]

People can bring change in others parents. I felt a little scared and guilty. As I sat down near Logan, guilt filled my head. I could feel heat building up in my head as I lay in the snow.

I feel like a little little kid that was about three years old. I was not that excited big kid, I felt like I was going backwards in life, like I was going from nine to three.

I am the kind of person who gives up easily when something like a mistake happens. I try to never mess up or do something wrong so I'm too hard on myself. Unlike Camilla, my little sister, or Logan, my younger friend. Why am I the only one who feels like it's all my fault? I always seem to take the fall for everything. Why do I care so much; I'm just a kid?

Growing up can have a rough color. Kids think that growing up is so great and so simple but they have no idea what they're in for. Growing up can feel really good but it does not happen fast and its not as easy as it looks. It's like a train where at every stop you get a little farther in life. I still remember when I thought growing up was so easy and so fast and I accidentally bumped into a man and his kid. After that I felt scared and little and did not sled again. So growing up can be great but it isn't as easy and smooth as it really looks.

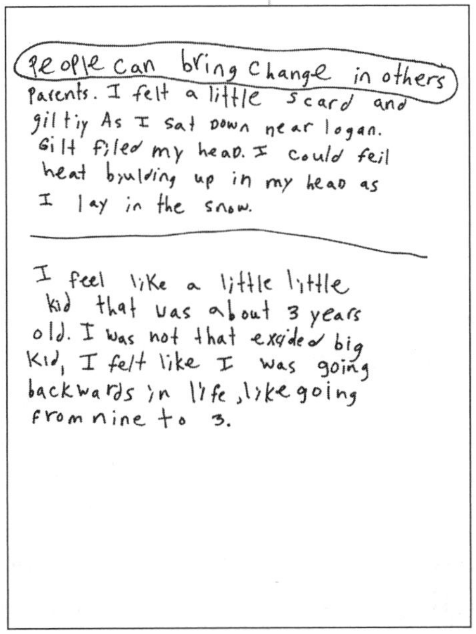

People can bring Change in others parents. I felt a little scard and giltiy As I sat Down near logan. Gilt filed my head. I could feil heat bqulding up in my head as I lay in the snow.

I feel like a little little kid that was about 3 years old. I was not that excided big kid, I felt like I was going backwards in life, like going from nine to 3.

Fig. V-1 Francesca's notebook entry

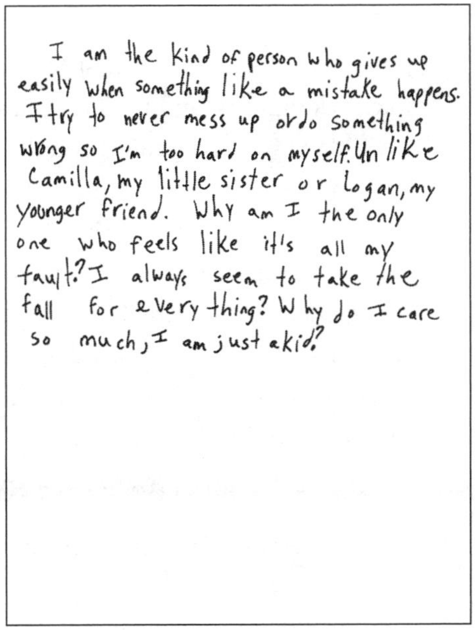

I am the kind of person who gives up easily when something like a mistake happens. I try to never mess up or do something wrong so I'm too hard on myself. Unlike Camilla, my little sister or Logan, my younger friend. Why am I the only one who feels like it's all my fault? I always seem to take the fall for every thing? Why do I care so much, I am just akid?

Fig. V-2 Francesca's notebook entry

Ask students to share their own essay-like writing, born of narrative entries.

"Francesca's ideas are taking on new growth-rings of meaning, growing like a tree grows. She began with an experience on the sledding hill, and she's used that experience to think about how quickly her big-kid strength can vanish. She's pondered why she beats herself up, and she thinks grown ideas not only about herself but about growing up in general. Her writing has shifted from a detail about sledding to broad insights about life. This is what essayists do."

"Would each of you share with your partner an entry that you wrote based on one of your personal narratives? If you haven't yet done this, would you do it now, out loud, writing in the air so you get a chance to feel what this work entails?"

Growing up Can Have A Ruff color. Kids think that Growing up is so great and so simple but they have no Idea What there in for. Growing up can feel really good but it does not happen fast and it's not as easy as it looks. It's like a train where at every stop you get a little farther in life. I still remember when I thought Growing up was so easy and so fast and I accidentally Bumped into a man and his kid. After that I felt scared and little and did not sled again. So Growing up can Be great but it isn't as easy and smooth as it really looks.

Fig. V-3 Francesca's notebook entry

HOMEWORK *Writing from Earlier Entries* Writers, remember Naomi Shihab Nye's poem "A Valentine for Ernest Mann," where she writes that poems hide in everyday places like sock drawers, and unlikely places like in the eyes of a skunk?

Today I want to remind you that it's not only *poems* that hide. *Issues* hide as well. They hide in the seemingly small events that haunt us, that resurface over and over in our minds.

Tonight, write an entry in which you step back from the hurly-burly of life and say, "There's a bigger issue here." That's important not only for life, but also for writing. I recall a fifth grader named Daniel who longed for a cat. Finally, after lots of preparation, he brought his case for a cat to his mother and she snapped back at him, 'Daniel, I don't have time for a cat.' Later, Daniel wrote about that moment in his notebook. He recreated the moment with his mother, recording her retort.

"Daniel, I don't have time for a cat."

But this time, Daniel added on. Here's what he wrote.

In my mind, I thought, "That's why I need one." I need a cat because I want someone who has time for me, who's there for me.

Daniel's next entry was about how, ever since his family moved from a little apartment in the city to a big suburban home, the rope that held his family together has been strained to the breaking point. His father leaves the house early, returns late. He and his brother no longer share a bedroom. His mother is busy all the time with the community. *All* of that was lurking behind Daniel's initial entry about wanting a cat! This is what I mean when I say, "Issues hide." The writer who questions, probes, and connects can find the real issues that lurk behind minor heartaches, behind an argument over whose turn it is to take out the trash. Do that work in your writer's notebook tonight unless you, as a writer, have plans that take priority over this, in which case, follow your own plans.

TAILORING YOUR TEACHING

If your children need support before they can benefit from this minilesson . . . by all means revisit it. There are few minilessons in the series that matter more. Give your children an extra day or two in which to reread their prior writing and to write entries about that writing. The minilesson that might mean the most to your children is one in which you say to them, "Last night at home, I decided to try my hand at the work you all did here in school yesterday. So I remembered that writers can reread a story we wrote earlier, and then ask questions of that story." Here you can recall the specific questions. Then tell the children that you tried this, and show them your text and teach them whatever insight about the initial event you gleaned from doing this work. If an insight doesn't leap to mind, show them how you can look for insight by asking yourself, "Why is this event in my life important to me?" Then talk and write about ways in which the event matters.

If your students are having trouble making decisions about which piece to choose or about what matters most in a particular piece . . . they may be paralyzed by the options, especially if they are fluent and prolific writers. If this is the case, you may want to narrow their task a bit by structuring their work more. You might begin this lesson by saying, "Writers, last night I decided to do the same work I asked you to do. I went back through my notebook and reread my entries. I was trying to catch the thoughts I was having so that I could start a new piece. But it was hard to do! I ended up reading through old entries. It reminded me of when I had to clean out my huge box of photographs. I wanted to throw some away, give some away, and put some in albums. But I spent hours just looking through the photos and remembering the moments and the people in them. I never got my work done. That's what happened when I was rereading through my notebook. I'd read an entry and then I'd stop and begin to remember times in my life, and the next thing I knew it was midnight! Time to go to sleep! This morning, on my way to work, I thought about what could help us with this situation and I tried it again before you guys arrived. Here's what I learned. First, we just need to pick an entry. So if you have several entries that really matter to you, just pick one of them! No big deal. You can flip a coin if necessary! Then reread that piece, and list out the thoughts you're having. I put a sticky note on the bottom of the page and, as I reread, I jotted quick notes to myself. Then, once again, I had to make a quick choice. I think I came up with five ideas from rereading my piece about when my dad came to the basketball game and yelled "Lukers!" So again, I just had to pick one to write an entry about. It was hard, and I was having trouble deciding, but then I just made a decision. You know what helped? I realized that I have my whole life to write, and so I can write about those other entries and those other ideas I have in the future. For now, it was important for me as a writer to just pick something!!"

For the Active Engagement part of this lesson, you could give students a timed minute or two to choose the entry they want to work off of and have them put a sticky note on the bottom of the page. Next, ask them to reread it and jot the thoughts they are having. Finally, tell them to make a quick pick of the idea they want to work on. You can ask them to tell their partner which idea they've chosen and to say a thing or two they plan on writing about it.

If your students struggle with the multilayered task of rereading entries, picking one to probe, and then generating an essay narrative from it . . . you might want to make the task a bit smaller by adapting an idea from *Writing Down the Bones*, by Natalie Goldberg. In her book, Goldberg suggests taking a poetry book and opening up to any page. She tells writers to grab a line, write it down, and keep writing off of the line. For the purposes of the essay unit, you might suggest to students that they pick an old narrative entry and find a line to copy on the next blank page in their notebook. "Writers, pick a line that is sort of meaty, a line that seems to be telling you, 'Say more here.' Then write, write, and write some more off of that one line." Chances are your students will pick a line that matters to them, and the writing that they do off of the line might help them generate a piece that has significance.

MECHANICS

Although much of our teaching at the start of this new unit will support children as they work with expository writing, we will also want to continue to support children's ongoing development as writers and spellers. Developmental instruction needs to be tailored to support specific groups of children. It's important to ensure that children don't interpret the shift to a new genre as an invitation to stop using the conventions of grammar or the spelling rules they've learned!

To help plan your teaching of spelling, take an inventory of your class. Look at whether your students have mastered these challenges:

- Do they represent all the sounds they hear in a word?

- Do they spell most high-frequency words correctly?

- Are their short vowels correct most of the time?

- Do they use generalizations in ways that lead to correct (and sometimes to incorrect) spelling? For example, do they add final "e"s when they should, by logic, be necessary?

- Do they understand generalizations pertaining to word endings, such as doubling a final consonant before adding the ending?

If you sit with a stack of children's work and a set of questions such as these, you'll soon form a list of names of children who need help representing all the sounds in a word and spelling most high–frequency words correctly. Those children will no doubt also need help determining whether to double

the final consonant in a word before adding an ending, but such help might overwhelm them at this point. Once you have formed small groups and have an agenda for each group, then you simply need to be sure of how and when to teach whatever you wish to teach. You'll want to rely on a good book to help you plan your spelling instruction. I suggest Snowball and Bolton's *Teaching Spelling K–8*, Marten's *Word Crafting,* or Wilde's *You Kan Red This!*

In addition to keeping records of each child's knowledge of conventions, you will also want to know at which stage of the writing process the child uses that knowledge. For example, does this one child insert commas correctly in her final drafts, but not yet use them correctly in her very rough notebook entries? If so, this suggests that commas are still challenging enough and new enough for her that using them requires conscious, deliberate, focused attention. Encourage this writer to begin to draft with commas, even if she doesn't use them absolutely correctly. You want her to learn that what she at first does towards the end of the writing process then moves forward in the process, becoming an acquired habit that is incorporated into drafting. It is important that children begin to use conventions with automaticity in early drafts. So guide children to apply their knowledge in a stage of the writing process that is one step earlier than whatever you see. Coach them into the new groove by helping them get the feel for using that knowledge more quickly as they write. If you are seeing the same level of control of conventions in all stages of a child's writing process, that could be a sign that the child is ready for more teaching—she may be able to push herself further at the end of the process.

GETTING READY

- Your own or a colleague's non-narrative notebook entry to demonstrate finding a thesis
- Student entry to illustrate the process of drafting a thesis
- List of questions for assessing a thesis, written on chart paper
- Student entry to illustrate the process of reviewing and revising a thesis
- See CD-ROM for resources

FINDING AND CRAFTING THESIS STATEMENTS

Prepare yourself. Over the next three days, *your children will spend all their time drafting and revising what will amount to a frame—an outline—for their essays. Today you'll teach them to draft and revise a strong, clear thesis. In the next session, they'll plan topic sentences and paragraphs to support their thesis. And then, in the following session, one which is especially optional, they'll talk and free write about their plan and then reconsider it in light of what they discover they really want to say.*

You'll definitely want to do this writing work along with your students. There won't be a great volume of writing in the next few days, but you and your children can learn far-reaching lessons about logical thinking if you do this work alongside each other. By trying the same things that you ask your students to do, you'll get an insider's feel for why this work is harder than it looks, and for how you can help children do it more effectively.

Before you proceed, I suggest you read aloud some of the essays provided on the CD-ROM, paying attention to the thesis statement and the topic sentences for each one. These essays may seem simple and repetitive, even dull. I promise that although the products may not seem as luscious as other writing you've seen across this series, the lessons in logic and language that you and your children can learn through this work are crucial and long lasting.

The work you launch today may not occupy children for a full-length workshop. Very skilled and experienced writers could invest weeks in today's work, but many children will find themselves done in short order. Because the next session's workload is gigantic, you can't collapse the two days into one. Instead, rely on conferring and small-group work to support revision, and be prepared to end today's workshop a bit earlier if children seem to be finished.

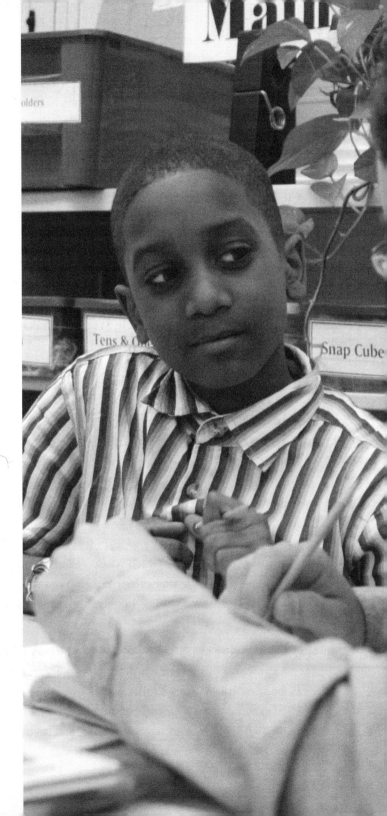

MINILESSON

Finding and Crafting Thesis Statements

CONNECTION

Connect the work of today to work writers did in previous units.

"Writers, earlier this year when we wrote our personal narratives, we collected entries in our notebooks for a week or two and then looked back at everything we had collected and chose a seed idea that we developed into a major piece of writing. Our notebooks are again brimming with possible seed ideas that could be developed, and now we want to select one that could become an essay."

Name your teaching point. Specifically, teach children that writers reread to find a seed idea, in this instance called a thesis.

"Today I want to teach you that when I reread my notebook to select a seed idea for an essay, what I'm looking for quite literally is a seed *idea*. When we wrote personal narratives, we used whole entries as our seed ideas—they were really seed *stories* rather than seed *ideas*. But when we write *essays*, it helps if the writer has an idea—or a claim—that the writer wants to advance, that the writer wants to explore or defend."

"Sometimes we find our seed ideas in the pages of our notebooks, but sometimes the idea we want to address isn't yet crystallized on the page. That's why we reread our notebooks and ask, 'What is the big thing I *really, really* want to say?' Then we write our claim, or our thesis (that's the term essay writers give to this claim), in a sentence or two."

"So, writers, today I hope you learn that each writer needs to reread his or her entries to find (or invent) a seed idea, which is also called a *claim* or a *thesis*. We write that seed idea in a sentence or two. Before we begin to develop our seed idea, our thesis, we try it on for size, asking, 'Could I imagine writing an essay about this? Is this what I want to say?'"

TEACHING

Demonstrate the way essayists try a few seed ideas on for size.

"I know you can imagine how writers go about rereading their entries, looking for seed ideas, because you've done similar work earlier this year. The only difference is that now we look for or write just *a sentence or two* that states the idea we want to develop. You can probably figure out how to reread looking for a seed idea; I'd like instead to show you how my friend Cory tried a few seed ideas on for size."

COACHING

The Connection usually begins by consolidating what we've already taught as a way both to review and to ready children to integrate a new bit of knowledge into their prior learning. Usually this means that the Connection summarizes the preceding minilessons. Sometimes, however, as in this instance, the Connection section of a minilesson refers back to (and prepares writers to build upon) the lessons they learned during parallel minilessons in earlier units.

Every new study carries with it new terminology, new vocabulary. In these sessions, I tend to tuck synonyms alongside the new terminology. Some of your children (including your English Language Learners) may need more explicit instruction in the vocabulary of the unit. For this unit, the terms include claim, thesis, evidence, idea, argue, persuasive, statistics, citations, parallel, support, counterarguments, outline, transitions, and bullets. All these terms will resurface in the later unit on Literary Essays.

If we want children to really attend to our minilessons, our teaching needs to be deserving of their attention. We can't say, "All eyes and ears up here, please" and then proceed to fill ten minutes with an elaborate demonstration of something the kids already know how to do! On the other hand, we do sometimes need to nudge kids to do some work they've learned previously. This minilesson, then, can provide a template for one way to handle this situation.

"After Cory read all the entries she'd written, asking herself, 'Which of these might make a good essay?' she found an entry she'd written about her friend Jen. It was a long entry; she reread it and underlined the two or three sentences that really captured her main idea about her friend. She underlined: <u>My friend Jen and I are so much alike.</u> She also underlined <u>Jen and I are close because we've been friends for years. We've been friends through the best and worst times.</u> She figured maybe one of these sentences could become her seed idea."

"Cory thought about building an essay around the first idea—that Jen and she are so much alike. She tried to picture what she might say in that essay. She said to me, 'It's true that we are alike, but when I think about writing an essay on that, I'm not sure that idea captures what I really want to say.' So Cory did what essayists do. She tried out the other idea, that she and Jen are close because they have been friends for years. She found that was better. But she still wasn't sure that was exactly what she wanted to say. I nudged her to ask herself, 'What exactly do I want to say about my topic?' That question led her to say, 'I want to tell about how good it is to have a best friend.' So she tried to write that in a sentence or two. She wrote, 'Best friends are like comfortable jeans.' She liked that, but she still tried writing her main idea another way. This time she wrote, 'The world is a softer place when you have a best friend.' She liked that best of all."

Debrief. In this case, point out that the seed idea is smaller here than in narrative, and it takes revision and projection into the future to settle on one.

"Writers, I hope you noticed that Cory first reread all her entries, then she found one she liked and underlined a few key ideas about it. When we are writing essays, our seed idea is not usually a whole entry, a whole story. We cull out a single sentence or two (or write a sentence or two) that really says what we want to say. I also hope that you noticed that Cory didn't just settle on her first version of a seed idea. She wrote a few drafts and asked herself, 'What exactly do I want to say?' and finally, after she imagined how several would go, she had a thesis she really liked and knew she had things to say about."

ACTIVE ENGAGEMENT
Ask writers to join you in helping one member of the class go through the process of crafting a thesis.

"Writers, let's practice this by seeing if we can help Joe settle on his seed idea. He's already reread his entries and he underlined this idea: '<u>Kids should be able to get exercise more often.</u>' I'm going to ask Joe to tell us what he *really* wants to say in his essay. Often our

Notice that each of these statements contains a subject and a point.

You'll also find times to bring a colleague into your minilessons. You can literally have someone coteach a minilesson, or simply tell the story of their work as I do here with Cory Gillette's work. Cory is doing some very complicated and important work here, drafting and revising her thesis. If you tell the story of another teacher's work, you can process what the writer is doing so the class can learn from both your colleague's mental moves and from your analysis. You can, of course, play both the role of the writer and of the teacher yourself, but be sure if you do this that you signal with your body language when you are being the writer and when you become the teacher.

As Cory revised her initial thesis statement, her thinking became more complex.

You can't expect children to see that the two different thesis statements each require different forms of elaboration, but you'll come to understand that the goal when writing a thesis is not one great sentence—it is, instead, a workable essay.

You'll be surprised to see that it is complicated to write a good clear thesis statement.

first effort at a thesis is vaguer and broader than the thesis we finally settle upon. Then would you work with your partner to see if the two of you can help Joe word his thesis in a way that really captures what he wants to say?"

Joe said, "See, I think it's not right that kids just eat junk food and watch TV and play video games. And I think kids need to exercise more. Schools should have gym more."

"So writers, the challenge will be to figure out how to consolidate Joe's main idea into a single sentence or two." I reiterated what he'd said. "Work with your partner, and then let's list some suggested thesis statements for Joe."

After a few minutes the class had compiled this list.

- Kids should be able to exercise more often.
- Schools should have gym more often.
- Instead of plopping on the couch, eating junk food, watching television, and playing video games, kids should get up off the couch and go exercise.

Reread each of the class' suggestions, projecting how an essay might go based on that particular thesis.

"These at first seem so similar, right? But if you project into the future and imagine how these theses might become essays, I think they'd be very different."

"'Kids should be able to exercise more often'—an essay from that thesis might name the reasons why kids should exercise more often. Maybe kids should do this because exercise is good for their hearts, their muscles—and maybe for their morale? Or there could be a different set of reasons why this matters."

"The next thesis, 'Schools should have gym more often,' is a little different, isn't it? That essay will need to defend why schools need to have gym—so maybe one reason is because exercise is important (that one part could tell about how exercise is important for kids' hearts, muscles, and morale, couldn't it?). Maybe another reason might be that kids are no longer playing out of doors during their free time; instead they are couch potatoes. Do you see how each thesis statement sets up a different plan for an essay?"

"Joe will probably draft other versions of a thesis statement, and that's the process all of you will need to go through today and every time you want to draft a thesis."

As you work with children, keep in mind that more general thesis statements are easier to develop but often lead to less stellar work. Nudge your more experienced writers, those who are game for a challenge, towards more specific thesis statements.

During the Active Engagement, it's often a reasonable option to ask children to work in partners, thinking through a way to help one child do whatever has been taught.

Elizabeth Lyon, author of A Writer's Guide to Nonfiction, *suggests (claims!) that there are three kinds of claims: of fact, of value, and of policy. She writes, "Claims of fact offer objectively verifiable data. Claims of value express approval or disapproval of taste or morality. They evaluate desirability. Movie reviews are a good example. Claims of policy suggest institutionalizing change as a solution to problems, such as 'There ought to be a law'" (Lyon 2003, p. 119).*

You'll probably find that your children aren't exact, precise readers; to many children all these sentences say the same thing. Help children to really read what's written on their own pages.

You will want to use a child in your own class, and the suggested thesis statements will then be very different. You'll find that often children suggest statements that have two or three branches in them—"kids need exercise and there should be more gym." Help children to prune these so the seed idea makes one big claim. This, in and of itself, will still be challenging to defend! You'll want to describe briefly the fact that each thesis leads to a different essay, although children will not tend to grasp this yet.

LINK

Repeat the teaching point. In this case, explain how to choose and make a thesis.

"So, writers, from this day forward, remember that after collecting ideas for a bit, the time will come to make a decision. Specifically, if you are writing an essay, after developing a bunch of entries and ideas you'll want to reread and select what is, quite literally, a seed idea. To do this, reread your entries and find or write sentences that get to the heart of your intentions. We usually write our seed idea, our claim, in at least six or seven different ways until we have the words and the meaning right. Today, each of you will want to begin rereading your entries, selecting a seed idea, and then you can draft and revise a thesis statement." *[Figs. VI-1 and VI-2]*

You'll notice that on this particular day, the minilesson is designed to channel every child to do the same work. This is unusual.

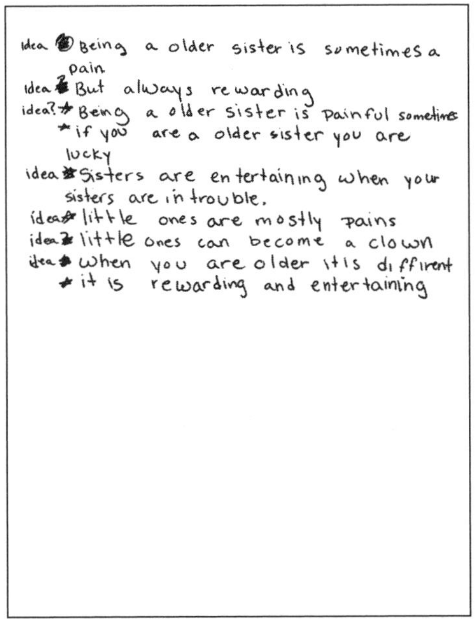

idea # Being a older sister is sometimes a pain
idea # But always rewarding
idea? * Being a older sister is painful sometimes
* if you are a older sister you are lucky
idea # Sisters are entertaining when your sisters are in trouble.
idea # little ones are mostly pains
idea # little ones can become a clown
idea # when you are older it is diffirent
* it is rewarding and entertaining

Fig. VI-1 Various seed ideas

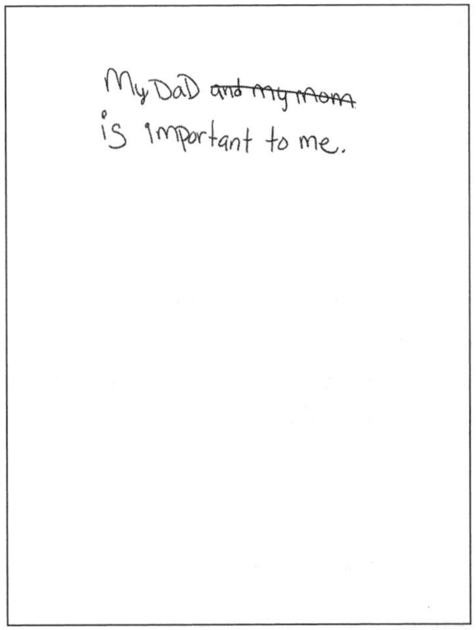

My DaD ~~and my mom~~
is important to me.

Fig. VI-2 Randolio's thesis

WRITING AND CONFERRING

Crafting Thesis Statements

Your minilesson probably did not feel particularly confusing to you, but the work you've set out for kids today and especially over the next few days will pose lots of challenges for them. These challenges are best addressed through one-to-one conferences and small-group strategy lessons. I recommend you look ahead to tomorrow's minilesson and the write-up on conferring in that session, and today, as you work with children set some of them up to have success tomorrow. I'd especially do this with some of your strugglers.

In terms of today's work with developing a thesis statement, you can anticipate that some kids will write and select questions rather than statements. Teach them that instead of writing, "Why do I love my dad so much?" they need to make a stand, to claim a position: "I love my father because he makes me improve myself." Some children will resist making clear, concise statements and instead hedge their claims: "One of the reasons why I love my dad is that some of the time he doesn't let me be anything less than my best." Help writers who hedge to create a lean, clear thesis that doesn't waffle.

MID-WORKSHOP TEACHING POINT *Checking Thesis Statements* "Writers, can I stop you? I hope you understand that your entire job for today's workshop is to write one sentence. You might think 'Whoopee! Not much work today!' But what I want to teach you is that it is crucial that today be your most intense, hard-working day of the unit. Your job is to work hard at writing and revising your thesis. To do that, you need to be willing to say, 'No, that's not quite it,' or 'Let me try writing another just to be sure.' So let me teach you two ways to go about revising your thesis statements."

"First, I mentioned to you earlier that after Cory and other writers have written a few possible thesis statements, they ask themselves questions and use those questions to help them revise those all-important sentences. These questions should nudge you, as well, to revise."

"Then, too, sometimes when you reread your entries, looking for a sentence which could become your thesis, you find that no one sentence really captures the complexity of what you want to say. Alejandro, for example, reread his notebook and found an entry he'd written about his friendship with Mike. He figured this might be a topic he'd like for an

continued on next page

Questions Writers Ask of Theses

- Is this topic something I know and care about? Can I imagine writing about this general topic for the next few weeks?
- Is my thesis an idea or an opinion—not a fact and not a question?
- Is my thesis exactly what I want to address? Is it as specific as possible?
- Is my thesis a strong, clear claim?
- Is there only one claim I'll need to support in this thesis?

Steer children away from a thesis that has two branches, as in "My mother and my father are important to me." That essayist would have to prove that both his mother and his father are important. It is simpler to start with one single claim. Then, too, sometimes a thesis is really making two points, as in this example: "Because children care a lot about their parents, sometimes they are embarrassed by them." There is nothing wrong with this thesis, but defending it poses an extra layer of writing challenge, because now the child needs to show not only that kids can be embarrassed by their parents, but also that this feeling is motivated by care. Later, writers can always address counterarguments or further claims, but for now, help children write straightforward, clean, crisp thesis statements.

Some kids will write a fact in lieu of a thesis. The child who writes, "My father picks me up after school," has written a fact, not an idea. I prompt children to go past the fact to an idea by asking "What are your ideas or your feelings about this?" Soon the child will have a thesis: "I love it when my father picks me up after school."

continued from previous page

essay, so he reread his entry, looking for a single sentence that summed up the entry and his feelings for Mike. *[Fig VI-3]* Listen."

> I have been thinking about my friendship with Mike. I thought that it is sometimes hard to be friends with Mike because he is interested in things that I am not interested in. For example, he is interested in movie making and I am not, he likes to make up comic book characters, he likes to play video games and I don't, he likes to watch the Simpsons and I don't. I sometimes have fights with him. For example, we play card games that he made up and he sometimes changes the rules in the middle of the game. On the other hand Mike is a good friend because the games that he makes up are fun.

"Alejandro realized that he didn't have one line that captured what he thought, because he had both good and bad feelings about Mike. So he thought, 'Maybe the one thing I am saying is that my friendship with Mike is complicated.' He wrote that down."

> My friendship with Mike is complicated.

"Then he tried to revise that idea by saying his feelings more precisely. He tried to compare the friendship to something everyone knows. Here's what he wrote next."

> My friendship with Mike is like a seesaw. Sometimes it is up and sometimes it is down.

"Then he tried to write this in a stronger fashion, adding in his emotions."

> It is hard to be friends with someone who is so different from me.

"You may need to do this kind of work to find or craft your thesis too."

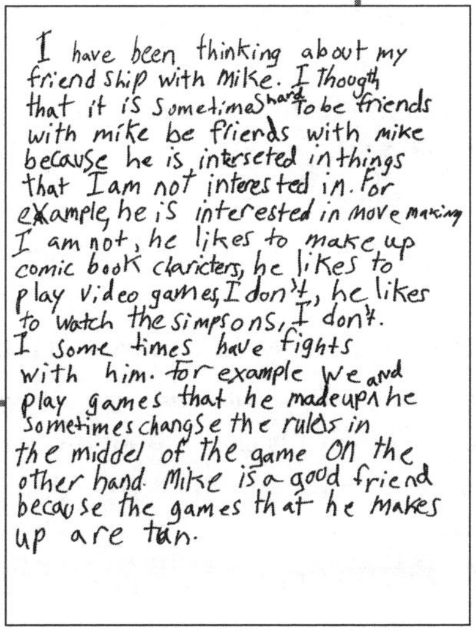

I have been thinking about my friend ship with Mike. I thougth that it is Sometimes hard to be friends with mike be friends with mike because he is intersested in things that I am not interested in. For example, he is interested in move making I am not, he likes to make up comic book claricters, he likes to play video games, I don't, he likes to watch the simpsons, I don't. I some times have fights with him. for example we and play games that he madeup he Sometimes changse the rules in the middel of the game On the other hand. Mike is a good friend becouse the games that he makes up are fun.

Fig. VI-3 Alejandro's notebook entry

SHARE

Let Small Stories Evoke Big Ideas

Ask writers to postpone closure on their theses, and to imagine another possibility. Teach them that writers sometimes begin with a powerful story, using it to generate an umbrella idea.

"Your thesis statement will frame all the work you do for the rest of this unit, so I want to suggest you devote this share session to imagining that your thesis statement could be altogether different than the one you've temporarily settled upon. So for today, you arrived at your thesis by rereading your notebook and searching for a sentence or two that named a big idea that matters to you. Later, as you write, you'll generate details that support this big idea."

"You could, on the other hand, arrive at a thesis by progressing in the opposite direction. Many writers find it helpful to begin with detail, a specific, and then write their way toward the big idea. Writers talk about the importance of "revealing detail," and I recently realized, with a start, that details can be revealing for the writer, not just for the reader. A revealing detail can help a writer realize a big idea. In this way, a revealing detail can shine a light on a larger concept for the writer."

Get children started rereading their notebooks, identifying a precious particle and developing an idea.

"Right now, would you sit quietly and just reread your notebook? Look for the anecdote or small story that catches your heartstrings or that makes your mind feel as if it's on fire. When you find this, reread that entry and consider that you may want to put this entry at the heart of an essay. To do this, you'll need to discover a big idea that comes from your small story. Try writing as a way to mull over the meaning of your anecdote. Ask, 'What does this little story really show about me? About life? About a particular topic?' Try asking, 'What surprises me about this?' Try writing about this one bit of writing, prefacing your words with a phrase such as: 'The real thing I want to say is . . .' Write several different entries in which you explore the big ideas that might be hiding within this bit of powerful writing."

"If doing this brings you towards writing that feels more alive and provocative than the work you already did, try to produce a seed idea, a thesis statement, that crystallizes your new thinking. You can use this as your thesis and, after this, you can use this pathway (going from small to big) to generate big ideas for yourself."[*Figs. VI-4, VI-5, VI-6, and VI-7*]

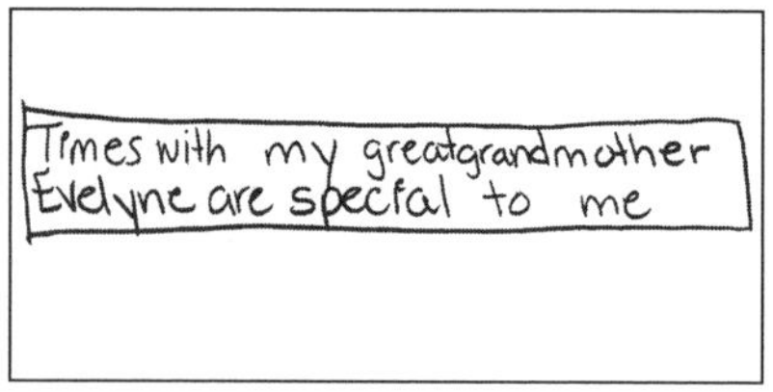

Times with my greatgrandmother Evelyne are special to me

Fig. VI-4 Sophie

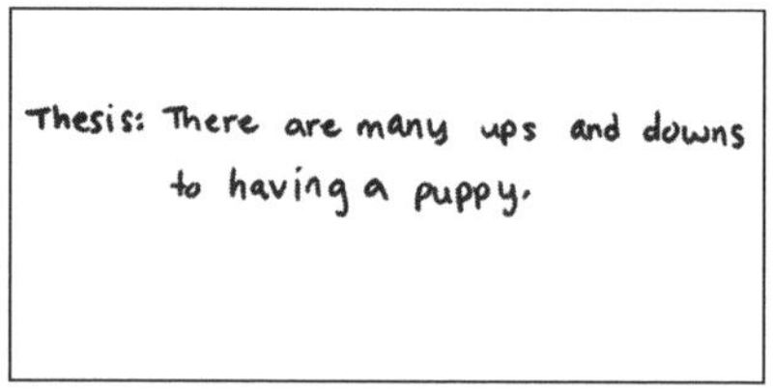

Thesis: There are many ups and downs to having a puppy.

Fig. VI-5 Elsie

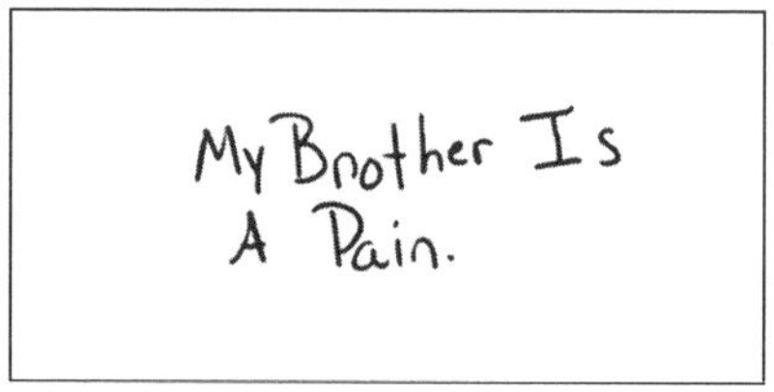

My Brother Is A Pain.

Fig. VI-6 Tray Sean

It's hard being a girl

Fig. VI-7 LaKeya

You can of course turn back to any of the minilessons in other units about finding and developing seed ideas since the process of finding and developing thesis ideas can be similar.

HOMEWORK | *Comparing Narrative and Expository Writing Processes* Writers, we haven't been talking a lot about the *writing process*, but I hope you realize that we're progressing through the stages of the writing process just as we did when we wrote personal narratives. Tonight, would you look back at our Monitoring My Writing Process checklist from our last unit of study, and think, "How is our process for writing essays the same as, and different from, the process we cycled through when we wrote personal narratives?" I'll send a blank chart home with you. Will you fill it out so that it accounts for the process you've experienced so far in this unit?

I'm also sending home our chart of the Qualities of Good Personal Narrative Writing. Would you think about this question: "Which qualities of good writing are shared in both genres? What qualities of good writing should we emphasize on a chart of Qualities of Good Expository Writing?" I'm sending home a blank Qualities of Good Expository Writing chart—please fill it out as well as you can.

The charts and lists that we make are ways to organize, consolidate, and make available all that children are learning so that they can draw on these strategies in the midst of writing time. If we want children to refer to charts, we need to do so in our minilessons, conferences, and small-group instruction. You may want to eventually turn some of these charts into checklists or rubrics, giving them to children to keep on hand as guides while they work.

Monitoring My Writing Process	First Piece	Next Piece
Gather entries		
Select and develop one seed idea		
Write an entry about what you are really trying to say		
Storytell to rehearse for writing		
Read published writing that resembles what I want to write		
Study published leads. Pay attention to what the author did and how the author did it. Let this influence your own writing		
Draft leads—try action, dialogue, setting		
Make a timeline		
Choose paper, plan story on pages, copy lead		
Write draft with each part on a separate page		
Reread and revise for clarity		
Draft endings—try writing with important ideas and images from the story, and with details that are reminders of the whole		
Revise and edit more now, or decide to wait until later, or not to revise		

To help you, I've also given each of you an essay that is worth studying.

Parent Pressure

By Harriet

Lately, I've been feeling like I have a huge weight on my back. I worry about every decision I make and every test I take. I feel like I always have to give 110 percent. I realize that I feel this way because I am under a lot of pressure from my parents. They put a lot of pressure on me in academics, sports, and even my social life.

My parents put tons of pressure on me when it comes to grades and tests. The subject doesn't matter. It could be math, reading, writing, gym, or drama! Any time I do anything at school I have to get a good grade. One time I studied really hard for a social studies test on the American Revolution and got three wrong. For two days my mom kept insisting that I didn't study. So on my next social studies test my mom timed me. I had to study one hour each night for four days. I was so nervous to take that test. My stomach felt like a million bees were buzzing inside of it! I didn't want to let my parents down.

Also my parents pressure me about my career. I had to get into a good elementary school. Now that I am there they say I have to go to a great high school, get a thousand scholarships, then go to a top college. It doesn't end there. I have to get another thousand scholarships to go to medical school. Then I have to study hard to become an incredible doctor. It feels like this pressure will never end. I am only nine years old!

My parents also pressure me athletically. My parents want me to be the absolute best in sports. In soccer they want me to kick the most goals, be the star. In swimming they want me to win every heat. They also want me to play a variety of sports like tennis, basketball, bowling, and golf. One time when I was playing soccer the star on the team, Cate, passed me the ball right in front of the net. I realized that if I made the goal my team would win. There was only a little time left. I could hear my dad cheering from the sides, "Go go go!" he shouted. "Kick it in!" I felt like time was slowing down. I was so afraid to mess up that I couldn't move. Suddenly a player from the other team kicked the ball from out between my feet. I never made a goal that game and I could tell that my dad was disappointed in me. There was too much pressure.

Finally, my parents pressure me socially. When I was little they wanted me to make the "right choice" when choosing friends. To be my friend kids had to be smart and never get in trouble. My parents really cared about the influence I got from other people. This was also true for my friend Angeli. Her parents only let her hang out with kids that got hundreds on tests. Angeli told me that she felt very limited with her friendships. She said there were a lot of kids that she wanted to have play dates with, but she wasn't allowed. She didn't want those kids to know that her parents wouldn't let her play with them. She didn't want to be mean. The pressure did not make her happy.

My parents put a lot of pressure on me and I hate it, but I realize that they probably don't realize how they make me feel. Adults can be oblivious to kids' feelings, but I also have never told them how I feel. Maybe if we talked about it they would understand that they don't have to worry about me. I always try my hardest.

Qualities of Good Personal Narrative Writing

- Write a little seed story; don't write all about a giant watermelon topic.
- Zoom in so you tell the most important parts of the story.
- Include true, exact details from the movie you have in your mind.
- Stay inside your own point of view. This will help you to write with true and exact details.
- Make sure stories tell not just what happens, but also the response to what happens.

TAILORING YOUR TEACHING

If your students have difficulty understanding what a thesis statement is and if they have trouble finding one in their entries . . . you might teach your students that we make thesis statements all the time in life. You can suggest to them that when they are trying to convince their parents about something, they often begin the discussion by making a thesis statement and then offering evidence to support it. "Dad, I need pierced ears. Here's why . . . " or "I have too many chores! I have no time for fooling around anymore."

Another real-life example you might share is that people make thesis statements when they argue. In arguments, people often talk in thesis statements and provide evidence to further the points they are trying to make. You could say, "Imagine you and your friend disagree about which sport is the best, and you tell your friend something like, 'Soccer is a better game than basketball.' That's a thesis statement that you'll have to prove by offering evidence that supports your claim. Right now, think about some arguments you've had or think about some things you've been trying to persuade your parents to let you do. Turn and tell your partner about the example you've come up with, but try to tell it by starting with the thesis statement."

Another way to approach this is to ask your students to consider a concern they have about school. You might say something like this: "Writers, you guys always come back from recess complaining that it's too short. Let's pretend we're going to write an essay about it to give to the principal. What is your thesis statement or claim?" You might have the students turn and talk while you listen in. "Writers, I heard lots of different thesis statements. Some of you said things like, 'Fourth graders need longer recess time after lunch.' I also heard some of you say, 'It's not fair that fourth graders have the same amount of recess time as third graders.' Hmm. A few of you said, 'More recess time will help fourth graders behave better in class.' Wow, what thesis statements. Each of those claims would be great beginnings for an essay—as long as you can supply evidence!"

From these examples, you might ask your students to go back into their notebooks and find a thesis statement that could turn into an essay.

COLLABORATING WITH COLLEAGUES

As you will have noticed, writing thesis statements is not easy for children. To better understand the challenges involved in creating a thesis statement, you might read this notebook entry with your colleagues, then together write several potential theses based on its contents. After a few minutes, come back together and compare what you have written.

> Our dad is quiet. My brother wishes he weren't. My brother's father-in-law is not quiet, and my brother spends almost all of his visiting time with his father-in-law and not with our dad. Our dad does not make a lot of phone calls to check in on us, his children. My brother's father-in-law comes over to his house most days. I see how well he knows my brother's house—he knows just how to move the door to the baby's room to keep it from creaking. Our dad gets lost on the way to my brother's house because he has been there so few times. My brother wishes our dad was different in so many ways. My brother forgets what our father did with him when he was little. Every Saturday, our dad would take my brother and me to the park to pitch to us until he was sore. Later that night, my mom would rub Tiger Balm into my dad's stiff arm. My brother's basketball team just won the championship. Dad heard about it from an acquaintance. My brother knows his wife's family so well, and he knows us less and less. I miss my brother.

When we tried this exercise, we came up with these possible thesis statements.

- Having a quiet father is hard.
- Quiet people have a difficult time maintaining relationships.
- Kids often wish their parents were different.
- Adult children don't value what was done for them as a child.

- Getting married doesn't expand your family, it shrinks it.
- People don't change just because you wish they would.
- People can really only have one father, not two.
- Adult children need to find ways to stay connected to their parents.
- My brother's hobby, basketball coaching, could repair the relationship between him and my dad.

As you look at this list or the one you and your colleagues generated, think about where a thesis statement comes from in relation to exactly what's written on the page as a notebook entry—then you can more easily help your children craft them. Sometimes we can form a thesis by taking a statement and attaching a judgment to it: "My dad is quiet" becomes "Having a quiet father is hard." Some thesis statements are a generalization based on the specifics in the writing. For example, "Quiet people have a difficult time maintaining relationships," generalizes the situation between this particular father and this son. Some thesis statements seem to come as potential solutions to problems: "My brother's hobby, basketball coaching, could repair the relationship between him and my dad." With your colleagues, you can find words to describe the ways in which different theses statements are created. However, this process of studying writing with colleagues and describing together what the writer has done can help your teaching of any stage of the writing process.

BOXES AND BULLETS: FRAMING ESSAYS

IN THIS SESSION, YOU WILL TEACH CHILDREN THAT ESSAYISTS FRAME THEIR WRITING BEFORE THEY DRAFT. YOU WILL DEMONSTRATE SOME STRATEGIES FOR DOING SO.

GETTING READY

- Simple example thesis that is easy to support with reasons, parts, or examples
- Class thesis statement
- Copies of two student essays from a past year, one set per child
- See CD-ROM for resources

Before you embark on today's session, you will definitely want to have a thesis in mind so that you can write your own essay along with your students. Unless you try your hand at this work, you won't grasp why and how it is challenging. To an outsider, the process described in this book may look simple, but it's vastly more complicated and more interesting than it appears from a distance.

Your goal today will be to help your children imagine several alternative plans or outlines for an essay. You will teach children that essayists sometimes support their thesis by providing reasons for a claim, sometimes by offering examples, sometimes by explaining how the parts of a subject support the author's point. Students will begin with their thesis statement(s) and then mull over the smaller points they want to make. Will they support the thesis by providing reasons? Examples? Kinds? By elucidating how the parts of the subject relate to the whole premise?

If you look closely at what your children do in response to today's teaching, you'll find this work is vastly more complicated than you ever imagined—and hence it will present you with lots of teaching and learning opportunities.

This session will not follow the usual pattern of a writing workshop. Instead of a ten-minute minilesson followed by a forty-minute Writing and Conferring, this minilesson will be a double-decker, with time for work interspersed throughout the extended minilesson. Let children know this plan at the start of the minilesson. As children sit around you in the meeting area, confer with individuals and small groups. Most of the lessons over the next few days will come from the ways you help writers confront and overcome difficulties. You'll definitely want to move quickly from child to child, helping them explore and learn from the writing that emerges on their pages. Perhaps you can have a small group of children gather around you during lunch or a prep period to give yourself extra time to read and think about their work.

Minilesson

Boxes and Bullets: Framing Essays

CONNECTION

Summarize the writing process your essayists have experienced thus far, referring to their homework.

"Writers, today marks a big day in our unit. Before we go forward, let's pat ourselves on the back for the work we've done so far. For homework, you thought about the writing process for us as essayists. We've been gathering entries by paying attention to things in our lives and thinking hard about them. Then we reread, asking ourselves, 'So what do I *really* want to say?' Then, we each wrote our seed idea as a thesis statement."

"I hope that right now each of you has a thesis that you feel fired up about, one that you can hold in your two hands like this." I showed the children how I held a construction-paper plaque containing my thesis between my two hands. "Right now, would you each write your thesis statement in a big box at the top of a clean notebook page?"

Name the teaching point. In this case, tell children that essay writers frame the main sections of essays before researching and drafting them.

"Today I am going to teach you that essay writers, unlike narrative writers, do not make a timeline or a story mountain and then progress straight into drafting. Instead we often pause at this point to plan (or frame) the main sections of our essay. We plan the sections of our essays by deciding how we will elaborate on our main idea."

COACHING

During a unit of study, we walk children through the writing process slowly, step-by-step, so that we can be present at crucial moments to lift the level of what children do. But we hope children will eventually be able to cycle through the stages of the writing process with independence, at whatever speed matches their methods and constraints. It's important, for now, to help children get an aerial view of the process, so they grasp the main contours of it and will be more ready to propel themselves through the process another time.

I have taught this session using fairly physical props, such as a construction paper "plaque" on which each child writes his or her thesis. When I do that, I'm trying to convey subtle messages through the use of materials. The plaque helps children to let go of their previous writing and give attention to their thesis. It helps them to feel as if they've made a commitment to a single thesis. The entire rehearsal and entry-gathering phase culminates in the commitment to this one- or two-sentence claim. I didn't do that today because for this class I felt having their boxed thesis and list of bulleted sections all on one page would be more helpful for them in conceiving the essay as a whole.

TEACHING

Show children that writers often elaborate upon a thesis by discussing the reasons for their claim.

"Let me show you how I consider different ways to elaborate on my thesis. For now, I will use a really simple (and not all that interesting) example. Pretend that my thesis is this: 'Bikes are fun.' My job is to think about what I really want to say about my thesis, and then to design categories or sections for my essay that match what I want to say. I'll first think of what I have to say." I role-played the part of the writer who does this thinking silently.

"Now let me think of how I could categorize what I have to say."

After just a bit, pause to debrief, pointing out the replicable steps you followed. Then continue to role-play the next steps in the process.

"Notice that I physically (or at least mentally) take hold of my thesis." I grasped my plaque labeled "Bikes are fun" with both hands. "Then I think of all I've written and thought about that topic and ask myself, 'What do I really want to say about bikes?' I'm considering whether I want to tell the different *reasons* they are fun, and I'm asking whether the ideas I have are *reasons*." Then I said, "Often I'm not totally sure, so I give it a try. Watch."

I shifted from the role of teacher to the role of writer. "Okay. My main idea is 'Bikes are fun.' I'm going to think about different reasons and see if those categories contain what I really want to say." I wrote my reasons in a bulleted list:

> Bikes are fun.

- Bikes are fun because you can do tricks on them.
- Bikes are fun because you can go places on them.
- Bikes are fun because you can fix them when they break.

Debrief by articulating what you did that you hope children will also do.

"I call this work 'planning out possible boxes and bullets.' As you can see, after I choose my seed idea and write it as a thesis, I always spend a while—sometimes an hour or so, sometimes less—imagining different possible sections I could include in my essay. I do this by trying out different 'boxes and bullets.' Each time I think, 'Is *this* what I really want to say?' So far today you learned that one way to develop a thesis, a claim, is by writing the different *reasons* for an idea, like I just did."

Notice that I settle for the most bare-bones thesis imaginable. You may be uncomfortable with this, in which case I encourage you to choose a more insightful thesis. The thesis I use here has advantages because it is so bland and uninteresting that my listeners' eyes and ears are drawn to the specific ways I elaborate on it, and thus to the focus of this minilesson.

I think silently because I don't want to add unnecessary detail and risk cluttering what will already be complex instruction. Never underestimate the dramatic effect you create by simply thinking silently for several seconds at the front of the meeting area.

There is nothing fancy about this example, but it is so simple and concrete that I think it works well. The more complex and specific a thesis is, the harder it is to think through these support categories.

It is challenging to defend a claim by discussing several reasons, but most claims can be supported in this way. Your children may not even need to consider other ways to elaborate. If you decide to teach only this one way to elaborate on an idea, you can tell children that once writers have made a claim they need to provide evidence (give reasons) why their idea/claim/opinion is true. You can, if you choose, ask your children to use the transitional word because.

ACTIVE ENGAGEMENT
Set children up to practice using reasons as a way to elaborate on a whole-class thesis.

"Why don't you try this? Just for now, pretend each one of you is in the midst of writing and your thesis is 'Working with first-grade reading buddies is fun.' Think for a minute about what you have to say on this topic." I wrote the topic on a construction paper plaque while the children thought silently. "Try asking yourself the same questions I asked: 'What if I thought of different *reasons* for this? Will that give me the categories that can contain my thoughts?'"

"To get yourselves started, I suggest you always repeat the stem of your thesis. So reiterate the stem (Working with first-grade reading buddies is fun), then add *because* and name one reason. 'Working with first-grade reading buddies is fun because . . . (this reason).' Then say, 'Working with first-grade reading buddies is *also* fun because . . . (that reason).'"

"Partner 1, write in the air to convey what you'd say are the main reasons why working with first-grade reading buddies is fun. Help each other if you get stuck." The room erupted into talk.

Listen in. Interject lean prompts that lift the level of what individuals do.

I pulled in to listen to children talking in partnerships. Leo said to his partner, "'Cause we teach 'em?"

I interjected, "Leo, the tone of your voice is important. Try saying your bullets as if each one is a claim, a pronouncement. I know you are just trying these out to see if they sound right and make sense, but use the voice of a teacher or a lecturer. And remember to repeat the whole sentence. Start 'Working with reading buddies is fun because . . .'"

" . . . we teach them to read."

I nodded and continued, repeating the thesis stem again and leaving a space for him to add a second reason. "'Working with reading buddies is also fun because . . .'"

" . . . we get to read cool books."

I nodded, gesturing for him to continue.

"And they look up to us."

I chose this whole class "exercise thesis" because it was a topic these kids knew about and one that would work for all the kinds of elaboration I want children to practice. You'll select a thesis that will work for your specific children—choose it with some care and plan on returning to the thesis often. Some teachers have found that "Fifth (or fourth) grade is challenging" works.

Instead of using a whole-class exercise text, you could ask children to try this work on their own theses. We rarely ask children to use their own work in the Active Engagement sections of the minilessons because that leaves them unable to initiate the work of the minilesson when they go back to their seats—they have already gotten started on the work. When I teach classrooms full of struggling writers, however, I am apt to use the Active Engagement time as a chance to get everyone to initiate the work of the day.

"Great, but repeat the stem. 'Working with reading buddies is *also* fun because they look up to us,' I said, and Leo dutifully repeated the sentence after me. "Now put it all together—say the whole thing to your partner," I said, and listened while he got started. "Working with reading buddies is fun because we teach kids to read. Working with reading buddies is also fun because we get to read cool books. And working with reading buddies is fun because the little kids look up to us."

You may find that you resist having your children repeat the stem of their thesis over and over. It runs against all our training for children to be so repetitive! If you decide to encourage children to word the stem differently each time, you'll be in good company. We tried this too. But we have come to believe that if children don't repeat their stem (at least during their first experiences with this unit of study), they end up with categories (bullets) that aren't cohesive. This disjunction becomes increasingly problematic when the main idea is elaborated upon in an entire paragraph that also doesn't align. I strongly recommend that you stop worrying that the topic sentences will be dull if children repeat the stem.

Spotlight what the child has done in a manner that demonstrates what you hope all children have learned to do.

I jotted down what Leo said onto chart paper. Then I said over the buzz of conversation, "Writers." I waited for silence. "At first when Leo tried to cite reasons for our idea, he said, 'Working with reading buddies is fun because we teach 'em?' but I told him he needed to use a teacher's tone, a lecturer's tone. He is making a claim. And he remembered to repeat the whole sentence for each point. Listen to what he says now." I read from where I'd copied his ideas onto chart paper.

In this unit, the work you do in response to kids' efforts will be especially important because the intellectual work of the unit has everything to do with muddling through the hard parts. So insert yourself into partner conversations and listen for what you can support and teach. You may find that you need to convene the whole class' attention several times, intervening to lift the level of children's work during the prolonged Active Engagement. For example, often a close look will reveal that two of the reasons a child has produced are the same, just worded differently—you could mention that now or save it for a later time. Perhaps the child's points don't sound aligned—you could adjust them subtly by repeating them, with small tweaks that make the child's language fall into parallel structure.

> Working with our ~~first-grade~~ reading buddies is fun.
>
> - Working with our ~~first-grade~~ reading buddies is fun because we get to teach them to read.
> - Working with our ~~first-grade~~ reading buddies is fun because we get to read really cool books.
> - Working with our ~~first-grade~~ reading buddies is also fun because they look up to us.

"Try your claims again and make sure you speak in a teaching voice, and that you repeat your stems. You can also trim them a bit so they go like this if you want," I said, and revised Leo's boxes and bullets so they looked (and sounded) like this:

Leo's actual words used the second-person "you." "Working with reading buddies is fun because you get to teach them to read." I've switched his pronouns to one I prefer: "we." It's not unusual for me to make tiny refinements before I spotlight a child's work.

Working with our first-grade reading buddies is fun.

- One reason that working with reading buddies is fun is that we get to teach our buddies to read.
- Another reason that working with reading buddies is fun is that we get to read really cool books.
- And, finally, working with reading buddies is fun because they look up to us.

This final revision is optional, of course. Eventually you'll want to teach children to use transition words such as these, but it needn't be now. Leave the child's work that you have spotlighted on display as a mentor text.

Try not to use too many words, to be too chatty, when your intent is to scaffold children toward independence.

LINK
Instead of sending children off to work at their desks, ask them to apply what you've taught to their own writing while they work in the meeting area.

"I would usually send you off to work now, reminding you that whenever you have a thesis and want to plan the categories in your essay, you can always consider whether the ideas you want to convey would fit into paragraphs in which you write, 'I think this because . . .' and then, 'Another reason I believe this is . . . .'"

You'll find that sometimes, for some thesis statements, elaborating by discussing kinds or examples will work better than reasons. So if several children don't find their content falls into the categories they establish by elaborating upon their reasons, then you'll definitely want to show these children that they can instead elaborate on their claims in ways I describe later in this mega-minilesson. And if your writers are experienced enough that you'd like to show more possibilities, then you'll also want to show other ways to elaborate.

WRITING AND CONFERRING

Framing Essays

The minilesson was over, but I didn't send children off to their work spots. "Instead of sending you off to try this with your own thesis statements, for today let's have a tiny workshop right here on the rug. Each of you has your thesis. Take a minute and ask, 'Can I think of different reasons—will reasons give me categories in which to write?' Write boxes (your thesis) and bullets (your reasons), as Leo did, in your writer's notebook." As I spoke, I pointed to Leo's thesis and bullets about first-grade reading buddies. "Remember to repeat the stem of your thesis over and over as Leo did," I said as I pointed to the repetition of "Working with first-grade reading buddies is fun because . . . " I told children to show their tentative plan to a partner. "Help each other. Talk about whether you actually want to write within the frame you've proposed. You need to be sure the categories hold what you want to say." As children worked, I moved among them.

I helped one child after another set up possible frameworks for an essay, and I encouraged nearby children to listen in as I worked with their classmates. I especially helped kids "try on" a variety of optional ways their essays could go. My conversations sounded like this:

"So what is your thesis, Diana?"

"My mom is important to me."

"That's such a huge, important idea. 'My mom is important to me!' What reasons will you provide?"

"I don't know. 'Cause she's nice?"

"Smart work. That definitely could be a reason why she is important to you. Can you say it in a whole sentence—and then keep going, listing another reason?" To show Diana, I said, "'My mom is important to me because she is nice. She is also important to me because . . . ' What else?"

MID-WORKSHOP TEACHING POINT **Finding Alternative Ways to Support a Thesis** "Writers, let's try *another* way to develop your thesis. Earlier I suggested telling my *reasons* behind the thesis. I could also consider whether the ideas I want to convey would fit into paragraphs in which I tell about different *kinds*. So watch me think about kinds of things to back up my thesis." Gripping the page on which I'd written my thesis, I said, "Okay. I'll go back to my main idea, 'Bikes are fun.' I'm going to think of all I've written and all I've thought about that topic, and then ask myself, 'Do I want to tell how different *kinds of bikes* are fun?'"

"I could write a paragraph about how *two-wheeler* bikes are fun, another one about how *tricycles* are fun, another one about how *bicycles built for two* are fun, and one paragraph about how *dirt bikes* are fun,'" I said, writing these in boxes and bullets format on chart paper.

> Bikes are fun.
>
> - Two-wheeler bikes are fun.
> - Tricycles are fun.
> - Bicycles built for two are fun.
> - And, most of all, dirt bikes are fun.

continued on next page

"She takes me places?"

"Okay, but say it in a whole sentence," I said.

I'm not worried right now about whether Diana's claims are especially original or specific. Although ordinarily I wouldn't accept something as vague as "My mom is important to me because she is nice," in this instance I keep in mind that I have asked kids to write *big ideas*. I have asked for generalizations. Although it is true that even big ideas often become more compelling when they are more specific, it can then be harder to elaborate on them when they are more specific. (For example, recently a child tried to work with, "Being a kid and not being able to drive till you are eighteen is hard.") So for now I don't necessarily push for more specificity than "My mom is nice." My goal is to help kids grasp the concept of an umbrella idea that is supported by several distinct and parallel subordinate categories.

As I worked with one child and then another, I often intervened when kids' categories didn't "go together." If a child said, "My mom is important to me because she is nice, my mom is important to me because she is patient, my mom is important to me because she got me a DVD for my birthday," I tried to help the child feel in his or her bones that those didn't match. The first two categories describe character traits, and they are fundamentally different from the last category. This gets more complicated when children's ideas are more complex. Tyrone, for example, had written: "I don't want to let my grandmother down" as his thesis, and his bullets were "by not taking care of the baby; she'd be all alone with no one to help her; so she isn't sad." To help this struggling writer understand why those three bullets didn't go together, I told Tyrone that if my thesis was "I like oranges" and my supports were "because they are juicy, because they are tasty, and [I said the next phrase in a way that accentuated that it didn't fit] because one day I saw an orange plant in a rainforest," people would say my categories didn't go together. To help a child recognize when things aren't parallel, I often point out, "This should sound like a song. Listen." For example, I read the claim "I like oranges because they are juicy/I like oranges because they

---

continued from previous page

"Why don't you try elaborating on our class topic by discussing different *kinds*?" I read aloud, "Working with our first-grade reading buddies is fun," and said, "Ask yourself, 'What if I think about different *kinds* of things—will that give me categories that fit with what I want to say?' Let's try thinking, specifically, about all the different kinds of work that you do with those guys. Talk with your partner and think through the different kinds of work that you and your reading buddies do that is fun." Soon I convened the group and shared Sophie's suggestions.

> **Working with our first-grade reading buddies is fun.**

- Telling our reading buddies to stop fooling around and to stay with us is fun.
- Teaching our reading buddies to read the words is fun.
- Reading great stories aloud to our reading buddies is fun.

continued on next page

Figure VII-1 Sophie's first draft of her boxes and bullets

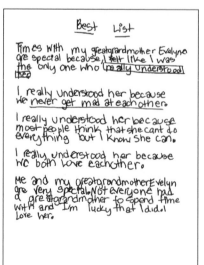

Figure VII-2 Sophie's second draft is more specific than her first draft

are tasty" with rhythm and intonation that accentuated the fact that the first two bullets matched. Then I read the third bullet ("I like oranges because one day I saw an orange plant in a rainforest") in a way that caused dissonance. To help the child construct a revised bullet, I almost always go back and reread the first two bullets in a song-like way and then get the child to construct a third statement that fits rhythmically alongside the other two. As I do this work, I also show children that in the end we can collapse topic sentences so that, for example, my thesis about liking oranges, can, in the end, look like this: "I like oranges because they are juicy, tasty, and healthy."

Children seem to grasp the point when I use a very obvious example. Tyronne, for example, could see that my original sentences about oranges weren't aligned, so he rewrote them to say, "I like oranges because they are juicy, because they are tasty, and because they are beautiful on the tree." With some help, Tyrone went back and revised his claims about his grandmother: "I don't want to let my grandmother down or else she'll be all alone, she'll have no one to help with the baby, and she'll be sad."

continued from previous page

"In a minute you'll have a chance to see if it works for you to think about different *kinds* of things related to your claim. But first I want to teach you another way to plan categories. As you've already learned, writers sometimes write *reasons*, we sometimes write *kinds* —but we also sometimes write *parts*." I demonstrated, saying, "Watch me recall my thesis (bikes are fun) and ask "What if I think of different *parts*?" Soon I'd mentioned that the wheels of bikes are fun, the handlebars of bikes are fun, and so forth. Then I pointed out that sometimes writers write about different times, or instances their claim has been true, to support it.

"So writers, let's go back to our desks where we can really concentrate. You'll be writing lots of different possible boxes and bullets in your notebooks so that you can figure out which way best matches what you really want to say," I said, gesturing to Leo's example, which showed the layout for this strategy. "Some of you will elaborate on your idea by discussing *kinds*, some will discuss different *reasons*, some different *parts* or *times*. Writers always try several ways to support a thesis, and we try wording whatever we come up with in lots of different ways until we feel we've hit the nail on the head. The important thing is to try several variations, and after each one consider, 'Is this what I want to say?'"

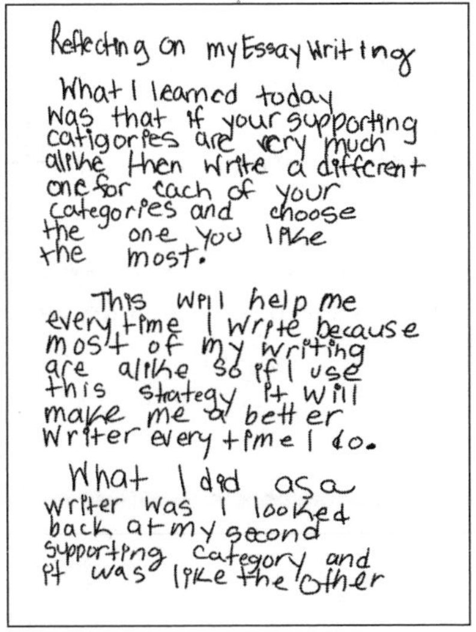

Reflecting on my Essay Writing

What I learned today was that if your supporting catigories are very much alike then write a different one for each of your categories and choose the one you like the most.

This will help me every time I write because most of my writing are alike so if I use this strategy it will make me a better writer every time I do.

What I did as a writer was I looked back at my second supporting category and it was like the other

Figure VII-3 Sophie explains, in this entry, what she learned from a conference that led to her next draft of boxes and bullets

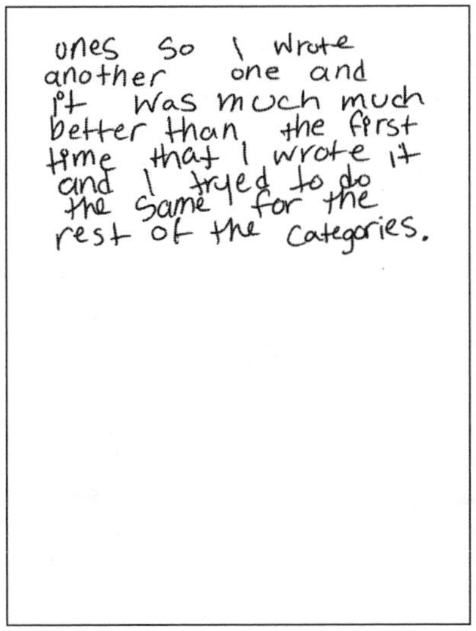

ones so I wrote another one and it was much much better than the first time that I wrote it and I tryed to do the same for the rest of the categories.

Figure VII-4 Sophie's entry page 2

SHARE

Revising Thesis Statements

Teach students that revising their thesis statement is an option when they have difficulty supporting it.

"Today you have been figuring out how your essays will go by deciding how you will support your thesis statements. I saw all of you trying this out. You decided whether you wanted to talk about the *reasons, kinds,* or *parts,* and you made sure that you had enough to say about the categories you selected. I noticed that some of you were really struggling to find bullets that support your thesis. When a writer has trouble supporting a thesis, one option is to revise the thesis statement."

"I want to share what Vianca did while she was trying to plan her essay. Her original thesis was 'Playing sports is fun,' and she planned to discuss how sports are fun for kids and grown-ups. When she thought about finding the evidence for this essay, however, she realized that she didn't want to write about *grown-ups* playing sports! So she decided to revise her thesis. Her new thesis is 'Playing sports is fun for kids.' She took one of her topic sentences and made it into her new thesis. In Vianca's case, this made her thesis more specific."

Have students go back to their plans to see if this strategy might be helpful to them.

"Can you share your current plans for your essay with your partner? Make sure to discuss the choices that you have made. Also, check your thesis. Will you have a lot of evidence to go with your topic sentences? Does your thesis match what you plan to say about it?"

If you believe that children have already revised their thesis statements well enough, you may want to use this share time to again emphasize the importance of building essays with parallel supporting paragraphs. You could list thesis statements and then supporting paragraph ideas, each with one that is off-kilter, so that children can learn to spy the ones that need revision.

> Sometimes I hurt peoples feelings
> • Sometimes I hurt peoples feelings to get back at them.
> • Sometimes I hurt peoples feelings to fit in.
> • Sometimes I hurt peoples feelings because I am man.
> • Sometimes I hurt peoples feelings when I am cranky.
> • Sometimes I hurt peoples feelings when I am having a hard time.

Fig VII-5 Olivia's thesis statement and possible support ideas

HOMEWORK *Checking Thesis and Support Alignment* For homework tonight, practice being a reader of essay drafts. I've made copies of the work two students wrote in my class last year. Pretend these are your essays, and ask, "Is the support material really aligned to the claim?" If it isn't, think about what you'd suggest the writer do.

For example, you'll see that Shanice claims, "I'm proud of my cat." One of her reasons is "I'm proud of my cat because she just had kittens." Think about the topic and think about the point that Shanice's support material needs to advance. Now read this entry and think, "Does this support Shanice's claim?"

> For example, one morning I woke up to a screaming noise.
> It was the sound of a baby kitten. I looked under my
> bed. My cat was giving birth. Later on I found out there
> was four baby kittens and we were giving them away.
> We were only keeping the mother and a brown kitten.

You'll probably agree that although yes, much of this *is* about the fact that the cat had kittens, it does not support the fact that Shanice is proud of her cat. Think, then, about how Shanice could have revised her writing to solve this. One of her friends suggested she revise her writing like this:

> For example, one morning I woke up to a screaming noise.
> It was the sound of a baby kitten. My cat was lying
> peacefully and being a perfect mother. I didn't even
> know she was old enough to be a mother. She is young to
> have babies and I'm proud of her.

Tonight, read the essays I'm sending home with you in just this manner, and carefully consider whether the support material is really aligned to the points.

If your students are struggling to support their thesis statements . . . you could teach them that writers can revise their thesis statements by either making their subject more specific or making it more general. Recall the Share when Vianca made her subject more specific by revising from "Sports are fun" to "Sports are fun for kids." "Sports" is a very big topic, so she narrowed it a bit by making it more specific to sports for kids. When the thesis statement is very broad, it can be paralyzing for young writers to decide which approach to take in order to support it. For example, in Vianca's case she could have talked about playing different kinds of sports, reasons that playing sports are fun, being a spectator at sporting events, and so on. If the thesis is this broad and if there are so many evidence options, it's easy for the young writer to develop supporting evidence that doesn't quite fit together. Consequently, the essay may veer wildly from point to point.

Conversely, writers who are having trouble supporting their thesis statements may want to make their subject more general by opening it up. For example, Alexa was trying to find support for her thesis statement, "Violent television is bad for kids." She couldn't find enough reasons that supported this statement, so she made her subject more general. She changed "violent television" to "television." Her new thesis reads, "Television is bad for kids," and she easily came up with evidence to support her idea.

In a minilesson, you might model a struggle to support one of your thesis statements, and then demonstrate how making it broader or narrower can help a writer develop evidence that supports it. For the active engagement, you might use a student's thesis statement that needs some revision and ask the students to consider how they'd tweak the statement to more easily support it.

ASSESSMENT

You will definitely want to spend time this evening poring over the work your children have done. You'll probably want to categorize children so that tomorrow you can gather those who need a particular kind of help and give them that support right away.

Some children will profit from help developing *parallel* bullets. For example, John's plan was as follows:

> I'm proud of myself because I'm a good baseball player.

- I have good sportsmanship.
- I know the game well.
- Characteristics of a good baseball player.

Once he'd lopped off the final bullet and revised the third bullet to "I have good skills," he was stuck because he couldn't imagine anything more to say! He was dead set against settling for only two categories, and ended up realizing he could divide his second category (I have good skills) into more specific points:

> I'm proud of myself because I'm a good baseball player.

- I'm good at bat.
- I'm good in the field.
- I'm good as a team member.

Similarly, Estefan realized these categories weren't parallel:

> My dad is important to me because ...

- I have fun when we play baseball.
- He makes sure I get a good amount of sleep so I am ready for the next day.
- He shows me math.

He worked on making them match, and ended up writing:

> My dad helps me ...

- with baseball
- with math
- with daily life

Other children need to consider what they've said very carefully, checking to be sure their words are precise. Sarah wrote:

> My dog is like my best friend.

- He keeps me company.
- He understands how I'm feeling.
- He licks me all over.

She realized that her best friend doesn't lick her at all.

The most common problem, however, was that bullets often reiterated the same point, as in Takuma's example:

> Without my grandparents, I would have felt lonely.

- It's hard to play alone.
- It's difficult and lonely not to be able to talk to others.
- It's hard to be walking all alone.

SESSION VIII

LEARNING TO OUTGROW A FIRST THESIS

IN THIS SESSION, YOU WILL TEACH CHILDREN THAT WRITERS FREE WRITE AND ASK QUESTIONS IN AN EFFORT TO OUTGROW EARLY DRAFTS OF A THESIS STATEMENT.

GETTING READY

- Story you can tell about a writer who discovered the value of postponing closure
- Notebook entries showing how children tried to push their thinking about their thesis statements
- Thesis you can use to demonstrate telling an essay aloud
- See CD-ROM for resources

An essay represents a mind at work. *Effective essays not only contain strong writing, they also contain strong thinking. From the start, then, we need to nudge children to think deeply as they write. It's easy to say that we will teach children to think deeply—but what might such instruction entail? We can't very well say, "Writers, watch me as I think deeply. Now I want all of you to think deeply."*

Typically, in our minilessons, we advocate a goal—a skill—and help children reach that goal by providing them with a small repertoire of optional strategies, each of which is, in effect, one set of step-by-step instructions a person might follow to reach that goal.

Today's minilesson aims to equip children with a set of strategies that may help them write more perceptive essays. A word of caution: Developing writers sometimes need to choose between writing thoughtful essays and writing tidy essays. If you are teaching inexperienced writers and this is their first experience with this essay unit, you may decide to detour around this minilesson, saving it for next year. Alternatively, you may use this as a strategy lesson only for your more agile writers. On the other hand, if your children are very experienced writers, you may teach this lesson and repeat another version of it later in the unit.

The lesson itself is not especially challenging, but it will nudge children to forgo generic (and easy-to-develop) thesis statements for more original, specific, and hard-to-develop claims. For many children, it is challenging enough to write an essay from a thesis at this level: "I'm good at baseball. I'm good when I'm in the field and I'm good when I'm up at bat." Proceed with this session if you hope your children will replace such a generic thesis statement with a more specific claim, such as, "Playing baseball well requires intelligence. When I'm at bat, I try to outwit the pitcher. When I'm in the field, I try to predict how other players will act." The latter essay is likely to be more perceptive, but it will also be more challenging to research and to structure.

MINILESSON

Learning to Outgrow a First Thesis

CONNECTION

Explain that writers postpone closure so as to *write* and also to *think* well.

"Writers, most of you drafted a thesis statement and plans for several support paragraphs in the two previous sessions. If you wanted to, you could probably write your whole essay in the next day or two. Especially once you are familiar with the expectations of this genre, you'll always have the option to either delve deep enough to write a provocative, ground-breaking essay or to whip up a quick, adequate essay. But for now, our job isn't to rush along as fast as possible. Instead our job is to take the time needed to learn along the way. And today I want to remind you that our goal when writing essays is not only to *write* well, but also to *think* well.

Name the teaching point. In this case, tell children that essayists revise early, using free writing to deepen thinking and outgrow their earliest claims.

"Specifically, I want to teach you that essayists don't wait until an essay is done before revising. Instead, we revise all along the way to make our words and our ideas as true, as significant, and as provocative as possible. Many writers use free writing as a strategy to help us do this."

TEACHING

Tell a story about someone who finished writing an essay, sensed there was more to say, and took the risk of revising the completed text.

"I want to tell you a story, a story that will end up being a lesson about writing. A few years ago, my father flew to a nearby airport to visit me. As we drove home from the airport, he told me, 'I finished writing my essay about my childhood.' I knew the text—it was a reflection on his childhood, written in part to pay homage to his parents for all they had given my dad and his siblings. As we drove, Dad explained that he had made copies of the essay for each of us nine kids and bound each copy professionally. He'd boxed up each copy to mail to us, too. Then, as Dad and I continued driving home, he said, 'But as I put the last manuscript into the last box, I realized *I left out a story.*' As he spoke, Dad punctuated each

COACHING

At the end of the unit, I will teach children to use all they've learned about essay writing in order to write quick, well-structured essays on demand when called to do so. They'll need to do this on standardized tests.

In New York City classrooms, where these units of study have been piloted, some teachers take a shortcut through this unit, arguing that in the end children need to write only the most bare-bones sort of an essay, and they need to write these very quickly. I question such a decision, believing it circumvents many teaching and learning opportunities, but it's a choice you can make.

Many writers and teachers argue vehemently against the restrictive, constrained form of a five-paragraph essay. They protest the notion that a writer decides early on what he will say and isn't allowed the journey of thought that is essential in creating thoughtful texts. This session's emphasis on writing to learn and on revising one's thesis is one of several ways in which I help children experience some of the musing, reflective, tentative, self-critical thinking that is at the heart of thoughtful writing.

Notice that this minilesson breaks stride. Instead of demonstrating or talking about a step-by-step strategy, this lesson advocates the importance of postponing closure in writing. I know that if I simply launched into this long story about my father without orienting the children, they might have sat there thinking, "Why is she telling us this?" I try to ease their minds by saying, at the start, "Sit back and listen. This will be circuitous, but in the end you'll see how it fits together."

word by banging on the dashboard of the car. '*I didn't just leave it out,*' he said. '*I boxed it out. Do you know why? Because it was just so sad. That's why.*'"

"My dad proceeded to tell me the story that he'd boxed out of his essay—a story of how, after he and his father won a sailing race together, the town circled him, celebrating by throwing him into the water, and how my dad resisted with feeble protests about having athlete's foot. Now, sitting beside me in the car, my dad continued, 'As we walked home, the water squeaking in my sneakers, my father didn't say a word to me. Not a word about the sailing race. Not a word about them heaving me into the sea.' Dad went on to say, 'The truth is, he didn't say a word about the athlete's foot or anything else. I'd failed him by not being the kind of boy who is thrown into the water with grace. And in our family, that wasn't okay. Failure wasn't okay. And talk—real talk—was rare. My father didn't say a word about the whole episode that day because, frankly, we couldn't talk about much of anything.'"

I shifted from storytelling that episode with my father to summarizing the events that ensued. I said to the children, "The visit with my dad ended, he flew home, and I waited to get the manuscript that he'd already boxed up to mail to me. Weeks went by and it didn't come. When I traveled home for Christmas, I asked my dad about it. His eyes twinkled. 'Look under the Christmas tree,' he said. There I found the long-awaited box, containing the manuscript. After I pulled it from the box, Dad directed me to a particular section. Reading it, I saw he had recounted the sailing race and the silence between him and his father after all, even though on the day of his visit to me, Dad had told me that the manuscript (without this story) had been professionally bound and boxed to mail. After retelling the sailing story, Dad had written this":

> The story, as I wrote it, fills me with intense sadness. The most important part of the story may not be the episode itself but the fact that I rejected it from the initial log. I didn't include it because it was just so sad ... for all I was given in my childhood, one thing was missing—a father who understood and cared for me, not just in a collective sense as one of his brood, but for me as a person.

Explicitly name the message you hope the story conveys. In this case, the message is that when a writer has the courage to resist premature closure and to revise, the writing becomes stronger.

"My father's final essay is more powerful because he had the courage to open the box and to mess up his original neatly packed manuscript," I said.

Notice that I refer to my dad's text as an essay. Really, it was a book-length memoir. I stretch the truth a bit to make my point to kids.

Readers who know my writing well may recall reading other versions of this story. I've told it often, each time angling it to make a different point. When I told the story in The Art of Teaching Writing, *my emphasis was that it's powerful to bring literacy home. When I told it in* The Art of Teaching Reading, *my emphasis was that we, as teachers, need the courage to outgrow our initial teaching ideas. This third version is a plea for writers to postpone closure of their writing.*

You may notice that I use all the narrative writing skills I teach children in order to write the little stories that are embedded in this minilesson. In the blink of an eye, I'll teach children that the first step to writing an effective essay is to collect miniature stories that illustrate the idea we hope to advance. As you read along through this story, take note.

"Writers know that courage matters. Writers resist the instinct for closure. We're willing to say, 'Wait. Is this *really* what I want to say?' We're willing to reopen our nicely completed thesis statements to try to be more precisely honest."

"And we try to be honest from the very start so that we don't end up, like my dad, reading the completed essay and feeling, in our bones, that we didn't really convey the true message we wanted to tell."

ACTIVE ENGAGEMENT

Tell children that you'll show a second instance in which a writer—this time a child—revised. Set children up to research and then to name the replicable strategy the writer uses.

"I want to show you one child's work and to ask you to join me in researching the specific strategies she used to outgrow her first thesis statement. We'll look again at Francesca's entry (and, more specifically, at her work from a previous minilesson). I'll describe a bit of what she did, then ask you to tell your partner what you notice that she's done that you could conceivably do as well."

"First, let me tell you a bit about the overall writing situation. Francesca found a personal narrative story she'd written about a time when she was sledding and accidentally crashed into a little child. When I approached her, she had already done the work many of you did last night, growing a big idea, a generalization. She'd settled upon this thesis."

> Grown-ups can really hurt a kid's self-esteem.

"She'd put her thesis through the battery of questions and decided it was clear, strong, and clean. But she felt uneasy about her thesis, partly because it seemed to blame grown-ups, and she wasn't sure she wanted to write an anti-grown-ups piece. So Francesca got out a sheet of paper and began to restate what she really wanted to say."

Pause early on. Ask children to list two things the writer whose story you're telling has done that they, too, could do.

Although my recount of Francesca's writing process had just begun, I nevertheless paused and said, "Turn and talk with your partner. List two things Francesca has done that you could also do as a writer. Talk about each thing and be specific. Make sure you are giving yourself advice on how to write more honest, true essays."

This minilesson tells the story of my father revising a completed text, and you may therefore wonder why I tell it now when each writer has merely written a thesis sentence. Why am I pushing revision when children have just begun to draft? The reason is that it's most likely that they'll revise in substantial ways if revision begins early. Then, too, the thesis and the plan for the essay control all that follows. They are crucial. Aristotle was right when he said, "Well begun is half done."

I like speaking of the qualities of good writing using terms such as courage and honesty. I do believe that there is a thin line between writing well and living well.

The Active Engagement section in this minilesson has an extra job to do. So far in this minilesson, children have only fleetingly heard about one specific strategy (free writing) they can use to accomplish the goal (early revision) I've advocated. The minilesson has been high on inspiration and low on instruction. Children will need me to offer more how-to help in this section.

By now, you should realize that asking children to research what a writer has done and to name what they see is one of the common choices for this section of any minilesson. It's never an ideal active engagement because the children aren't actually getting a chance to do the work—they are instead talking about it—but sometimes this seems to be the best course.

You may be surprised that I no sooner began telling Francesca's story than I was saying, "Turn and talk. What do you notice?" This is deliberate and common. I want children to listen with alertness, expecting that they'll be called upon to make meaning. I don't want them to sit back in their seats and wait for meaning, significance, to jump up and bop them over the head.

The children talked, I eavesdropped, and then I asked for their attention. "I heard you say several things that Francesca did."

- She really looked closely at what she'd written.
- She gave her own words the truth test.
- She listened to her uneasy feeling.
- She was willing to mess up a perfectly okay, tidy thesis.
- Finally, Francesca tried to restate what she wanted to say.

It is unlikely that I actually heard children saying these points, and certainly not in this chronological order. You may decide to reiterate what your children do in fact say, or you may use this as a chance to restate what you hope children have deduced.

"I especially want to emphasize that smart, thoughtful writers don't just settle for words that are in the ballpark. We are willing to feel uneasy; we have the keen eyesight required to see little untruths and contradictions and problems hiding in the shadows and cracks of our own sentences, and we're willing to flush them out."

"Let me continue with my story of Francesca. She tried to write more, to say more, and to talk not only about sledding—the particular story—but also about her biggest topic, self-esteem. She wrote this entry."

> Your self-esteem pretty much stays the same in your life unless you really change who you are. The way you interact with the world controls how you feel. Say you were riding your bike all summer and you are about to show everyone, then you fall off. It may not change how you look at yourself if you have really good self-esteem. Self-esteem is very important to everyone on this earth. It is important to like yourself all throughout your life. Your self-esteem needs to be treated right. If people abuse you and make you feel really bad, your self-esteem can change. If you are not around people who care about you, your self-esteem (can) really change. You need to always want to grow up, but you need to know that it isn't really smooth.

Pause and ask children again to list two things the writer has done that they, too, could do. Generate a list of advice gleaned from eavesdropping.

"Turn and talk with your partner. Again, list two things Francesca has done as a writer that you could also do. Talk about each thing and be specific. Make sure you are gleaning advice that you can use as you think about free writing today."

The children talked, I eavesdropped, and then I reconvened the class. "I heard you say a lot of smart things."

- Francesca wrote really long about her original thesis. She wrote a full page.
- She really looked closely at what she'd written.
- She journeyed from one idea to another and related ideas as she wrote, hoping (probably) to move toward saying more true, more significant ideas.
- She became more and more willing to face the hard, and, in her case, the sort of sad truths about life. She started out saying, "Self-esteem is important" and ended up writing, "Growing up isn't smooth."

"Those are all things you too can do in your own writing, aren't they?"

LINK
Restate the teaching point and describe upcoming work.

"Today, then, and whenever you write an essay, remember that many writers deliberately try to take a journey from one thesis to another. We do this to make our thinking more powerful. I'd love to have you put the exact wording of your thesis aside, as Francesca did with her early statement, 'Grown-ups can really hurt a kid's self-esteem,' and free write so you can rethink what it is you want to say about your topic. After you've written long, you'll reread what you've written, then again lift out your seed idea and write it as another draft of your thesis."

I will often say, "I heard you say . . ." and I do incorporate what I heard into my report. But I'm apt to have thoughts about what I want to cumulate for kids, and if I didn't hear a child make a point that I want emphasized, I nevertheless add it to the list.

I am pushing the students to write quickly here. I don't want them to think through every word before they put it on the page. I want them to write and write and then go back and mine their writing for emerging ideas.

WRITING AND CONFERRING

Aiming Toward Your Precise Meaning

If you see (or anticipate) that several children will need your help, cluster them together and teach a strategy lesson that gives them extra practice and support. Perhaps you'll see that one child in the group has already settled on a thesis. For example, I saw that Chris' thesis was "My dog is important to me." I convened a small group of kids who I knew all needed a bit more practice pushing themselves past their first ideas. I suggested that together they help Chris rethink his thesis. "This doesn't mean it's not a good thesis—it is! But writers shouldn't be afraid to make our best ideas even better." Then, to bring the whole group in on the work, I said, "Remember, Chris will be trying to say the same general idea, but he'll aim to be more exact and more honest. Pretend you are Chris. You want to say that your dog is important to you, but you want to be more exact. Tell each other, in twos, what you might say. Keep talking and thinking (pretending you are Chris and that your dog is important to you) until you have something more true, more specific to say."

I listened as they said, "My dog is my friend," "I'd die if I had to lose my dog," and "My dog is like a brother to me."

Intervening, I said, "What I do, as a writer, is I write my thoughts down, and then I reread them, looking for the one that seems more precisely true." I asked Chris which of the statements rang especially true. He said, "My dog is like a brother to me," and wrote it. Then I told all the children, "Now you need to explore *that idea* like you might explore a patch of forest. Instead of turning logs over to see the bugs underneath them, turn words over. Ask, 'What exactly do I mean by . . .' and choose a word, any key word. Open it up. Try more precise words. Then do that again with other words you are using." Soon the children had said, and Chris had written:

> My dog tags along behind me like a little brother. He's like Velcro. He's like a tag-along little brother because whenever I go anywhere, he seems to say, "Take me." He's like a tag-along little brother also because he's never the one to go first.

MID-WORKSHOP TEACHING POINT *Writing with Insight and Honesty* "Writers, today I find myself admiring your *thinking*. Many of you are asking tough questions of your own first ideas. You are saying to yourself, 'Is this *exactly* what I mean?' and trying to be more precise. Listen, for example, to the way Rebecca pushed herself to be more truthful. She began with this thesis."

> My grandfather and I have a good relationship.

"This is what she wrote next."

> My grandfather and I have a good relationship. But I don't think it is good enough because he hates noise and he hates my brother and me fighting. I know my grandfather well, but I don't like him much. I like him, but I think he yells because his back is hurting. My grandfather can always find something to tell me to stop doing.

continued on next page

"Wow, you are getting more and more precise!" I said. "Keep it up!" Then, turning to all the children, I reiterated the steps we'd just taken and launched each one into similar work.

If I spend some of my time working with small groups of children, this then can free me to spend the rest of my time in one-to-one conferences. When I asked Rie how she was doing with her boxes and bullets, she looked at me a bit nervously and muttered something about wanting to do this right. Glancing at her papers, it was clear she'd been revising—or struggling. Every page contained lots and lots of crossed-out lines. Meanwhile, her thesis was, "Making a mistake in front of a crowd frustrates me." Just before I'd approached her, Rie had crossed out the line, "Not only people laugh at me, I also laugh at myself." Rie overviewed for me her various

continued from previous page

I know I can count on my Mom for things, but this is hard for me to tell her about. I know I'll never be stuck with him, but I still can't stand him sometimes. It's hard to believe he's my Mom's dad.

"Rebecca started off writing in what could be called a cliché: 'My grandfather and I have a good relationship.' She's now writing with honesty that takes our breath away. 'I can't stand him sometimes . . . I can't tell my Mom about this.' My hunch is that writing the hard parts will help Rebecca *live with* those hard parts. Okay, back to your own honest writing."

attempts to create support categories for her essay, and each attempt struck me as a reasonable one (although sometimes the different categories overlapped). My real concern, however, was over whether it would be productive for Rie to spend weeks during the upcoming unit of study perseverating over why it is so utterly humiliating for her to make even a minor error in front of an audience. My concern was not that this would produce a flawed essay—it was that I'd like to see Rie use writing as a way to name her nemesis, and to look it in the eye. So I celebrated her willingness to revise and to write the truth, and then asked if I could teach her one thing.

"Rie," I said, "In class over the past few days I've taught you all one way that an essay could go. But the truth is there are other ways that writers sometimes structure our essays. Could I teach you a different template, a different pattern, for an essay—because I have a hunch it would work for you." Soon I'd explained that some essays make a claim—"It can be boring to be home alone"—which we support for a bit. But then we make a second claim, one that pushes off from the first. "Because it's boring being home alone, I've become an avid reader." Often these essays first highlight a problem, then propose a solution, as occurred in that example. Before long, Rie had new plans for her essay, which started this way: *[Fig. VIII-1]*

I hate to make mistakes in front of a crowd
because I always want to do my best.

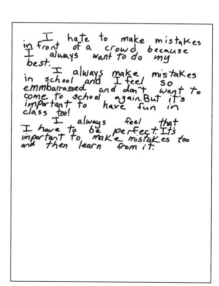

Fig. VIII-1 Rie trying to outgrow her first thesis

SHARE

Teaching as a Form of Rehearsing for Writing

Tell students you are about to ask them to say their essays aloud. Show them how to use their fingers to organize their thoughts before they begin.

"Writers, earlier this year you wrote stories, and to get ready for writing those stories you storytold them to each other. Soon you'll be writing essays, and it's also helpful to try talking about your essays to each other. I know you haven't yet figured out exactly what you'll write in your essays, but let's move forward anyhow. Right now, would you get ready to teach a course, to give a lecture, on the topic of your newest and truest thesis? To get ready, say your thesis aloud in your mind until you can imagine delivering it in a definitive voice to a whole roomful of students. Then plan across your fingers some of the points you could make to support your thesis, to teach your 'students.'"

Demonstrate by saying your thesis, and listing your supportive ideas across your fingers. Elaborate on each.

"My thesis is 'My father has been my most important teacher.' One point will be 'My father's been my most important teacher because he taught me to adore my work.'" As I mentioned that point, I gestured to my first finger. Moving to the next, I said, "Another point will be 'My father taught me that it's okay to fail.'" Then I told children, "I could, in a minute, give a little speech in which I announce my big claim, give my first reason [I gestured to one finger], and then talk a lot about it. Then I'd go to my second reason and talk a lot about it."

Ask students to plan and then tell their essays aloud.

"Would you, right now, take a minute to prepare a speech on your thesis?" I gave the children a few minutes. "Partner 1, will you pretend your partner is a roomful of listeners and give your speech?" I listened in as the children spoke with each other. Then I asked Partner 2 to take a turn.

This step has proven transformational. When I worked once with fifty teacher-researchers, just after they'd drafted tentative rough outlines for an article they wanted to write, and before they set to work on their lead paragraph, I gave them fifteen minutes to plan how they might lead a staff development workshop on the topic and asked them to give these instant workshops to each other. What a difference! I'm convinced that when we write as a form of teaching others, it's transformational to do some actual teaching in lieu of an early draft of writing.

This will be a great opportunity to see how well children understand what you have tried to teach them. Make sure to listen. If it seems that most are making points and organizing their information under these big ideas, you can listen for the finer points of their structure—are the reasons parallel in construction and importance? Are the reasons illustrated with precise and interesting details and stories? What you see your kids do will help you tailor your next day's teaching.

Supporting Theses in Various Ways For homework tonight, try this exercise. Practice using different kinds of sets of evidence to support one thesis statement. Read each thesis statement below and try supporting it using kinds, parts, reasons, ways, and finally, times when. Try to come up with three statements that support the claim for each of those kinds of support. If another way of supporting the thesis makes sense to you, of course try that way too!

Here's an example of a thesis followed by ways to set up evidence that could support it:

Essay Possibility #1 (Kinds)

Fifth graders work hard; we study, babysit our siblings, and help our parents.

Essay Possibility #2 (Parts)

Fifth graders work with three parts of themselves. They work with their bodies, emotions, and intelligence.

Essay Possibility #3 (Reasons)

Fifth graders work hard because we want to do well at school, because we want to please our parents, and because we want to develop skills.

Essay Possibility #4 (Places/Ways)

Fifth graders work hard. We work hard in school, at home, and during sports.

Essay Possibility #5 (Times)

There are three times when fifth graders' lives are filled with work. Fifth graders work before school, during school, and after school.

You may wonder what the impetus was for me to teach children that a writer can elaborate on her thesis by writing about reasons, parts, kinds, and so on. This is my attempt to take the lessons my son struggled to learn in high school and scale them down so they're accessible for children.

You may protest, claiming, "Why simplify high school-level-work and teach it to nine-year-olds?" But, of course, in the writing workshop as a whole we are constantly taking the strategies, habits, and goals of adult writers and finding ways to invite even five- and six-year-olds to "have a go" with those aspects of writing.

If your students need more practice using writing to grow ideas . . . you could decide to teach another minilesson on this strategy. It might begin like this: "Writers, I had a conversation with a friend last night that reminded me of the work we did in class yesterday when we free wrote to outgrow and revise our thesis statements. I had just gotten back from my swim class. I told my friend that swimming was frustrating. 'What do you mean?' she asked. 'Well, every time I feel like I am getting better, there is something new to learn.' 'What do you mean?' she asked. 'It feels like it is impossible to become a good swimmer.' I said. 'What do you mean?' she asked again. Getting a little annoyed, I answered, 'I guess that getting better at swimming is like getting better at anything in life. The more you know, the more you realize what you don't know.'"

"Later that evening I realized that as much as I was annoyed with her for repeating 'What do you mean?' over and over again, her question helped me figure out what I was trying to say. My first claim, 'Swimming is frustrating,' didn't fully represent what I was feeling."

"This strategy of asking repeating questions might be something that you can try with yourself on paper. Just write your idea, then ask yourself, 'What do I mean?' and try to restate it in a clearer, stronger way. Or do this with a partner if you are having trouble getting your words to match what you really want to say. And from now on, any time that you feel like your ideas do not match what you mean to say, try asking yourself clarifying questions until you feel like your writing matches what you really think."

If you feel that in order to revise their thesis statements, your children would benefit from a clearer understanding of the qualities of an effective essay . . . you might tell them what you admire in the work of one essayist, and ask them to note what they admire in the work of another. For your part, you might say something like, "Writers, last night I was reading a book of essays by one of my favorite authors, Barbara Kingsolver. She usually writes novels, so I was very interested in reading her essays. I was thinking about you guys the whole time I was reading! I noticed that the essays in Barbara Kingsolver's book had a couple of characteristics that made them so interesting to read. First, it felt like she knew what she was talking about. She chose to write essays on topics that she knew quite well. Her essays sounded smart! Then the other thing I noticed was they had a kind of passion. I could tell that she really cared about the topics in her essays. It's like her essays had brains and heart—knowledge and passion." Then, of course, you'd want to give children a similar opportunity to name what they admire in the work of an essay they've previously studied. You could then say something like, "Today I want us to think about the thesis statements we've come up with to see if, like Barbara Kingsolver, we have chosen to write about topics we know and care a lot about."

COLLABORATING WITH COLLEAGUES

For homework the other day, you asked your children to consider which qualities of good writing pertain to both narrative and expository writing. You also asked them to think about the qualities of good writing that are especially important for essayists. These questions merit your attention as well.

Earlier in this series, I quoted Lucille Clifton, the great American poet, who said, "We cannot create what we cannot imagine." When helping children write well, it is terribly important that we and our students are guided by a clear vision of what we are trying to create. During our earlier work with personal narrative writing, we helped children write with focus and detail, and we encouraged them to "show, not tell." Do those same qualities pertain to expository writing?

If you or your colleagues pore over op-ed editorials, feature articles, essays, and persuasive letters, trying to ascertain what makes some of this writing especially strong, I suspect you'll find that specificity is crucial when the aim is to be convincing. You know this already. If you phone a friend, and the person who answers says something vague like, "She's not here. I don't know where she is. Why don't you call back?" you may well suspect your friend is avoiding you. But if that person responds, "She's driving Jimmy to his Boy Scout meeting. It starts at 7:00 p.m., so she should be back by 7:20 p.m.," then you don't doubt the veracity of this response. Specificity elicits trust.

In narrative writing, details can stand on their own. In expository writing, details are provided and then "unpacked," or discussed. That is, in expository writing one expects that examples will be linked in an explicit way to ideas. In fact, details and anecdotes and examples usually abut generalizations or citations.

Cohesion is another important quality of good expository writing. Of course, cohesion is also important in stories. In a good story, the beginning, the middle, and the end all relate to each other. Characters don't come and

go from nowhere. Cohesion is equally important in a good essay—any one part of the essay needs to relate to the whole of the essay—but the techniques for creating cohesion are different in expository than in narrative texts. I often tell children that the need for cohesion translates into the fact that it's important for them to write sentences throughout their essay that refer back to the thesis. But it is also true that expository writers create a sense of cohesion by repeating a word or a phrase from the thesis often. Certainly at the end of any chunk of text, readers expect to be told how this new information advances the essay's premise.

I've found it very helpful to read books written for high school and college students on the essay and on nonfiction writing. For example, I love poring over Richard Bailey and Linda Denstaedt's *Destinations: An Integrated Approach to Writing Paragraphs and Essays*. It's a textbook for college freshmen and clearly light years beyond reach for elementary students, but I'm interested, for example, in their description of cause-and-effect, comparison, and definition essays. Linda and her colleague, Laura Shilling, have helped me think about expository writing.

They suggest that to write a cause-and-effect essay, for example, a student might generate ideas by asking questions that elicit causes: Does this thing have one or more causes? Does it have one or more effects or consequences? Does it help to think in terms of reasons for this thing? On the other hand, to help write a definition essay, a student might ask questions such as: Does this thing have components or parts? What are its origins? How does it change over time? (Bailey and Denstaedt 2005, p. 300).

Find books like this one and share them with your colleagues. You'll find your minds and conversations soon buzz with possibilities.

COMPOSING AND SORTING MINI-STORIES

IN THIS SESSION, YOU'LL TEACH
CHILDREN TO WRITE, ANGLE, AND
UNPACK MINI-STORIES THAT SUPPORT
THE IDEAS THEY WANT TO ADVANCE.

GETTING READY

- Colored file folder for each student
- Several manila folders for each student (one per supporting topic sentence)
- Your own thesis, topic sentences, and supporting list of true stories
- One story you've developed to support a topic sentence
- Colored file and manila folders labeled for your own essay
- Class thesis and supporting topic sentences from the preceding minilesson, written on chart paper
- Guidelines for Writing Essays chart
- See CD-ROM for resources

I remember the first research report I ever wrote. My older brother and sister had each written reports, so I knew in advance that I'd need to buy index cards, a file box, and pens of different colors. I traveled by bus to the big library in the center of Buffalo, spending several Saturdays surrounded by books, proudly accumulating index cards full of information.

Now when I write nonfiction books, I no longer record information on index cards. But I do still collect bits and pieces of related information: quotes, stories, examples of student writing, data, and ideas. Later, when I prepare to write, I lay the bits alongside each other, noticing that two citations say almost the same thing, that this one text illustrates that citation, that some of my sources contradict each other. I realize some people do most of this work on the computer, but I still rely on the old-fashioned system of collecting, sorting, making headings, and so forth.

In order to bring children into the realm of writing that is organized logically instead of chronologically, it is crucial that they have opportunities to manipulate their information in physical and concrete ways. When teaching children to add and divide numbers, we initially ask them to combine and share buttons or blocks. In similar ways children benefit from physically manipulating bits of information and ideas. In this way, they can grasp that two chunks of data are similar, that one story literally fits under a main idea, that a large pile can be divided into two smaller piles.

In this session, you'll teach children a system for collecting information and ideas, and then you'll help them start collecting and filing the materials they'll need to support their theses. For now, you'll teach them to collect stories that illustrate their ideas, knowing that this is a task they should be able to do with confidence and skill.

Your teaching needs to rally children to rely upon what they already know about writing stories, and to help them with the new challenge of angling (and unpacking) their stories to support their main ideas.

MINILESSON

Composing and Sorting Mini-Stories

CONNECTION

Tell children that the boxes and bullets they wrote in the previous session will provide the frames for their essays.

"Have you seen the huge building they are constructing down the block? I walked by it this morning and saw iron beams; they formed the shape of the building. In the last session, all of us worked on creating the iron structure for our essays. Most of you have chosen the boxes and bullets that will be your iron beams. From looking at the structure you've made, you can imagine your essay. Others of you are still working on this."

"The builders will soon truck in materials and begin to fill in the parts of the building outlined by the iron beams. They have pictured in their minds what the building will look like when the walls are in place, and they will bring in materials that will fit around the structure they have erected."

"Once you have the iron structure for your essay, once you have at least a tentative plan for your boxes and bullets, it is time for you (like the builders down the block) to cart in the materials you will need to build your essay. Before builders or writers can truck in a lot of building materials, they need to decide where to store those materials so the stuff that belongs in one part will be separate from the stuff that will make a second part."

Explain that writers use files to store the materials that will fill in the frame of an essay. Provide an example.

"Builders create piles; writers make files. I've put a stack of colored file folders and a much larger stack of manila folders at the center of each table. I suggest that you write or tape your thesis across the top of a colored outer folder. Don't make your letters too large or bold, because you may alter your thesis as you proceed—so save space for future revisions. Then, in the same way, write one of the support sentences you've chosen—writers call these topic sentences—along the top of each manila folder. Then set each of these topic-sentence folders inside your thesis folder."

COACHING

There are lots of advantages to using a metaphor in a minilesson. We're trying to teach abstract and complicated ideas. Sometimes a metaphor can make our ideas more concrete and memorable. It is important, however, to avoid using multiple metaphors. We can't one day liken the frame of an essay to the frame of a building and then the next day suggest that an essay is shaped like a butterfly with separate but similar wings or like a three-leaf clover or a tree with branches. You'll see that I return often to this session's metaphor, that an essay is like a building, and that I generally return later to any metaphor that I use in a minilesson. Before you choose a metaphor, then, be sure it can be sustained across more than just one minilesson.

Sometimes it is tempting to use the minilesson as a time to tell your students what you'd like them all to do. It would have been easy to state as my teaching point, "Writers, today I want to show you how I'd like you to organize and collect writing. You're each going to make three files . . . " But I guard against letting minilessons become occasions to simply assign work to children, and I carefully watch my wording so that I am teaching children strategies that writers use often rather than nudging them to jump through a particular set of hoops on a particular day. Watch how I circumvent a teaching point that merely assigns today's work so as to hold to the principle that minilessons are occasions for teaching a strategy or an idea children can use often.

"You'll remember Andy's essay in which he claimed that parents' fighting affects kids very much (see CD-ROM for complete essay). His skeletal plans had looked like this:"

> Parents' fighting affects kids very much.
>
> - Parents' fighting makes kids yell for things.
> - Parents' fighting makes kids choose sides between their parents.
> - Parents' fighting makes kids start not trusting people.

"He wrote his thesis," I pointed to it, "on a blue folder." Then, showing that his blue outer folder contained three inner manila folders, each labeled with one of Andy's bulleted sentences, I said, "Look how Andy created three different folders so he had separate places in which to collect and store the materials he planned to use when he was ready to build each of his three body paragraphs."

"Whenever you write a non-narrative piece, one that will require a lot of materials, a lot of information, it helps to set up a system for gathering and collecting the materials you'll end up assembling."

Name your teaching point. In this case, tell children that writers collect (among other things) mini-stories that illustrate our ideas.

"But today what I want to teach you is this. The most important materials writers collect when writing essays are—stories!"

TEACHING
Demonstrate that writers bring knowledge of personal narratives to this new task, only this time we collect and write mini-stories that are angled to illustrate the bulleted topic sentence. First we generate stories to support our claim.

"The good news is this: You can use all that you already know about writing good stories to help you collect powerful materials in your folders. Watch how I go about collecting stories in my folders, stories that could fit into the plan I've made for my essay. Here is my plan for my essay."

> My father has been my most important teacher.
>
> - My father taught me what it means to regard a job as a hobby.
> - My father taught me to love writing.
> - My father taught me to believe that one person can make a difference.

Some teachers use pocket folders instead of file folders, with the inside-the-cover pocket set aside to hold drafts of the title and introductory paragraph, and with one-half of a pocket folder (yes, each child needs a folder with one-half of another folder set inside it!) providing a place for materials that will end up becoming the first and second body paragraphs. Then the final pocket can be for either just the third body paragraph or for that and also, eventually, the concluding paragraph.

I could have made this sentence the teaching point. If your students risk being on instructional overload, you may decide to do so. It is reasonable to devote a minilesson to teaching children that writers need to set up systems for assembling their materials. The problem with this teaching point is that the work involved won't keep kids busy for the whole workshop. Therefore, I move on to introduce what is essentially a second teaching point—the notion that stories are some of the most important materials that writers collect.

"To get myself writing a story that relates to my thesis, I take one of my topic sentences, one bullet—I'll take 'My father taught me what it means to regard a job as a hobby'—and I ask myself, 'What true story can I think of related to this?' Let me list several." I then began jotting quickly on my clipboard and saying aloud what I wrote.

- On the last day of summer, Dad and I sailed together. He confided that he couldn't wait for vacation to be over so he could return to work.

- On Christmas mornings, my father always goes to the hospital carrying a waffle iron, ready to make waffles for the doctors and patients. I asked why he didn't send someone else. Dad admitted that he liked going to work. "It's my hobby."

- When Dad was a kid, he heard a book about Louis Pasteur read aloud. Dad said, "Listening to that read-aloud, I realized that the research which Pasteur loved so much was his job." Until then, Dad had always thought a person's job was a chore. Dad vowed that he'd grow up to love his job.

Select one story, recall the process of writing stories well, and draft.

"Next, I will choose one of the stories. Before writing it, I need to remember what I know about writing focused stories. I'll make a movie in my mind of how the story unfolded, starting at the beginning. When I write the story, I'll also keep in mind that it needs to highlight one particular idea—in this instance, that Dad taught me what it means to regard a job as a hobby. I know from the start that I'll play up the parts that make this a story about Dad loving his job. I also know this needs to be a tiny story." I picked up my clipboard and began writing (and voicing).

My dad regards his work as his hobby. For example, on Christmas mornings, right after the presents have been opened, my dad always goes into the kitchen and begins the one bit of cooking that he does all year. He stirs Bisquick and eggs in a huge bowl and sets off for the hospital, leaving us to finish Christmas without him. For Dad, Christmas mornings are not just a time to be with family, they are also a time to serve hot waffles to the medical students and patients. When I asked him once why he didn't send someone else with the waffles, he told me he loves being at the hospital on Christmas mornings. "It's my hobby," he said.

I could have made my point in a briefer fashion, but when I write about topics that really matter to me I find it hard to be brief. I think children can tell when we are authentically engaged in our own writing, and they respond in kind. So I decided to forgive myself for offering examples that are longer than is ideal. You'll notice that I jotted this writing on my clipboard, not on chart paper—the advantage of the clipboard is that I can scrawl and abbreviate (and, if necessary, prepare a cheat sheet ahead of time to remind me of what I want to say).

It is very powerful to write detailed stories that carry gigantic ideas. The writer Richard Price once said, "The bigger the issue, the smaller you write."

I worked on this story before I met with the kids, trying to keep it brief, to make sure it was a step-by-step story, and to highlight the sections that illustrated my main idea. I tried to be explicit about the connection between this example and the overarching idea. I deliberately used the phrase, 'For example . . .' You will, of course, want to write your own story. Bring your dad into your teaching! Look ahead to Session XIV, when you'll want to use the draft you write today again.

Debrief, highlighting the process and pointing out that you told the story step-by-step rather than summarizing it.

Then, pausing in the midst of the story, I shifted away from the role of writer and into the role of teacher. "Writers, I hope you saw that I collected this mini-story outside my notebook on loose-leaf paper. I did that because now I'm going to put the mini-story in the folder titled 'My father taught me what it means to regard a job as a hobby.'" I did this.

"I hope you also noticed that to get myself started telling a story, I rewrote my claim and then wrote 'For example . . .' Writers don't always use those exact words, but for today, use the phrase 'For example . . .' or 'One time I . . .' Finally, writers, I hope you noticed that when writing a story, I asked myself, 'How did it start?' I made a movie in my mind of what happened and wrote the story in a step-by-step way."

ACTIVE ENGAGEMENT
Set children up to try this while writing in the air. Ask them to write a story that can be embedded into the whole-class essay.

"So let's practice doing this; it's a lot to remember. Pretend it is writing time and I've said, 'Okay writers, time to work. Off you go.' Pretend Leo's bullets for 'Working with our first-grade reading buddies is fun' are your bullets. Remember Leo suggested," I turned back to the boxes and bullets from the preceding day's minilesson, "that the essay could be framed liked this:"

> Working with our first-grade reading buddies is fun.

- One reason that working with reading buddies is fun is that you get to teach them to read.

- Another reason that working with reading buddies is fun is that you get to read really cool books.

- And, finally, working with reading buddies is fun because they look up to us.

It's important to notice that although there is one teaching point in a minilesson, we often tuck instructive comments throughout the minilesson. My goal is to pack any minilesson with enough good stuff that an alert student can learn, learn, learn. How else can I justify taking up students' writing time?

I am scaffolding kids so the writing they produce will end up clicking into a nicely structured written essay. Asking kids to use specific transitional phrases such as for example and one day may make you uneasy—it made me uneasy at first. But I've seen that once children have successful experiences writing essays, they use the forms we teach with increasing flexibility. Of course, you must discard any parts of these lessons that make you uneasy, finding your own ways to teach whatever you decide your children need to learn.

Notice that this piece about reading buddies threads its way throughout much of this session and this unit. If you teach a classroom full of struggling writers and you are always working to just get your kids producing more volume of writing, you may want to revise many of my minilessons so that this component of the minilesson becomes a time for kids to work with their own texts. You could, for example, ask each child to take his or her first topic sentence, and to think of a story illustrating it, signaling with a thumbs up when they have that in mind. Then coach partner 1s to say their bullet points again, to add for example, and to tell the beginning of the story starting with what exactly they did first.

"Assume these are your bullets. Now, you're at your workspace, ready to start. You have your boxes and bullets. What do you do next to get yourself organized? Tell your partner." They talked for just ten seconds. "Writers, I heard most of you remembering that when any of us plan to work on an essay, it helps to set up a system for sorting the materials. Specifically, you talked about getting folders ready before you start assembling the materials, the data."

"Stay with me, because now this gets harder. Let's say that you have labeled your folders. Now you want to begin collecting some entries, some materials that you'll put in those folders. Let's say you decide to start by collecting stories for the folder labeled 'One reason that working with reading buddies is fun is that you get to teach them to read.' You'll get a piece of paper. You'll copy the bullet and then write, 'For example . . .', and you'll probably add a time phrase. So you might write, 'One reason that working with reading buddies is fun is that you get to teach them to read. For example, one morning . . .' and then keep going, telling a mini-story. In this instance, your story needs to illustrate that it's fun working with reading buddies because you get to teach them to read. So think of one time when it was fun teaching your buddy to read. Partner 1, write in the air to your partner."

As you recall, the early section of this minilesson mentioned the importance of setting up a system for gathering materials, and only later did it highlight the fact that writers can collect stories that elaborate on their topic sentences. I need to be sure the children keep the first point (the need for systems) in mind, so I tuck in this reminder.

Some teachers describe the materials that get collected in this phase as mini-stories, suggesting that they can often be just three to four sentences long. Mini-stories need a sentence to begin the story, one or two sentences to tell what happened, and an ending sentence to wrap up the story and relate it to the main idea of the essay. You'll see that I decided not to highlight brevity just yet, but that was an option I considered.

Listen in on your children's work with partners. Intervene to lift the level of what individuals are doing. Then debrief.

As the partners turned to talk, I listened in. After a moment, I heard Diego say, "I taught my buddy the /sh/ sound 'cause she was going /s/."

"Class. All of you, I need your attention. Diego just said, 'I taught my buddy the /sh/ sound.'" Then I said, "The reminder I'm going to give Diego is one that probably pertains to many of you. So listen closely." Looking at Diego, I said, "Diego, while I don't question that you *did* teach Sari the /sh/ sound, you have not told this as a story yet! For now, we're writing stories to illustrate our points—another day we'll quickly list examples. To write a story, remember that you need to go back to that day in your mind (and if you don't remember it exactly, make it up). How did the moment when you taught Sari the /sh/ sound start? Use the words I gave you—'For example, one morning . . .' to get yourself started."

It's very likely that your children, too, will shrink their stories, bypassing the beginning to get to the middle. There's logic in this—the one sentence Diego has told spotlights the time in the episode that fits with his point. For Diego to tell this as a story, however, he needs to provide the windup that precedes the climax. Of course, sometimes people end up providing too much windup! I believe that is a small price to pay for the vitality and honesty that real stories add to writing.

Diego started again, while the class listened. "For example, one time Sari was reading a book about a sheep's car getting stuck in the mud. She read the words *sheep shove* so it sounded like *sheep sove*, and she was stuck. I said, 'Sound it out,' but she didn't have the right sounds."

"Now you are telling this as a story, Diego!" Turning to the class, I said, "Try again; this time ask yourselves that question, 'How did it start?' and tell your example like a story. Use the phrase *for example, one time* or *for example, one sunny day* to get yourself started telling this as a story."

LINK
Restate the teaching point and remind students of the metaphor you established earlier describing their upcoming work.

"Writers, the builders have built their iron beams, and most of you have built yours as well. Once builders and writers have constructed a frame, it's time to gather the materials needed to fill in around the girders. Builders will truck in boards and cinder blocks; as writers, we build with words. Today (and whenever you have built an iron structure for an essay) begin to cart in materials—stories—to build your essay. When you write stories that will be tucked into essays, remember to use everything you already know about writing powerful stories."

You'll find that when the challenge is to tell a story in such a way that it illustrates a point, writers often delete the beginning of the story (which therefore means the story is not a story after all). For example, if my topic sentence is, "It is dangerous to drive to work," I could "tell the story" of yesterday's near accident by cutting to the chase in a way which relates to the topic sentence, saying, "Yesterday, I was almost in an accident." But that is not a story. To tell this as a story, I need to tell the start of the story, angling it towards the point I wanted to make: "Yesterday, I drove to work as usual, drinking coffee, talking on the cell phone, and steering around potholes. Suddenly . . . " That's an angled story!

WRITING AND CONFERRING

You will have your hands full today. First, you'll need to help any child who hasn't yet arrived at a workable thesis buttressed by several support statements, to finalize that work. If a child is still struggling, help out. For example, I am apt to say, "What do you want to say about losing your grandfather? Tell me what this meant to you."

Then the child will talk: "Well, I felt hollow. Because he was sort of, not really a grandfather; it was as if he was my age. Plus he was like a father."

I'll nudge the child on, murmuring, "Say more."

The child says, "I didn't have any tears in me. I didn't want to talk about it."

Listening, I will try to grasp the main categories the child seems to want to address, and then I will say these back to the child. "So do you want to write, 'When I lost my grandfather, I felt sad,' and then write about the *kinds* of sadness? You could write, 'I felt hollow, I felt silent, I felt...' Or, on the other hand, do you want to write, 'When I lost my grandfather, I lost a friend, I lost a father ...' (and write the different kinds of roles he played in your life?) Or do you want to write, 'When I lost my grandfather, this was a huge blow to me. For example, I . . . ; for example, I . . . ' It's up to you because you are the author, you are in charge."

You may ask, "Aren't you doing the child's work for him?" and the answer is partly yes. The child, however, is probably oblivious to the fact that I am giving him a piggyback ride across the high water. The child will probably think he has done the work independently, and meanwhile I will have helped him begin to be comfortable with the new text structure. There will be lots of other occasions for the child to do this work alone without scaffolds. For me, the question is not whether or not I helped the child; the question is whether my help lifts and supports the writer beyond today, and I think that setting up writers who struggle a bit for future success qualifies.

> **MID-WORKSHOP TEACHING POINT**   ***Angling Stories to Support Theses***   "Writers, can I have your attention? Eddy and I just discovered something important that I suspect pertains to many of you. Eddy's thesis is that he loves to spend time with his parents. In one of his folders, he's collecting material to support the idea, 'I love to spend time with my parents when we go on vacation together.' He collected a story about staying overnight in a hotel with his parents. I want you to listen to the story he collected, and see if you can discern the problem that Eddy faces (and I suspect many of you face as well). Listen."
>
> I love to spend time with my parents when we are on vacation together. For example, one time we went to a hotel in New Jersey. First we went to the zoo in the hotel. It had really cute baby animals. Then I went swimming. Then I watched three TV shows.
>
> "Eddy, tell the kids what you discovered," I said.
>
> "I realized I left my parents out!"
>
> *continued on next page*

Today you'll also want to confer and lead small groups to help children gather stories that illustrate their ideas. You'll find that when children reach for stories that illustrate an idea, usually the idea comes at the end—the climax—of the story. Children, therefore, often bypass the setup and windup sections of their stories. When Jay Jay wanted to tell a story to illustrate that he loves being with his father because his father teaches him roller skating moves, he wrote:

> One day my father taught me a skating trick and I like him cause he did that.

I helped Jay Jay see that he needed to back up and tell how the story started (though now the problem became the other extreme—too much windup!). Soon Jay Jay's story went like this:

> One sunny Sunday, my dad came and picked me up to go to his job at the Skate Key. On the way I asked him how to do a 360°. When we got there, he said, "Jay Jay put your skates on." He putted his skates on. He did it first then I did it next but I fell on the floor. My head was...

Often children will tell a story without developing the part that illustrates the bullet point, the topic sentence. When I see this, I often say to the child, as I said to this child, "Would you box the part of this story that goes with your bullet point?" Then I state the child's bullet point, the statement labeled on the folder. In the example above, Jay Jay decided that only one line of his story, "He did it first then I did it next," advanced his idea which was, "I love being with my father because he teaches me skating moves."

continued from previous page

Nodding, I added, "Eddy made a really important discovery. If his story is going to illustrate that he loves vacationing with his parents, then he needs to angle his story about staying at the hotel so that the story shows that he likes to stay there because he gets to be with his parents! Listen to Eddy's next version of this story." [Fig. IX-1]

> I love to spend time with my parents when we vacation together. For example, one time we went to a hotel in New Jersey. First we visited a zoo that was in the hotel. It had really cute baby animals. My Mom loved the baby sheep so much that she pretended she was going to sneak it up the elevator to our room. My Dad and I had to drag her away. We were just joking. Then we watched three TV shows; one that was my choice, one that was Mom's, one that was Dad's. We usually don't watch each others' shows.

"Right now, before you do anything else, would each of you reread one of the stories you have collected and talk with your partner about how you could rewrite that story so that it really highlights whatever it is you need to show? Then rewrite that one entry, that one story. I'll be admiring the revisions you make."

> I love to spend time with my parents when we vacation together. For example, one time we went to a hotel in New Jersey. We visited a zoo that was in an hotel, I had really cute baby animals. My Mom. loved the baby sheep so much that she pretended she was going to sneak it up the elevator to our room. My Dad and I had to drag her away. We were just joking. Then we watched three TV shows; one that was my choice, one that was my Mom's, one that was Dad's. We usually don't watch each others' shows.

Fig. IX-1 Eddy's revised story

I typically then ask children to take the underlined/boxed section and write a long paragraph just about that. Jay Jay wrote this to insert into his original paragraph: [Fig. IX-2]

> My dad whirled so fast—fast like a roadrunner. I couldn't see him. He jumped in the air. I thought he was going to fall back. Bang with his strong skates. I thought his wheels popped off. My eyes were spinning fast like I got dizzy. I thought that he fell headfirst into the floor. I thought he broke his leg when he came down.

The story tells more about Jay Jay's father as a skater than about the fact that Jay Jay loves his father because he taught him the 360° and other moves, but I let this go and moved on to teach one other tip. Once children have written a story, I often teach them to add a sentence at the end of the story that refers back to their bulleted reason. For example, Jay Jay's story at first had ended this way:

> I fell on the floor. My head was bloody.

I taught Jay Jay that essayists try to add a sentence at the end of a story that links back to the topic sentence (I love being with my father because he teaches me skating moves). Jay Jay added:

> I came to in the locker room, still thinking how I love my Dad for teaching me skating moves.

The ending makes all the difference! Now he'd accumulated material in his folder which read like this:

> I love being with my father because he teaches me skating moves. One sunny Sunday, my dad came and picked me up to go to his job at the Skate Key. On the way I asked him how to do a 360°. When we got there, he said, "Jay Jay, put your skates on." He put his skates on. He did it first. My dad whirled so fast—fast like a roadrunner. I couldn't see him. Bang with his strong skates. I thought his wheels popped off. My eyes were spinning fast like I got dizzy. I thought that he fell headfirst into the floor. I thought he broke his leg when he came down. He did it first, but next I did it. I fell on the floor. My head was bloody. I came to in the locker room, still thinking how I love my Dad for teaching me skating moves.

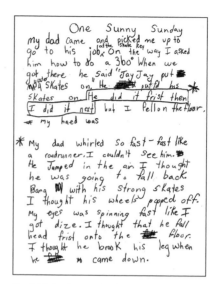

Fig. IX-2 Jay Jay's revised story about his father

SHARE

Honing Supporting Stories

Share your realizations about the process of essay writing to practice evaluating a piece of writing for what qualities are there and what qualities are missing.

"Writers, you've each collected a story that supports one of your topic sentences."

"As I've worked with you today, I've realized that together we have figured out a bunch of guidelines to follow as we write our essays. I've written them out for you here, so you can refer to them whenever you want."

Guidelines for Writing Essays

- Essayists frame the main sections of their essays.
- Essayists revise early, using free writing to deepen thinking and outgrow their earliest claims.
- Essayists set up a system so we can sort and compose material to support our ideas.
- Essayists collect and write mini-stories that are angled to illustrate our topic sentence.

"Now you've collected mini-stories to illustrate the ideas you want to advance in your writing. And what stories these are! We've learned guidelines for writing stories to support our ideas, too."

Never underestimate the power of story as the conveyer of ideas. Many sections of the Bible are written in stories—parables, often—and these stories convey ideas. How lucky we are that Melville didn't write a book about whaling in general, but instead wrote about one man and one whale. And how lucky that Jane Austen didn't write about pride and prejudice, but instead wrote about one man and one woman struggling with and against their pride and their prejudice (Zinsser 2004, p. 107).

Guidelines for Writing Supporting Stories for Essays

- Writers usually include a transition into the story.
- The story needs to have a beginning, middle, and end.
- The story needs to be told to especially reveal the part of it that illustrates the thesis and bullet points.
- At the end of the story, it is usually wise to include a sentence that refers back to or repeats the main idea of that paragraph.

"Writers, let's listen to Tony's story and notice which of these guidelines he's followed and which he can still follow." *[Fig. IX-3]*

> Drawing is really fun. I can express myself in drawing. One time I was mad at a kid for bothering me. Instead of settling it in a violent way, I controlled myself; for a minute I thought about all I knew about drawing. Then I took out a paper and a pencil. I drew him running around, screaming, with snake hair, a rat's head, and a slow turtle body. Drawing helps me express myself.

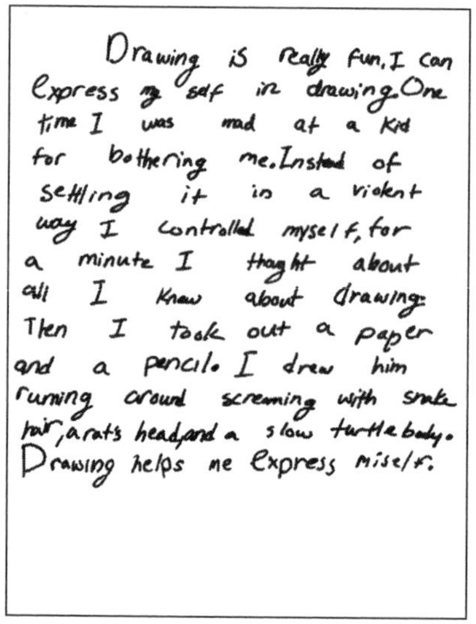
Drawing is Really fun, I can express my self in drawing. One time I was mad at a kid for bothering me. Insted of settling it in a violent way I controlled myself, for a minute I thaght about all I knaw about drawing. Then I took out a paper and a pencil. I drew him runing around screaming with snake hair, a rat's head and a slow turtle body. Drawing helps me express miself.

Fig. IX-3 Tony struggles with spelling, but he successfully uses a story to illustrate his idea

"Let's look next at Olivia's story," I said. "She's written two different stories, and although it's possible that she could bring both these stories into her essay, she will probably need to decide which one better illustrates her topic sentence, which is, 'Sometimes I hurt people's feelings to fit in.' Let's listen to one of her stories, and think—as we did with Tony's entry—whether her story matches our guidelines for writing stories to express our ideas." I read one of her stories aloud. *[Fig. IX-4]*

> Sometimes I hurt people's feelings to fit in.
>
> An example was at lunch one day. I was sitting with a cool group of kids trying to get with the conversation. I put down my sandwich. I looked at everybody around me. I was sitting with them ready to make my move to be their friend. They talked about people who were geeks.

"I know somebody who plays with Polly Pockets," I said. They looked at me and said, "Really? Who?"

"Alejandra," I said. They looked at me and said, "Come and play with us."

"Ok," I said feeling so happy inside that I was going to play with them.

I got up to go line up with them but I ended up face-to-face with Alejandra. I could see tears in her eyes. She turned around and left. I knew I had hurt her feelings. I felt bad inside, like someone punched me in the stomach.

"Come on, Olivia," I started walking to them. But instead of feeling really happy, I felt really sad because I had just left my best friend out.

"Olivia!" I started running towards them.

Sometimes you can be so eager to fit in you hurt people.

Ask students to assess their writing using the Guidelines for Supporting Stories chart to see what work to do next.

"Writers, can you take a minute and look through your own writing? Talk with your partners, referring to the chart. How do your stories fit our guidelines and how might you revise them?"

Fig.IX-4 Olivia's story is angled to support her idea

HOMEWORK *Angling Oral Stories* Writers, remember how much better our stories became after we rehearsed them, telling them before writing them down? Tonight please practice angling another story to support one of your points. Tell it to someone before you write it down. Try telling the same story a second time, even if you need to recruit your dog as your listener! Once you are happy with how the story sounds, write it down. I'm enclosing copies of our guidelines for telling stories to support ideas. Use those guidelines to help you revise your story. Bring it tomorrow and file it in the appropriate file.

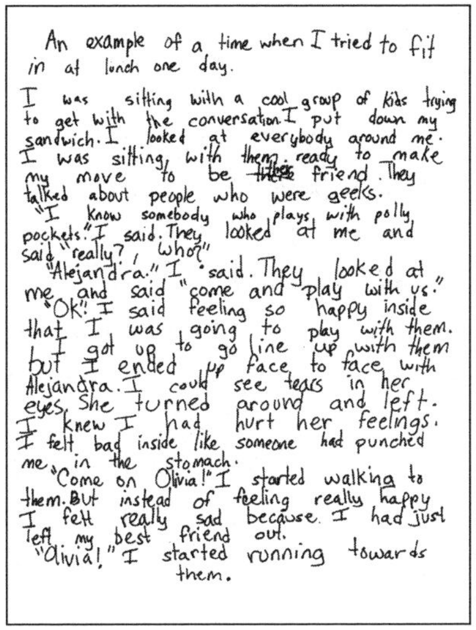

If your students need a push into revision . . . you might tell them a story like this: "Writers, yesterday at lunch I was talking to my colleagues about writing. As we ate our sandwiches we shared our experiences with revision. After a lot of discussion we realized that writers need courage to be good revisers. When we figured that out, it was like a light-bulb went off in my head! I realized that this is what had made revision so difficult for me for so long. I would go to revise and find myself physically tightening up because I was so afraid to lose what had taken me so long to write. I would make teeny tiny changes to my old ideas and then I would reread what I'd written and wonder why it had not gotten any better. Writers, all that time I didn't realize that what I really needed was courage. I needed the courage to erase and make big changes. I needed courage to trust that I could write better. I needed courage to believe that my first work was not my best work. Finding that courage has changed my writing so today I want to tell you: be brave writers!"

If your students are writing supporting ideas that are too long, too detailed, or too much like personal narratives . . . you'll probably need to revisit the difference between telling a story as a personal narrative and using a story as a way to support a claim. One of the ways you can demonstrate this is to show the difference between the two in your own writing. It helps to have a focused personal narrative entry that you've adapted so that it can work as a story within an essay paragraph. You may decide to show the two pieces of writing side-by-side so students can see and name the differences themselves. Inevitably, you'll notice that the thesis-supporting text is shorter, leaner, and to the point, whereas the personal narrative entry offers the reader the whole story.

For Active Engagement, during the lesson, you might decide to have your students go though their notebooks and find an entry that could, if it were leaner and more to the point, support one of their claims. Each writer could tell their partner about plans for revising that entry.

ASSESSMENT

When you look at your students' work, pay attention to goals that span all units. For example, you will want to carefully watch your children's fluency as writers. As the year progresses, you should see that your kids now write much, much more than they wrote at the start of the year. Watch them closely and you will notice that some children get the idea for a paragraph in their heads, and then tuck their heads down and write, write, write until that unit of thought has been written. Others think of a sentence and then write until that thought is on the page. Yet others think of a word, write it, reread, and only then think of the next word! You might be tempted to excuse these differences as being simply a matter of speed, but actually it is crucial to help children think and write in longer units of thought. If children are not writing quickly and with fluency, they are not apt to elaborate, to spin out believable stories, to write with details, or to develop convincing ideas. This means that you need to actually push kids to write faster and for longer stretches. Ask all your students to record where in their notebooks they start and stop writing each day in school and at home. Help them to join you in looking for trends related to their volume of writing.

If children's writing stamina (and the resulting volume) is a priority for you, you'll want to look across all the notebooks from a class, dividing them into two piles: strong stamina and weaker stamina. There might be a third pile for intermittently strong stamina. I suggest you record the names of kids in each group; then during writing time convene the group that most needs your help and teach them a strategy which you hope can help them write with more stamina. You'll also want to set up a structure to check on their progress. If the problem persists, you may need to work with some children outside of class time to address the issue (and to signal to the writer that progress on this front is nonnegotiable).

When you study student work, you may notice predictable problems that crop up in children's writing, and group those children who could profit from a specific kind of help. For example, I find that when children write about ideas, their writing often becomes repetitive because they circle back to say something again and again, hoping perhaps to clarify. Teach these children to reread their writing immediately after they've written it, deleting cumbersome iterations of an idea and leaving only the clearest version in place. Allow them to feel great about brief, clear writing.

You may find some children have regarded this unit of study as an invitation to write in bland, obvious generalizations. Encourage them to write more specifically and to say more in a sentence—usually when they write an idea using more words, they write with more specificity. Help them reach for more precise language. Coach them to push past words like good and fun toward words that name their feelings more exactly.

Notice whether the child uses any of the transition terms one would expect in non-narrative writing. Does the child use phrases such as *one reason, for example, I also think, it is important that, also, because, on the other hand?* If the child is not using any of these transition words, determine whether the child is instead using words such as *next, after this, and then*—transition terms one expects to see in narrative writing. If children aren't using transition words at all, this may or may not be a sign that they are not elaborating on or developing their ideas. Remember, using transition words is not our goal! Thinking of whole ideas in varying relationships to one another is our goal, and using certain transition words is one indicator that children are doing that. Children can use transition words without understanding or intentionally creating relationships between ideas, and they can leave out transition words while still creating these relationships.

SEEKING OUTSIDE SOURCES

IN THIS SESSION, YOU WILL TEACH CHILDREN THAT WRITERS SEEK OUTSIDE SOURCES, SOLICITING OTHER PEOPLE'S STORIES, TO SUPPORT THEIR IDEAS IN ESSAY WRITING.

GETTING READY

- One incident from which you have written two stories: one that illustrates your topic sentence, one that illustrates a different point

- A few sentences from an interview that support a bullet point from the class story, written on chart paper

- Example of a child's story and topic sentence requiring revision to support the main idea

- See CD-ROM for resources

When I studied writing with Donald Murray, he told me that I needed to learn that I could put other people's voices and stories into my writing. For several years, all of my articles had been about my own teaching, and Murray was determined for me to expand my repertoire. "Think of a story you'd like to tell," he said to me, "that is not your own story. Then phone people and say, 'I want to write your story. Can I come visit you? Can I talk with you?'"

Three days later, I set off on a four-day trip to visit teachers across the state of Vermont who'd studied in the National Writing Project's summer program at the University of Vermont. Looking back now, I laugh to realize that my first steps into the world of investigative journalism had been cautious ones, for I hadn't exactly explored a topic too far afield from my area of expertise! Still, I learned a lot from traversing the state, gathering the stories of people I did not know, as told in their own voices.

Now it is important to me that we nudge youngsters, too, to include stories and quotes from people they have interviewed, as well as the voices of people they meet in the pages of books. William Zinsser said, "Whatever form of nonfiction you write, it will come alive in proportion to the number of quotes you can weave into it as you go along" (Zinsser 2001).

How important it is for writers to learn to listen. Byrd Baylor, the author of the children's book The Other Way to Listen, tells the story of an old man who teaches a young child how to listen. "Do this: go get to know one thing as well as you can," he advises. "Don't be ashamed to learn from bugs or sand or anything" (Baylor 1997). The old man's advice can aid your students as they begin the journey to support their thesis statements. Invite them to look around, to listen hard, and to be collectors of stories.

MINILESSON

Seeking Outside Sources

CONNECTION

Remind children that authors collect and angle stories to highlight the idea we want to convey. Show that a familiar shared story could have been angled differently, conveying a different idea.

"Writers, in the previous session you learned that as writers we collect stories, and then we write those stories in such a way that we highlight the idea we really want to convey. For example, I wrote a story about how on Christmas mornings my father used to leave us for the hospital, where he cooked waffles for the doctors and patients. I angled the story to show my dad's dedication to his work, but I *could* instead have written about the fact that on Christmas mornings, I have often felt swamped with cleanup chores, partially due to Dad's trips to the hospital. I *could* have written this":

> When the living room was a sea of torn wrapping paper
> and empty boxes, my father would head out of the
> house, leaving us to clean up. He was adamant that he
> needed to cook waffles for the people at the hospital.
> So my brothers and I were left to lug load after load of
> trash to the garage.

"However, if I'd written about my Christmas morning job overload, this would not have advanced my thesis about my dad loving his job. The details about our living room being a sea of torn wrapping paper and the loads of trash would not have been aligned with my point; they would not have provided supportive evidence for the idea that Dad taught me what it means to regard a job as a hobby! I hope you have learned that when we write stories—stories we hope will become part of our essays—we need to keep in mind the messages we want to convey, and we need to tell the stories in ways that make readers *feel* our messages."

COACHING

You will notice that today's Connection is much more extensive than usual. I practically reteach the preceding minilesson. I do this from time to time when I think the preceding lesson was particularly new or complicated. Another option could have been to spend a day revisiting the previous session's instruction, and only then move on to the new teaching.

Notice that I revisit earlier stories, using a familiar story in a new way to make a new point. Again and again, you'll see a particular story thread through four or five minilessons. I do this so that children can focus on what is new about my story, and about today's teaching point, instead of focusing on the story's content. For the same reason, when I use children's literature to illustrate a teaching point, I try to choose stories with which students are already familiar.

Notice, too, that I once again highlight the feature I want children to notice in writing by juxtaposing a "do this" example with a "don't do this" example. I present contrasting examples as a way to bring a particular feature into focus.

"When I wrote the Christmas morning story, I kept in mind that it was supposed to provide evidence that Dad loved his job; now I'll underline sections of my story that I hope bring out that idea."

> I remember on Christmas mornings after the presents had been opened, my dad always went into the kitchen and began <u>doing the one bit of cooking that he did all year.</u> He stirred Bisquick and eggs in a huge bowl and set off for the hospital, leaving us to finish Christmas celebrations without him. <u>For dad, Christmas mornings were not just a time to be with family, they were also a time to serve hot waffles to the medical residents and patients.</u> When I asked him once why he didn't send someone else with the waffles, <u>he told me he loved being at the hospital on Christmas mornings.</u> "It's my hobby," he said.

"In a similar fashion, yesterday you all angled your stories to convey certain ideas. When Jay Jay looked back at a story he wrote to illustrate that he loves spending time with his father, Jay Jay realized that he hadn't yet made the point, so he rewrote the story. Listen to his first draft and then to the revised version of it."

> *1st Draft*
> One sunny Sunday my dad came and picked me up to go to his job at the Skate Key. On the way I asked him how to do a 360°. When we got there he put his skates on. He did it first then I did it next but I fell on the ice.

> *Revision*
> I love being with my father because he teaches me skating moves. One sunny Sunday, my dad came and picked me up to go to his job at the Skate Key. On the way I asked him how to do a 360°. When we got there, he said, "Jay Jay, put your skates on." He put his skates on. He did it first. My dad whirled so fast—fast like a road runner. I couldn't see him. Bang with his strong skates. I thought his wheels popped off. My eyes were spinning fast like I got dizzy. I thought that he fell headfirst into the floor. I thought he broke his leg when he came down. He did it first, but next I did it. I fell on the floor. My head was bloody. I came to in the locker room, still thinking how I love my Dad for teaching me skating moves.

A third move I make in this minilesson, one I make in many minilessons, is that after I state a general rule or an overarching idea I follow it up with a very specific example. Notice that this shift from big idea to specific example is a mainstay of any essay—and it is a mainstay also of any course of study! If you feel as if this genre is not home terrain for you, think again—because much of your teaching follows the structures of an essay.

This is Jay Jay's first year in a writing workshop. He has lots of trouble spelling conventionally, but he has already learned a gigantic amount about the craft of effective writing. One of the interesting things that you will no doubt see with your kids is this: it is not that hard to teach a struggling writer the craft of effective writing. Strugglers like Jay Jay can learn to angle their stories and to recap a main idea after they've told a story that they hope illustrates that main idea. But it is less easy to teach strugglers to write with strong spelling and complex sentence structures. Their learning on this front will be incremental, not exponential.

Notice that I used a student sample as well as my own sample in the Connection. This is more examples than usual, and more teaching in the Connection than usual.

"All of you, like Jay Jay, are learning to reread your stories, checking that you highlighted whatever matched your main idea."

Name your teaching point. In this case, tell children that essay writers often collect stories from outside sources.

"Today I want to teach you that writers of essays are collectors, collecting not only *our* stories but also stories of others, as long as these stories illustrate our main ideas."

TEACHING
Teach children that writers can rely on outside sources, on other people's stories, to support their ideas. Present an example.

"For example, Caleb's been working on collecting stories that illustrate his thesis that when learning sports, practice makes perfect. Caleb has lots of stories from his own life—we all know Caleb spends lots of time practicing sports—but he decided to search for stories from other people's lives as well, and to put those in his folders. I want you to notice, in this story about Michael Jordan, specific things Caleb does to highlight his point that, in sports, practice makes perfect. Listen and notice that Caleb's stories are shaped like stories. He tells about Michael Jordan encountering a problem, then struggling, then resolving the problem. Even though he writes mini-stories, his stories follow the same story arc that Keats uses to write *Peter's Chair*. Listen." [*Figs. X-1 and X-2*]

> As a kid, famed basketball player Michael Jordan was heartbroken when he heard that he had not made his high school basketball team. He was so heartbroken that that summer he spent most of his free time on the basketball court, practicing. And guess what? The next time he tried out for that team, because of all that practice, he made the team, and was one of the best players.
>
> Michael and most other athletes will tell you that the key to their success is mostly practice. When you're practicing, someone else isn't, and when you two meet up, who's going to be better? You: the person who was practicing.

It is easier to recall bits of information when those bits are nested in familiar concepts or otherwise related to what a person already knows. I try to make my new point easy to remember by showing how this new lesson relates to and extends the previous lesson. I do this sort of thing often.

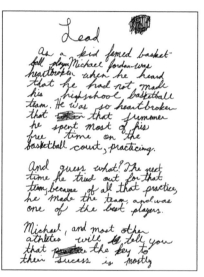

Fig. X-1 Caleb collects anecdotes to support his thesis

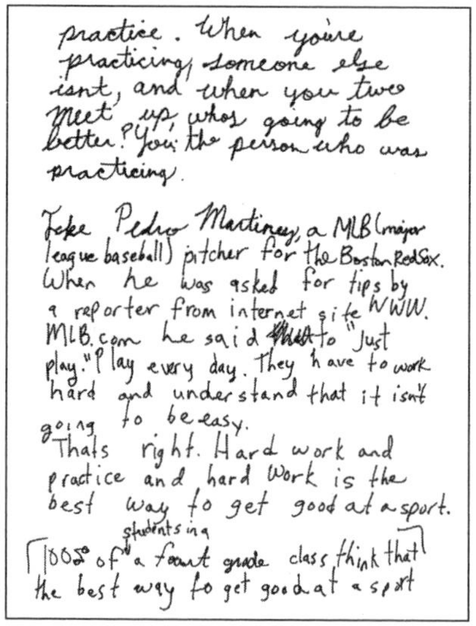

Fig. X-2 Caleb's anecdotes illustrate his thesis

"Did you notice that Caleb's story started like stories often do, with Caleb telling the problem Michael Jordan had, and then Caleb shows how Michael Jordan tried—and eventually resolved—his problem. But the other important thing I hope you noticed is that after telling the story, Caleb did just what Jay Jay did when he wrote about his father teaching him to roller-skate. Caleb came back and talked about how the story goes with his main idea. Listen again." I reread it, stressing the last paragraph.

"Sometimes when we go to collect stories from others, we end up collecting quotes more than stories, as in this next example. But again notice how, at the end, Caleb talks about how this bit of information connects with his idea, which is that practice, in sports, is important."

> Take Pedro Martinez, a MLB (major league baseball) pitcher for the Boston Red Sox. When he was asked for tips by a reporter from Internet site www.mlb.com, he said to just play. "Play every day. They have to work hard and understand that it isn't going to be easy."
>
> That's right. Hard work and practice and hard work is the best way to get good at a sport.

"Did you notice that Caleb connected this story to his claim at the end as well, almost as if he were saying, 'Notice this story really builds my case!' It's like the story is evidence in a trial, and Caleb is the lawyer, showing people that the evidence proves the case."

ACTIVE ENGAGEMENT
Ask students to use the class piece to practice seeking outside sources and writing them into an essay.

"So let's try it on our class essay about first-grade reading buddies. Imagine you are writing a page to go into your folder labeled 'Another reason that working with reading buddies is fun is that you get to read really cool books,'" I said, holding up the folder with that label. You need some stories to support that bullet point, don't you! Now pretend you interviewed Randolio to learn whether he thought the first-grade books were cool. I did that, and I wrote down what he said right here." I pointed at the chart paper on which I had transcribed Randolio's comments about books.

Notice how I am really slowing down this instruction. This work is not easy, and I am teaching it by sharing an example rather than by demonstrating. I want to make sure that my students are seeing and hearing what I want them to notice. For this reason, I make a great point to share the example in a way that highlights the aspects I want highlighted. In this minilesson I am doing what I taught kids to do in the preceding lesson: I am telling a small story and angling it so that it illustrates my point.

In high school English classes, students learn that you can't make a claim, cite a passage from a text to illustrate that claim, and call it a day. Instead, it's important to write another sentence or two that digs into the passage, discussing specifically how this citation relates to the claim. Elementary school students can do a junior version of this if they learn to write about how their story illustrates their thesis.

Over and over you'll notice that to set children up to efficiently practice what I've taught, I do 80 percent of the necessary work, leaving just a bit for them to do. The part of the endeavor I leave for the children exactly matches what I've just taught them to do. I usually get them started doing this, almost as I might help a child get started riding a two-wheeler.

A lot of books have parts that pop up and squeak and quack and all. I love the ones that have sound effects. Once my buddy had a pile of books. He opened the first one and it mooed and neighed. It was so funny. The second book played "Old Susannah." The third one didn't make sounds. He also had a book with a wheel that spun around.

"What part of Randolio's comments would you quote to support that bullet point? Partner 2, write in the air, saying aloud to your partner exactly what you'd write if you were quoting the section of Randolio's comments that make your case. What part of his comments prove that working with reading buddies allows you to read really cool books?"

The children did this, and I listened in. "I love the way you let some parts of what Randolio said drop away," I said, "but most of you aren't quite finished. You forgot to talk at the end about how Randolio's comments fit with the claim that working with reading buddies is fun. Pretend you ended by saying, 'Randolio's buddy, for example, had a pile of books. One mooed, another played "Old Susannah."' How could you explicitly connect this [I pointed to the line about first-grade books being cool because they have sound effects] to your topic sentence? Turn and talk. Write that final sentence in the air to your partner and then go off to your own writing, keeping this in mind."

Notice how I don't let children leave the meeting area until they have connected their comments with their claim. I am tucking this in here because I know this is an area where many students struggle. I want it to become habit for them.

WRITING AND CONFERRING

Checking That Stories Match Topic Sentences

Whether your writers are collecting their own stories or retelling the anecdotes of others, there are a few predictable lessons you'll teach them as you confer and work with small groups. You'll need to teach children to angle their stories to make their point, and I've discussed this already. You'll also need to teach children to reread whatever they collect in their files, asking, "Does this really support my topic sentence?" Often the evidence will be only tangentially related to the topic sentence.

For example, I pulled in and listened to Emily, whose thesis was "December is fun." One of her topic sentences said, "December is fun because of Christmas parties." I taught her to underline the two or three key words in her topic sentence, and she underlined *December, Christmas parties,* and *fun.* Then I told her that what I do to check that my material matches the point, the meaning, is that I reread my material and ask whether the information is related to each of the key words. So Emily read one of the stories she'd collected aloud, checking to see whether it supported the three things she'd decided were key (*December, Christmas parties*, and *fun*). [Fig. X-3]

> One time that <u>December</u> was fun at a <u>X-mas party</u>. Me, my cousins, and my sister were eating <u>Christmas dinner</u> in my room and when we finished we decided to play this game on my bed. We put pillows under my bed and against the wall, then we would all sit in the crack and the bed would move forward fast and we would drop down fast and land on our pillows.

"It goes with my point?" she said, her intonation suggesting she wasn't sure.

"Let's check. For this to 'go,' it needs to be about December. Is it? Yes. It needs to be about a Christmas party—is it? Yes. It needs to be about the party being fun—is it?"

"Yes?" Emily asked, but on closer inspection she realized that although she'd described a game that she does indeed find to be fun, she hadn't made clear to readers that the game was a lot of fun (and in fact, because the game involved crashing from the bed onto the floor on one's butt, she could not assume readers would just 'know' that this was sheer joy).

<u>MID-WORKSHOP</u>
<u>TEACHING POINT</u> ***Showing** and **Telling*** "Writers, can I have your eyes and your attention? I have a quick but very important tip for you. As you are rereading your essays to make sure your stories prove your claims, you can also reread checking for something else. Remember how we've talked about how writers show, not tell? The truth is, essay writers nearly always both show *and* tell! As you reread what you've written, check to see that every story you've collected has times in it where you tell—outright explain what's important—and also times when you show—describe how something goes. You already know how to show—by making a movie in your mind and describing what you see and hear and sense. Emily is going to tell that her Christmas party was fun by saying that's where she and her cousin invented some of her favorite games. She's going to show it was fun by describing how they were laughing while they were playing them. You can show *and* tell in every essay you ever write, and that will make your essays all the more powerful."

> one time that December was fun at a X-mas party. Me, my cousins and my sister were eating christmas dinner in my room and when we finished we disided to play this game on my bed. We put pillows under my bed and agaist the wall then we would all sit in the crack and the bed would move forward <u>fast</u> and we we would drop down <u>fast</u> and land on our pillows.

Fig. X-3 Emily's notebook entry

I complimented Emily on the way she angled her story, even though she hadn't done it perfectly. In my compliment, I walked her through the steps of angling, naming each turn she took or should have taken. "I love the way you didn't just tell your story any ol' way. Instead you said, 'I better make it clear this was a Christmas party,' so you put that fact up front in the story. And later you reread to check that key words—or key ideas—were in your example." This made my compliment reteach the process. Then I reminded her she always needs to reread the stories she collects to be sure they illustrate every important part of a topic sentence—she still needed to make clear that the party was fun. I suggested she could come right out and say something like, "Many of my favorite games are those that my cousins and I invented during those Christmas parties."

As you confer with individuals and teach small groups today, keep in mind that not only will you want to teach children to show and tell, but you'll also want to draw on all that your children have learned during the launching and personal narrative units of study. Be sure the old charts of Qualities of Good Narrative Writing are displayed in a prominent place, and be sure to remind children that they can draw on those early lessons, that they were indeed lessons that were meant to last a lifetime.

When I drew my chair alongside Rie, she told me she'd already written a story to support each of her topic sentences. Her stories were each brief—no more than half a page. "I'm impressed that even your tiny stories actually feel like stories," I said to her. Then I pointed out, "One thing I try to do is vary the length of my stories." I suggested she look them over and decide on a few stories to tell with more detail. Rie decided to stretch out this story, which she hoped illustrated the idea that she hates to make mistakes in front of a crowd. She'd written: *[Fig. X-4]*

> I was in Japan in school waiting for my test score. My teacher was really shocked. "Rie!" he called, "You got sixty!" I was shocked about what I heard. I usually got ninety or hundred or ninety-five. Kids started to laugh at me. I felt my face grow red. I heard kids whispering and I heard an insult name.

This is her new version of it: *[Fig. X-5]*

> I wasn't happy doing a test because the teachers in Japan says the test score out loud. "Rie," called out a voice. It was my teacher's voice. I knew that I wouldn't get a hundred percent. I went up front. He said my score out to the class. "Rie, you got sixty." My jaw dropped open. I couldn't believe my ears. I usually got ninety-five or ninety. I saw everyone giggling in front of me. I wanted to cry. But I was in school. Everyone would laugh at me even more. I wished if only I had magic powers and I disappeared.

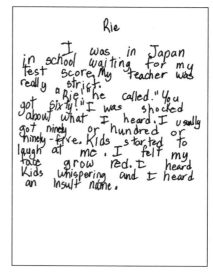

Fig. X-4 Rie's notebook entry (first draft)

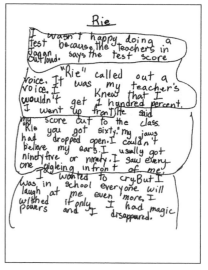

Fig. X-5 Rie's revised entry

SHARE

Checking That Stories Support Topic Sentences

Remind writers that they need to angle stories to support their topic sentences. Present an example of a student's story and a topic sentence, and describe how the writer checked his alignment and then revised his story to support his claim.

"Writers, I want to remind you that we need to check to be sure that our stories address our main ideas. Alejandro realized today that this is hard to do. At first, he thought, 'My story definitely supports my idea.' His topic sentence is 'Mr. Lee is a great teacher because he taught me how to do art.' His story is all about learning to do art. Listen, and see if you think Alejandro's example illustrates his point that Mr. Lee is a great teacher because he taught Alejandro to do art."

> We made self-portraits. We used tissue paper to make the color of our skin. We glued the tissue paper on to the picture of our head. It looked like skin. We made eyes using wax . . .

"At first Alejandro said, 'My story matches my main idea because it *is* all about doing art.' But then he said, 'Wait a minute!' and he reread. 'Now I get it,' he said. 'My thesis is "Mr. Lee was a great teacher (for all these reasons)," but in my self-portrait story, Mr. Lee is missing!' So Alejandro rewrote the story this way."

> Mr. Lee taught us new art techniques. For example, he taught us that when we want to show skin, we can use tissue paper. Mr. Lee knows a lot of tricks like that. He taught us that to make eyes . . .

Ask partners to reread their own and their partner's stories, checking to see if their stories support their topic sentences.

"Writers, would you each reread your thesis statement with your partner and underline the two or three key words, the parts that need to be supported by your story. Alejandro will need to underline *Mr. Lee* (the subject), *taught* (what he did), and *taught us new art techniques* (the specific point). Then look together at your stories and see if they illustrate all these parts of your topic sentence. If they don't, help each other revise the story so that it does the job you need it to do."

It is very easy to give data just a cursory glance and to say, "Of course that supports the claim." But often, when one really looks, there are problems that need to be addressed.

The truth is that I had conferred with Alejandro and helped him realize that no, his example did not exactly support his claim. When I tell the story to the class, though, I leave myself out of it. I act as if Alejandro first thought his story matched his claim, and then on his own came to the realization that he'd left Mr. Lee out of the story. I do this because the contrast between his first, problematic version and the revised one brings home the point I am trying to make. Because I erase my role from this and act as if Alejandro, on his own, thought, "Wait a minute!" and revised his initial idea, I'm able to tell the "before" version without it seeming like a public insult. This is a very common way for me to show an example of a child traveling on a path that I hope other children will travel. I use the story not just to praise but also to teach others what they can do.

HOMEWORK *Waiting for More Stories That Illustrate Your Ideas* I know at home tonight, stories related to your topic sentences will come to the surface of your thinking. That happens to every writer. We live with a topic, waiting on it. Eudora Welty once said that we sit, waiting for stories like we wait for a mouse to emerge from a hole in the wall. Don Murray says that all writers need to wait. "Waiting takes time, time for staring out windows, time for thinking, time for dreaming, time for doodling, time for rehearsing, planning, drafting, restarting . . . for moving closer, backing off, coming at it from a different angle, circling again, trying a new approach" (Murray 1989, pp. 22–23). And Kafka had, over his writing desk, just one word: wait.

So as you travel home, wait for related story ideas to emerge. As you walk into your home, wait for a related story idea. When you tell folks at home what you are writing (and do that—talking helps ideas come out), wait. The stories will come, just as the mouse comes out of the hole. Plan to write two or three stories, each on separate sheets of paper, because you'll file these in your folders, each telling a different story related to a different topic sentence. Combined, do a total of a page and a half or two pages of writing—which means you'll need your stories to be efficient ones!

TAILORING YOUR TEACHING

If your writers are having some trouble angling their narratives to support an idea . . . you can demonstrate that sometimes it helps to write the story, keeping in mind the main idea, almost as one would hold onto a mantra. You could say, "I want to show you how I create my narrative, repeating phrases to remind myself the meaning I want to highlight in my story, almost as if it is a mantra. First, I create my mantra. If my thesis is 'Friendships are complicated' and the topic sentence is 'Friendships are complicated at school,' the mantra might go, 'friendships . . . complicated . . . school,' 'friendships . . . complicated . . . school'. Okay, now I have it. Now I am ready to write my story about the time I saw my friend Emily cheating on a test." Then I'd write, stopping every once in a while to say the mantra out loud. "Did you see how I took the subject of the thesis, 'friendship,' and the main idea about friendship, 'complicated at school,' and recited this over and over as I wrote out a narrative?"

MECHANICS

When you read over the writing your children do under the auspices of this unit, you will probably notice that at least a few children are trying to make their essay entries sound more objective, formal, and academic than their narratives. Chances are good that this well-intentioned effort will create lots of new issues involving mechanics and grammar.

First, you may see children writing unnecessarily in the passive voice and using abstract rather than concrete and specific words. A college student who is trying to be impressive might get caught in convoluted sentences such as: "The influence exerted by leaders upon the citizens extends to voting and . . . " Children can create their own versions of this: "A true friendship contains being helpful, showing that you understand and care, not being made fun of, and laughter. The obstacles in a friendship can be hurtful, but they also teach you a lesson about yourself and about your friends, and how to handle a situation like this later . . . "

If your children are trying to write like this—stop them! Teach them first of all to trust simple sentences in which a doer does something. The power in a sentence comes from the active agent, the subject, and from the actor's action, the verb. Sentences will always work best if they contain a clear, forceful, imaginable subject. "My best friend, Kara . . . " will work better than "Friendships contain . . . ."

In Session I, for example, you read Adam's entry in which he mulled over classmates' reactions to a disease. Notice Adam's struggles with pronoun agreement:

People shouldn't judge people by what they look like. When kids are discriminated by what they look like they are treated very cruelly. It is really mean to do this because you don't really know this person. For example, let's say someone wears a shirt with a stain on it and everybody doesn't want to be your friend because they think you're dirty. The person who did not want to talk to you could have been your future best friend. When I was in kindergarten in this school a lot of people avoided me because I am bald. It took me a long time to make friends. It is harder to go into a new school if you have something different like I do. Before people judge people by what they look like, they need to tell themselves, "What would I feel like if I was that kid? With everybody staring at me and nobody talking to you." Then you look at you and your friends, with everybody admiring you and including you. Then you go over there to the "different kid" and include him and talk to him.

Notice, too, that some of your children will probably struggle with *anaphora*—the use of a pronoun to reference an earlier noun. Take this passage:

Leo made errors, including telling the joke to his brother. He was embarrassed. Now that he'd told one, he needed to tell another.

Is "he" intended to be Leo or his brother? Is "one" intended to be "one person" or "one joke"? Is "another" a person or a joke?

The author of an expository text must use pronouns to represent not only nouns—people and objects—but also *concepts*. For example, I might write a whole paragraph describing the architecture of a minilesson. Later in my discussion, all of that information would be contained in the simple phrase *the architecture of a minilesson;* moreover, the information might later still be referenced in the tiny pronoun *it.* This means that pronouns carry a heavy cargo!

Many times, however, the writer needs to use synonyms or repeat the noun (rather than use a pronoun) to avoid an unclear referent. Watch Ali, a proficient fifth grader, struggle with the new demands of expository writing. I put her intended meaning in parentheses:

My brother is his own person. Sometimes it is kind of hard *to tell a thing like that* (to discern that he has this character trait) when *they* (people) are little. But he is almost nothing like me, my mom or dad. *That* (my brother's uniqueness) is something I love about him. In some aspects of his personality he is very much the same (as others in the family).

It's important that we, as teachers, are able to look at our students' writing and recognize and categorize their miscues. Then we need to prioritize our instructional plans for responding to these miscues. If a child hasn't yet studied the concept of pronoun reference, it's probably not reasonable to try to devise lessons on anaphora. But it may make sense to ask these children, when they *read* expository texts, to notice that over and over again an entire paragraph or page ends up crystallized into a single term that is then referenced later by just a pronoun. When reading these lines:

The network of canals forms an irrigation system. Irrigation systems are vital to the success of a farm. These systems . . .

the reader needs to draw mental arrows backwards in the text.

From Irrigation to network of canals. From these to Irrigation.

Some readers do this without requiring direct instruction, but others need us to explicitly teach these reading and writing moves.

CREATING PARALLELISM IN LISTS

I love to make lists. I list my priorities for a day, a week, a vacation, a year. I list the names of flowers I've planted in my garden. I list names for the dog I'll someday get. I list books I've read and books I want to read. I list places I'd like to visit someday. I list the days when my son will be away, and the days when he'll be home again.

Lists reflect the human instinct to collect, sort, order, and select. When we cannot physically gather in our arms all the flowers we've planted and line them up on the counter, we list their names, and those names make the flowers present. Simply by naming them, we conjure them up: dahlia, daisy, lily—yes, I've got them all in my garden.

During today's session, you'll help children make lists that may help their essays. There are lots of possible ways to teach this concept. You could share your own propensity to list and to collect, and share also what you know of your children's similar tendencies. One child collects baseball cards, another barrettes. Both children spend time sorting these into categories. Writers do similar work.

Specifically, today you'll teach children to write what I refer to as "tight lists," or lists of items linked by a repeating phrase. The lesson, then, will be not only about lists but also about parallelism.

For writers, the challenge of this lesson will be to attend to both content and form. It would be easy to write tight lists of anything in the world—but remember, Rebecca's tight lists need to advance her claims about her fury with her grandfather, and Caleb's tight lists need to show that practice is essential to success in a sport. Trying to convey a meaning while writing within a tight list structure is like trying to tap your head and rub your belly at the same time—it is not easy. Try it and you'll see!

IN THIS SESSION, YOU'LL TEACH CHILDREN THAT WRITERS STRUCTURE INFORMATION TO SUPPORT A CLAIM IN THE SAME WAY AGAIN AND AGAIN. WRITERS CREATE PARALLELISM THAT CAN BEGIN IN A LIST.

GETTING READY

- Example of published writing where author used lists ("I have a dream" speech by Martin Luther King Jr. used in this session) on chart paper
- Your own topic sentences and supporting lists to illustrate use of repeated phrases and parallel wording
- See CD-ROM for resources

MINILESSON

Creating Parallelism in Lists

CONNECTION

Remind your students that writers collect material, especially stories, to use in their essays. Spotlight the work of one child in a way that serves as a model for all children.

"Writers, over the past few days you learned that while builders build with plasterboard and lumber, writers build with words. Before we can draft our essays, we need to collect the materials we might use to build our boxes and bullets. You have already collected stories, and some of you used phrases such as *for example* to get yourselves started writing step-by-step stories. Diego did this when he wrote about Sari getting stuck trying to read the phrase *sheep shove*, and Caleb did this when he collected stories about Michael Jordan and Pedro Martinez."

"Emily, for example, collected a story to support her idea 'Having a dog is a big responsibility.' She wrote the story in a step-by-step way with a lot of detail, and those details make the story enthralling. Listen to it."

> Having a dog is a big responsibility because when they are adults they are playful. For example, one day when I was sleeping my dog woke me up in the middle of the night to play. She was bouncing all over the place. She barked, then jumped on my bed and started wiggling all over. I pushed her off and she jumped back on. I got up, walked her to her dog bed, and put her to sleep. It took a long time, but it paid off.

"Do you see how Emily highlighted the parts of the story that show that dogs are a big responsibility because they are playful? And she continued, writing one more tiny story that also illustrates her main idea."

> This also reminds me of when I was in the park. I saw a boy walking his dog. It looked like the dog was walking him. He was yelling at the dog, then he took out a ball. The dog started jumping all over the place. He threw the ball, the dog got it, he threw it again, the dog got it. He put the ball away and the dog walked him home.

COACHING

I know this unit can be complicated. One day children learn to write personal stories; another day to collect less-personal anecdotes; and on another day they learn to write lists. I try to consolidate all they've learned so that it feels simple and portable. I do that here when I say builders build with plasterboard and lumber, writers with words.

I've tried to immerse children in examples of the sort of thing I hope they write. But meanwhile I've slowed down my minilesson by including a fairly long example in the Connection phase. You may decide to streamline this lesson if you don't believe your children need the immersion.

"I know you have more stories in mind and you'll continue collecting them in your files. Once you get started writing stories, more and more examples will float to the surface of your mind."

Name your teaching point. In this case, tell children that sometimes writers collect lists of examples.

"Today I want to teach you that when writing essays, writers sometimes collect examples that we do not stretch out and tell as stories, but that we instead list."

TEACHING
Illustrate the importance of lists by referencing the parallel construction in a well-known speech.

"Listen to one of the most famous pieces of non-narrative writing in the world. I have a copy up here on the overhead so you can read along."

"You will surely have heard this text before—it is Martin Luther King Jr.'s 'I have a dream' speech. The whole speech is not structured exactly like the essays we are writing, but we can learn from studying the way Martin Luther King Jr. uses *lists* to support his idea. I want you to listen first to a bit of his speech, and then watch how I (as a writer) go back and study what this author has done in order to borrow his techniques. Then we'll move to a second bit of King's speech and you'll have a chance to name the techniques you see him using that you can emulate."

> We have come to this hallowed spot to remind America of the fierce urgency of now . . . Now is the time to make real the promises of democracy; now is the time to rise from the dark and desolate valley of segregation to the sunlit porch of racial justice; now is the time to lift our nation from the quicksands of racial injustice to the solid rock of brotherhood; now is the time to make justice a reality for all of God's children.

"Listen to how King has one main idea here—that it is urgent to work toward civil rights *now*. Then he gives example after example of that main idea, telling what we need to do now. His examples echo each other. The key words are repeated so they sound like a

This is an odd Connection. I elaborate about the stories that writers sometimes tell, but then instead of incorporating this somehow in my point for the day I just end that topic and shift to another. I simply say, "Writers also do something else," pushing off from the first kind of writing to a second kind. The minilesson might have been better had I brought some of the content from this session's introduction into it, or pointed out the significance of lists within the classroom. By this time in the year, you will have lists of strategies, lists of qualities, lists of tools. You may decide to point out these lists, and then suggest that essayists are teachers of a sort and, like all teachers, we rely on lists to consolidate a lot of information.

Note the way I try to orient listeners at the start of the Teaching component of a minilesson. I want children to know what I'll be doing and why, and I also want them to know what they'll be expected to learn and to do. I began deliberately adding bits of orientation after visiting hundreds of classrooms where I sat among the children in the meeting area listening to a minilesson, and often found myself disoriented as the teacher launched into a story or an example. Readers can skim the page and see from subheadings and other text features where the text is going, but listeners have none of those supports. It's helpful, therefore, if speakers give us a bit of orientation.

Notice that I sometimes use exemplar texts that are not exactly essays, and in those instances I use the larger umbrella term of non-narrative to describe those texts.

song." I reread several of them, accentuating the repeated phrase. "They all start with the same phrase—*Now is the time to…!*"

Ask children to watch as you use the techniques the author used to write a tight list pertinent to your topic.

"So let me try to borrow some of these techniques and use them for this idea: 'My father taught me that one person can make a difference.' So let me see . . . " I reread my sentence.

> My father taught me to believe that one person can make a difference.

"I'm going to take the stem of this claim. Maybe if I repeat it, I can jog my mind to come up with a list of examples."

> My father taught me to believe that . . .

"I need to come up with things that fit under the idea that one person can make a difference. And I need to remember to write with details."

> My father taught me to believe that . . . that . . . one person could start a hospital clinic . . . that one person could rally all the members of a family to write their memoirs, that one person could turn a rainy drab day into an adventure, that one person could change the spirit at a hospital . . .

"Do you see how I took a key phrase and repeated it? Some of the lines I've come up with aren't all that great, and some sort of repeat each other, but I think I've got some good stuff here." I put the entry in the appropriate file folder.

ACTIVE ENGAGEMENT
Remind children that to learn techniques for their own writing, they can study the writing of a published author. In this case, they can study parallelism.

"I hope you noticed the way I took just a bit of what Martin Luther King Jr. had written and I read it again. Then I asked myself, 'So what has Martin Luther King Jr. done that I can do too?' Whether you are writing a story or an essay, it always helps to study the work of the pros. Let's each try to do that with the copies of King's speech that I've given you. Would

Above all, I want children to sense the rhythm of King's language. You may decide that King's writing is too complex to serve as a mentor text for your children. You could use "Hairs," a passage from Sandra Cisneros' wonderful anthology The House on Mango Street, *as a more accessible example, or "Alone," a chapter from Jacqueline Woodson's* From the Notebooks of Melanin Sun. *Alternatively, you could choose any great picture book or poem that relies on repetitive lists. Search for titles by Charlotte Zolotow if you are looking for a picture book that's written as a list—she's written dozens of wonderful ones!*

Say this with intonation that signals children to fill in what could go next.

It is important to notice that I don't start with a neat mental list and then record it. I write what I refer to as a stem of a sentence, and in this instance it is the stem of my topic sentence. Only then do I generate and record one idea for how to complete the sentence. After I've written one idea, I push toward a second idea. I find that simply repeating the pattern generated by the first line makes it easier to produce a list than trying to pull a full-blown list out of the air. Simultaneously conceiving of both the pattern and of the elements that will fill the pattern is quite difficult. "When you catch someone a fish, they eat for a day. When you teach them to fish, they eat for a lifetime." I'm trying—lightly—to demonstrate the process of learning from a mentor text while also showcasing the way this writer used lists.

you and your partner take the next paragraph, read it aloud, then try to name *specifically* what King has done that you can do too?"

> With this faith we will be able to work together, to pray together, to struggle together, to go to jail together, to stand up for freedom together, knowing that we will be free one day. And this will be the day.
>
> So let freedom ring from the prodigious hilltops of New Hampshire; let freedom ring from the mighty mountains of New York; let freedom ring from the snow-capped Rockies of Colorado; let freedom ring from the curvaceous slopes of California . . . And when this happens, and when we allow freedom to ring, when we let it ring from every village and every hamlet, from every state and every city, we will be able to speed up the day when all of God's children, black men and white men, Jews and Gentiles, Protestants and Catholics, will be able to join hands and sing in the words of the old Negro spiritual, "Free at last. Free at last."

"Once you and your partner have got an idea for something that Martin Luther King Jr. has done that you could try, would you use the technique you admire and work together, planning a list that you could insert into our class essay."

Reiterate your writing process, highlighting the steps you hope writers will take as they write lists for their essays.

"Remember that whenever you decide to write a list, you also need to figure out what the stem of your list will be, because this is what you'll repeat and this is the part all the items in your list have to match with." I held up the folders, each displaying a topic sentence. "You could, for example, take this folder—'Working with our first-grade reading buddies is fun because you get to read really cool books'—and you could decide to list particular books. You could say, 'You get to read *Where the Wild Things Are*' and then say a phrase about that book; 'You get to read *Toot and Puddles*' and say a phrase about that one. *Or* you could choose a different stem and write, 'The books are cool because they have magic.' 'The books are cool because they have great pictures!'"

Alternatively, you could work with a different folder, a different topic sentence, and write, 'My reading buddy taught me this. My reading buddy taught me that.'"

If children need more support, I'll either read the paragraph aloud to them and ask them to talk in pairs about it, or I'll read it first, and then ask one of the partners to reread it aloud.

This is a long excerpt. You may want to read it aloud to help your children read it and hear its rhythms. You may also select just a part of it as your example. Alternatively, you may select a text that will be easier for your children to read. Picture books are full of examples!

Sometimes it can be a little jarring to take great works of literature and give their structure more attention than their content. Then, too, it can feel jarring to study magnificent writing and then apply a facet of it to everyday writing. However, I feel it is appropriate to do this in the classroom at times, for several reasons. First, nearly every text we study is one whose content is already familiar. We are not honoring form over content; we are simply continuing our study of the text by also studying its structure.

Second, we need to bring great literature and literature about great topics into the classroom at every opportunity. Even if the focus of our study is not the content of a piece of literature, some children will learn things from the content. Why not have the literature in the classroom be the most important literature we can possibly study? Last, as we've heard, imitation can be the sincerest form of flattery. Even the most awkward and ordinary bit of prose written to emulate a great work can be seen as a tribute to that great work. Our children and their work deserve the best writing we can bring them. Perhaps then, someday, they can create work that teachers across the country bring into classrooms as classic and heroic writing.

LINK

Restate the teaching point. Remind writers that today and always, essayists collect not only stories but also lists that illustrate their ideas.

"So writers, builders use cinder blocks and lumber. Writers use materials too, and so far you have learned that writers use stories. Today you learned that writers like Martin Luther King Jr. also use lists."

"The final point I want to make is that often we can choose to put the same content into *either* a list or into a story. When you think of an example today, think, 'Should I stretch this out as a story? Or should I combine it with other examples and write it as a list?' Both have their challenges, and today you'll probably write both lists and stories. But I would not write the same content over and over, in different forms. Make choices."

"Stories take a while to write because they are long, but lists also take a while to write because you need to work on many drafts so that you word them in ways that are parallel, concise, and make sense. I can't wait to admire and help you as you do this new work! Off you go."

Toward the end of a minilesson, I often try to put the day's teaching point alongside earlier teaching points, and, if possible, show how they are related. In this instance, I refer back to the metaphor of writers as builders because this conveys the main concept of this minilesson. I also remind children that writers make choices, and that they can draw on previous teaching points as well as today's point.

It's not wise for a child to write the exact same content in a list and then again in a story. If a child is writing that his mother cares for him and he wants to say that she gives him Tylenol, penicillin, and cough medicine, the child needs to decide whether to write that in a list or in a story—but not to put the same specifics into both forms. The child may try it both ways and choose the way that seems to work best, but in the end an essay can't contain the same content, written twice, each time in a different format.

WRITING AND CONFERRING

Making List Items Parallel

Any time we read students' writing or have a conference with one child, we need to ask ourselves, "Is this a lesson to teach one child—or should I pull in another writer or two?" As we read over our children's work, then, we create groups of kids. We think to ourselves, "Emily and Chris are both having trouble with . . ." and then later we pull them together and teach them a strategy we suspect will help them both. The following is an example of a strategy lesson I often teach in the wake of this minilesson.

"I gathered you together because I want to show you a trick I discovered when I was trying to make the items in my list parallel to each other. It's not easy to make them parallel, is it? I've noticed you guys are struggling with that, and you're not alone! So let me tell you what I learned from working on a list to go with my claim, 'My father taught me what it means to regard a job as a hobby.'"

"I had already written, 'My father doesn't just *like* his job, he *loves* his job.' When I read that line over, I knew it had a certain snap. I liked it. I didn't intend for the line to come out that way—I just wrote what I thought, and then I reread it and liked it. So I looked closely at the sentence to see if I could write more sentences in the same pattern. I noticed it has two parts, and they echo each other."

My father doesn't just like his job, he loves his job.

"So I built the next item on my list in the same way. I knew it had to go something like this: 'My father doesn't just *bing*, he *super-bings*. My father doesn't just like (something), he super-likes (something).' You see how it had to go? So I this is what I wrote:"

My father doesn't just care about his patients, he identifies with his patients.

MID-WORKSHOP TEACHING POINT *Revising Lists* "Some of you are having some trouble getting started on a list. You aren't sure what to use as the repeating stem of the list. One thing to do is to think of a story, tell it to yourself in your mind, and then ask, 'How can I write this information—or the important parts of it—as a *list* and not as a story?' So listen to a story Eddy could have written to go with his general idea, 'I love spending time with my parents,' and with the specific idea (and folder), 'when we vacation together.' Remember his story? You've heard it before, but this time listen so you can tell your partner what Eddy could *list* instead of *storytell*." [Fig. XI-1]

I love to spend time with my parents when we vacation together. For example, one time we went to a hotel in New Jersey. We visited a zoo that was in the hotel. It had really cute baby animals. My Mom loved the baby sheep so much that she pretended she was going to sneak it up the elevator to our room. My Dad and I had to drag her away. We were just joking. Then we watched three TV shows; one that was my choice, one that was Mom's, one that was Dad's. We usually don't watch each others' shows.

continued on next page

I love to spend time with my parents when we vacation together. For example, one time we went to a hotel in New Jersey. We visited a zoo that was in an hotel. I had really cute baby animals. My Mom loved the baby sheep so much that she pretended she was going to sneak it up the elevator to our room. My Dad and I had to drag her away. We were just joking. Then we watched three TV shows; one that was my choice, one that was my Mom's, one that was Dad's. We usually don't watch each others' shows.

Fig. XI-1 Eddy's story

"Do you see how I followed the pattern of the first sentence I wrote? I started with the same phrase, *'My father doesn't just . . .'* and then I put in *'care about his patients.'* I knew the next part had to be something that tells he does more than just care about them, he 'super-cares' about them. And the phrase I chose was *identifies with his patients,* because that is so much more than caring."

"LaKeya did this too. Would you read this aloud and listen for the pattern, the song, in her words, and then look closely and point out to each other what she did that you could do as well." *[Fig. XI-2]*

> Being a girl is hard because we go through a lot of changes, and have mixed/sensitive feelings. I can be happy but in a moment I can be mad. I can not care how I look and then in a moment I can look in the mirror every minute. I can feel thin and then all of a sudden my rear end is getting bigger. I can smell good one moment and then the next moment my armpits stink.

"Now, each of you, try making a list or revising the one you've started to put into your own essay. Remember that first you reread what you've written or you find a line you like, then you study what you did in that line to see if you can make another like it. I'll be right here helping you while you get started."

continued from previous page

The partners talked, and then I intervened. "I heard you finding lots of ways to do this, and of course there is no one right way. Theo first tried this."

> At the hotel, my family went to the zoo. At the hotel, my family watched TV. At the hotel, my family rode the elevator.

"But then he realized he'd left out the part about the family doing this *together* (which is, of course, the main idea!). He also left out all the interesting details. So he tried it again and this is what he came up with."

> I loved spending time with my parents when we stayed at a hotel. Together, we watched three TV shows (one that each of us had chosen). Together, we visited the hotel's zoo (where my Mom tried to sneak a baby lamb onto the elevator). And together we...

"Do you see that Theo has come up with a way for Eddy to repeat the important parts—that he, his mom, and his dad did these things *together*—and he has also included the details that bring his story to life? Coming up with this list isn't easy; Theo tried the list first one way, then another, then another. If you are working on lists that you can include in your folders, I should see draft 1, draft 2, draft 3 as you try your lists one way, then another, then another."

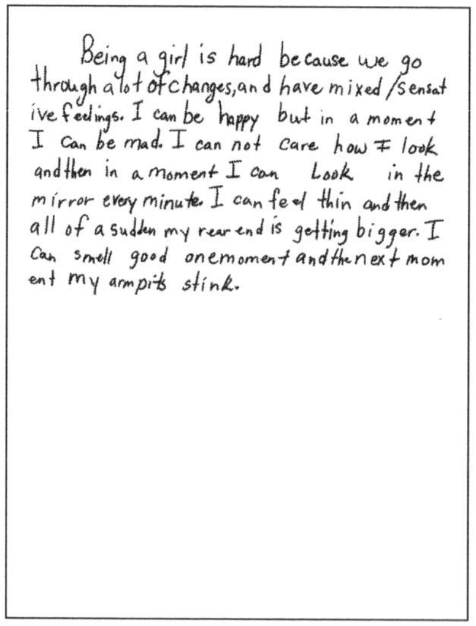

Being a girl is hard because we go through a lot of changes,and have mixed/sensat ive feelings. I can be happy but in a moment I can be mad. I can not care how I look andthen in a moment I can Look in the mirror every minute. I can feel thin and then all of a sudden my rear end is getting bigger. I can smell good onemoment andthenext mom ent my armpits stink.

Fig. XI-2 LaKeya's lists

SHARE

Balancing Details and Parallelism

Name the problem that you have noticed. In this instance, children are so focused on parallelism that they forget the importance of honesty and detail.

"You are writing your lists in patterns and that is great, but you know how sometimes when we try to write poems that rhyme, we get into trouble—our poems end up having almost nothing *but* rhyme? Well, some of you are writing *lists* where one sentence matches with the next, but it's as if you are so worried about matching your words that you forget all you know about good writing! When you are writing a list (as when you are writing anything!), it is important to try to write well."

Showcase sections of an exemplar text that can teach the importance of using active verbs and precise details.

"There are a few qualities of good writing that you especially need to remember as you work on gathering lists. First, your word choice matters. If possible, write with precise, active verbs (or action words) and very specific nouns (or name words). King could have written, 'Let freedom *sound*,' but instead he wrote, 'Let freedom *ring*.' He could have said, 'From *north* to *south*,' but instead he wrote, 'From the *snow-capped Rockies of Colorado* . . . from the *curvaceous slopes of California.*'"

"The other thing that matters a lot when you write lists is using *specific* details. When Eddy wanted to write a list about staying in the hotel with his parents, this meant that he'd need to squeeze his whole long story into items in a list. He was probably tempted to leave out the details about watching one television show that he chose, one show that his mother chose, and one that his father chose. He was probably tempted to leave out the detail about his mother wanting to adopt a baby lamb, but Eddy wisely knew those details were the strongest part of his writing, so he kept them."

"Sometimes when writing a list, the details can't fit into sentences that sound just right—in that case, sometimes writers decide to keep the details and let go of the parallelism. That's the decision Jamile made when he listed examples to show how his pets are good entertainers, and I think his decision was really wise. Listen." *[Fig. XI-3]*

> I think pets are good entertainers. My little sister has tea parties with my dog; he has carrots and she has bread. I read with my dog and he shares his thinking with me. Most of his thoughts have to do with snuffle, snuffle, snuffle.

This share deals with an issue that we see in writing workshop all the time. We teach a strategy, students approximate it, and then they overuse it, to the exclusion of everything else. This is part of the learning process. Rejoice that your students are approximating, because then you can teach them how to make choices as a writer, pulling from a variety of strategies.

I decided to refer back to the text I used in the minilesson because I wanted to be able to make a quick reference. You can choose any piece. Also notice that my second example is a child's. I like to put a professional writer's text alongside a child's text as a way to elevate the work all children are doing.

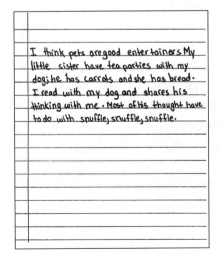

Fig. XI-3 Jamile's list does not have parallelism; he opted instead for details

"The items in Jamile's list don't perfectly match each other. He decided that content mattered more than sound, and he was probably wise to make that choice. I call this an elaborated—not a tight—list."

Debrief by naming what you did that is transferable to another day on another topic.

"So when you work on your lists, try to remember that strong action words and specific, precise nouns matter (it is better to say 'from the snow-capped Rockies of Colorado' than 'from the north'). And try to remember that even when you are squeezing a whole story into a sentence or two, you need to leave in the details like the dog eating carrots at the tea party and Mum wanting to sneak a baby lamb up the elevator to her hotel room!"

"Right now, would you and your partner look over your lists, and think and talk about whether your effort to give your list a musical sound, with one line matching the next, may have dominated too much. Ask whether you have written the truth and used exact details. If you've sacrificed truth or detail, try rewriting your lists."

Specificity always helps.

When teaching children to write lists, after they do so in a way that repeats the stem over and over you may want to show them that writers can collapse our lists. Instead of writing, "My grandfather is precious to me because he teaches me card tricks. My grandfather is precious to me because he lets me stay up late," you can tell a child to consolidate and write, "My grandfather is precious to me because he teaches me card tricks, lets me stay up late, and (whatever else the child wants to say).

HOMEWORK *Finding the Specifics That Bring Pieces to Life* Writers, you are learning that writers don't just write with words, they write with information. Don Murray, the Pulitzer Prize–winning writer, once said, "Beginning writers often misunderstand this. Young writers often become drunk on their way to becoming good writers. They dance to the sound of their own voices. They try to substitute style for subject matter, tricks for content, ruffles and flourishes for information. It doesn't work."

"The writer who has a warehouse of specific, detailed, relevant information has the advantage over any other writer," Murray continues. And writers, you are collecting files full of information. So tonight, would you collect specific information related to your topic? Live like magnets. Last night Philip did this, collecting information about how cats can be a lot of trouble, and he recorded this detail on his clipboard: "My cat trampled over me when she was catching a fly." What a detail—and he has it in his files because even when he was at home, he lived like a magnet, letting things related to his topic stick to him. Would you all do what Philip has done? Carry a clipboard with you, and let things that relate to your topic stick with you.

TAILORING YOUR TEACHING

If your students are skilled at creating parallelism . . . you might want to offer them yet another example of it that is more complex for them to emulate. Martin Luther King Jr. uses parallel sets of opposites to make his point in the following excerpt:

> Now is the time to rise from the dark and desolate valley [dark, lifeless place] of segregation to the sunlit porch [light, social place] of racial justice;
>
> Now is the time to lift our nation from the quicksands [unstable, dangerous place] of racial injustice to the solid rock [stable, safe place] of brotherhood.

In a mid-workshop teaching point, you might show students this example and say something like "Look how King starts with a phrase—Now is the time—and then he makes a word pattern. The pattern is something like this: Now is the time to go up from the bad something to the good something. Can you fill in the pattern to make a new sentence that could have gone next? Tell your partner your sentence."

ASSESSMENT

When I was young, my older brother (whom I idolized) had a quote on his bulletin board that said, "I can live three months on a good compliment." I've sometimes thought that I've managed to live thirty years on good compliments! Sometimes I give workshops to teachers called *The Art of Complimenting Learners*. You'll recall that in every writing conference, after the teacher researches to understand what the writer is trying to do and has done, the teacher then compliments the child.

When I compliment a writer, I try to name what the writer has done that seems to be at the top of her game—what she's done that would serve her well if she does it (or tries to do it) forever. I'm particularly attentive to what the writer has been *trying* to do (even if she is only halfway there). Take this entry, for example, and think about how to compliment this writer.

> Worms are not just small creatures on the earth, or garden lepers. They can be your friend. Even though they can't interact with you or play with you, you can observe them for hours and write about them. They are very interesting pets to have and watch. Worms look small but they're pretty strong when they dig into the dirt.

So when I look at Lydia's entry about worms, I'm not going to say, "I love that you spelled *worms* correctly." This seems like no big deal for her. And it is not particularly helpful for me to encourage her to spell *worms* correctly for the rest of her life. But it could be helpful, it could be a powerful compliment, to make a statement like one of these:

- I'm really impressed that you can take something seemingly ordinary like worms and make it significant by writing about it.
- I'm really impressed at how much you've found to say about a worm. Lots of people would just say a line or two and then would shrug and think, "So what else can you say about a worm!" But you've really pushed yourself to think, then to think again, then to think some more.

- I'm really impressed that you looked hard at worms and tried to find true things and true words to say about them. Most people don't look at worms and think "strong," but you really cleared a space to think your own thoughts about your topic, didn't you? That is am amazing thinking quality you have shown here—finding your own associations and words for things!

I know that I'm often complimenting something that a writer tried but didn't completely do. I might also compliment something that a writer did accidentally, to help encourage the writer to do it intentionally the next time. I name the replicable process I suspect the writer went through en route to the results I see. For example,

- "I can tell you lived a writerly life, paying attention to details other writers would walk by—even to a worm! And it seems like you almost pretend to argue in defense of worms as you are writing. So you say, "People think that worms are just these slimy gross creatures, but they're not!" Then you give one reason (you can observe them) and another (you can keep them as pets). Later you come back to these arguments and say even more ("You can observe them for hours and write about them. They are interesting to watch . . . "). You even provided evidence by referring to how your friends learned by observing them."

Finally, I'd make sure to help the writer take this compliment personally. The adage goes, "Don't criticize me, criticize my actions." But when complimenting, by all means compliment me as a person! Then, too, I want to remind this writer and others who may hear the compliment that what she has done is transferable: "This is brilliant work! For the rest of your life, remember that you have a talent for finding meaning and majesty in small stuff that others would overlook, and, specifically, that you are great at rallying to someone's (or something's) defense."

Learning to compliment children in powerful, lasting ways is a skill that is worth mastering. Your colleagues, friends, and family will certainly appreciate any practicing you might care to do!

GETTING READY

- Example of writing (your own or another writer's) that needs to be revised for honesty
- Passages from class essay that can be revised for honesty, written on chart paper
- See CD-ROM for resources

REVISING TOWARD HONESTY

You'll probably find that once your children grasp *what is entailed in writing these very structured essays, it's as if the green light goes on and they are raring to go. And you may be tempted to bring this unit to an expeditious close. You may tell yourself that after all, in real life, children need to churn out thesis-driven essays within forty-five minutes.*

I want to caution you against encouraging your students to whip up quick essays and call it a day. This unit is a journey, and at every bend in the road you have extraordinary lessons to teach. The most important learning and teaching will happen as you and your students grapple with the complexities and challenges of thinking and writing logically. And the complexities are legion!

In this session, you'll alter your focus to teach a quality of good thinking. Specifically, you will emphasize that good writing and good thinking are honest. You'll highlight precise, clear, accountable, honest thinking. This is a complicated idea because it is also true that writers take poetic license (and therefore are not always exactly honest)! Writers strive to tell an honest experience that does not always match the exact events. We may combine two events that actually took place at different times or places, or we may allow a character to speak in direct quotes when we can't really recall the exact words used—but we do this in an attempt to convey a truth. And it is crucial for writers to yearn to represent truth on the page. The writer's intent to convey a meaning that is exactly true gives the resulting text a ring of reality, an authenticity and power that listeners feel.

It's important for a writer not only to strive to tell the truth, but also to be able to discern when writing isn't true. Ernest Hemingway once said, "Every writer needs a 100 percent foolproof crap detector." And William Zinsser suggested that often writers need to cross out their opening and closing paragraphs, because that's where we tend to do the most lying. As writers, we need to develop a critical eye to turn on ourselves. We need to read over our words with skepticism and doubt. "Is this exactly what I want to say?"

MINILESSON

Revising Toward Honesty

CONNECTION

Remind writers that they've been working on improving the quality of their essay writing, and then name the teaching point. In this case, tell children that writers also try to improve the quality of their thinking by aiming for honesty.

"Writers, yesterday we worked a bit on improving the quality of our writing, but today I want to remind you that when writing essays, it is even more important to improve the quality of our *thinking.* But it's not that easy to sit down, pen in hand, and *think* really well. What does it mean to *think well?*"

"To me, it means telling the truth, and that's the most important thing I do as a writer."

TEACHING

Tell a story of one time when you (or another writer) wrote first in easy glib words, then rewrote for honesty.

"Telling the truth is harder than you think. When I write, my words tend to fall into easy grooves. It's easy to write in words we've heard before, or to describe the way we assume things to be. When describing the snow, it is easy to write, 'I looked at the white snow.' It takes a mental effort to be sure I'm really saying the truth: 'I looked at the snow, speckled with ash.'"

"When I finished writing my first big book, *The Art of Teaching Writing,* I wrote my Acknowledgments. After I'd thanked all the people who helped with the book, I got to the final paragraph, to the place where writers traditionally thank their family members. I picked up my pen and wrote the words that came to mind."

> I want to thank my husband, John Skorpen, for not
> minding the long hours of desk work.

"Then I pulled back, read what I'd written about my husband not minding my work, and thought, 'This is a pile of baloney. John is *always* complaining that I work too much.'"

COACHING

In this session, I support honest and precise thinking. I'm convinced that when authors reach for the language to articulate something true, the intention to be honest brings power to a text.

This story is in The Art of Teaching Writing. *Many such books are filled with anecdotes and quotes that you can mine as you develop minilessons. The stories in your minilessons needn't all be ones that have happened to you. You can always say to children, "A writer I know told me that . . . " and retell stories you've heard or read.*

"So then I decided to try and write the truth (knowing I could always publish the sweet platitudes if I couldn't come up with anything better to say). I picked up my pen, held it near the page, and thought, 'So what *do* I want to thank John for?'"

"This time, I aimed to write the exact truth. Here's what I wrote."

> Although it is traditional to end one's Acknowledgments by thanking one's spouse for not minding the long hours of desk work, I want instead to thank my husband, John Skorpen, for calling me away from the desk. I want to thank John for the days of hiking in the Wind River Range and for the quiet adventures with our cat, dog, home, and family.

Debrief. Point out what you hope students learned from the story.

"The new version is a much better Acknowledgments because I have written with exactly true words. It takes mental energy to write the truth, and it takes courage, too. I always tell myself, 'I'll *try* to put the exact truth on the page—if I don't like what stares back at me, I can change it.'"

ACTIVE ENGAGEMENT
Set children up to practice rewriting with more honesty. Give them a few tiny excerpts that they could have written, and invite them to revise them for honesty.

"Let's practice this. You all have been writing a lot about working with reading buddies. I've put a few passages that some of you have written on chart paper. Would you pretend that you, personally, wrote these? Reread them, giving them the truth test. Ask yourself, 'Does this say the exact and precise truth of what I want to say about working with reading buddies?' If it doesn't, spend a minute working in your notebook to rewrite one passage until it is truthful. Here are the passages."

> Another reason that working with reading buddies is fun is you get to read cool books. I really love books like The Cat in the Hat and Mrs. Wishy Washy.

> Another reason that working with reading buddies is fun is that they look up to us. They think we are smart and important. They make me feel special.

Notice that I rely again and again on the very same form that we teach our students. I could have made sweeping comments all-about my experience writing the Acknowledgments section of The Art of Teaching Writing. I would then have summarized that process. Instead I retell the event in a step-by-step fashion, making characters speak, highlighting the problem and the solution. Try to do likewise with small writing moments you've experienced, and embed those narratives in your essays . . . and your teaching.

This Teaching section does not contain a demonstration, as so many do, but instead relies upon a story. Still, I set up the story and afterwards, debrief it.

As I mentioned earlier, Hemingway once suggested that to write well, we need a 100 percent foolproof crap detector. I've always loved the image of a writer rereading his or her text, moving his or her crap detector over the words like a divining rod, waiting for it to start crackling. I'm apt to tuck quotes like this into my teaching when the spirit moves me. Draw on all you know when you teach.

Convene the class. Point out that the new, more honest versions of their writing tend to be more specific and precise.

After children worked in their notebooks for a few minutes, I said, "Would you give me a thumbs up if you were able to rewrite one of these passages so that you were more honest? I'm wondering—how many of you found that you also became more specific? And how many of you ended up using more precise words, perhaps substituting a more exact term for *fun* or *cool*? I'm so interested to see that writing with honesty seems to have a lot to do with writing with specific and precise words. Would you turn and show your partner how you rewrote and rethought the writing so you could be more honest?"

LINK
Rename the teaching point. Remind children that they can draw on all they've learned as they continue to collect entries in their folders.

"So writers, I know that today you'll draw on all that you know as you collect entries for your files. You'll collect stories (using what you know about effective stories), and you'll collect lists. As you write—today and always—try to hold yourself to the goal of telling the truth."

Notice that at this juncture in a minilesson the teacher usually debriefs, but here children assume that responsibility. In this instance, I think that giving children the opportunity to reflect on what they've just done will cement their learning. You may decide to adopt this as a regular ritual in your minilessons. Just guard against minilessons becoming maxi-lessons.

Notice the cumulative quality of this section of a minilesson. I'm hoping to keep alive the fact that during any one day's workshop, writers will be drawing on all they've learned thus far.

WRITING AND CONFERRING

Reading Writing Closely

Over and over when teaching this unit, I have found that skills and strategies that sound simple when I talk about them in minilessons prove to be vastly more complicated than I'd ever dreamed possible when a child actually tries to do the work. Every minute of the writing workshop, then, is an intensely packed learning adventure. How important it is for you to draw your chair alongside children, welcoming the chance to see and to understand the difficulties the child is experiencing! Develop an attitude of welcoming signs of trouble. These indications of trouble are requests for help. They'll make you feel needed!

To spot signs of trouble, you need to scrutinize your students' work. Don't just scan a child's words. Take them in. Think, "What is this child trying to say and do?" Ask, "Is this writing basically working? What has the child done that I can name in a fashion that will transfer to other pieces? What isn't working? How can I equip the writer to handle this area of difficulty in this piece and in future pieces?" Consider Estefan's entry with these questions in mind.

My dad is important to me because I have fun when he teaches me baseball. One time my dad woke me up to tell me if I want to go play baseball. I said, "Ok, I'll get ready." When I washed up and got ready we went to the baseball field. There we got out the baseball bats and balls. At the baseball field, my dad was throwing fastballs, so I telled him to slow down. My dad said, "Alright, but you got to get used to fastballs." I said, "Ok, I will."

> **MID-WORKSHOP TEACHING POINT**   *Celebrating Writers Who Are Telling the Truth*   "Writers, can I stop you? Many of you are finding out that your writing becomes more powerful when you bear down and tell the truth. The great nonfiction writer, Milton Meltzer, says it this way: "The best writers of nonfiction put their hearts and minds into their work. In the writer who cares, there is a pressure of feeling which emerges in the rhythm of sentences, the choice of details, in the color of language." (1976, p. 21)
>
> "Listen to these places where you all are bearing down, trying to write the precise truth. This is what some of you have said."
>
> - I find that when I am sad, my dog is too. He makes me think feelings are contagious. (Jamile)
>
> - If you made your team lose, you feel responsible for your actions, but you feel like you have no power so you blame everything on yourself. (Felix)
>
> *continued on next page*

There are many things Estefan has done well:

- Estefan has adroitly shifted from stating a big idea (My dad is important to me) to telling a specific story, and he's done so using the transitional phrase "one time."

- Estefan has transferred what he knows about writing stories to this new work with essays. His story is told in a step-by-step, chronological way, and as a reader I can re-experience it. He includes dialogue and details.

- Estefan's story is generally about the idea he wants to convey. The part of the story that he has elaborated upon (his father's efforts to instruct Estefan) is the part that matches his idea.

In a conference with Estefan I'd probably choose just one or two of these points to compliment. In this case, because of what I know I will soon teach, I created a compliment by combining the second two points. "Estefan," I said, "I absolutely love the fact that you brought all you know about stories to bear on the miniature story you tell inside this essay! And, more than that, you knew to elaborate with precise details."

There are a number of qualities and strategies I could teach Estefan. Most important, I'd want him to realize that although it's great that he used all he knows about stories to write this one, we place special demands on the stories that we embed into essays. These stories need to efficiently and directly address the main idea of the essay. I'd teach Estefan that I reread the stories I write within nonfiction texts, pausing after almost every line of the story to ask, "Does this go with my main idea?"

When Estefan read his first sentence, asking, "Does this go with my main idea?" the answer was yes. It is really smart of Estefan to not just say that his dad woke him, but to say that his dad asked about baseball. I didn't point out to Estefan that he could have done even more to highlight the role baseball played in waking up. For example, he could have written, "I lay in bed and thought about how much fun it is to play baseball with my father. Even though it was early, I raced out of bed. I didn't want to miss this chance." I didn't bring out this point because I felt it wasn't something that Estefan could learn to do on his own just yet—and because I had less subtle instruction in mind. Estefan and I noted that yes, his first sentence pertained to his main idea. But as Estefan read on, pausing after each sentence to ask, "Does this further my

continued from previous page

- Imagine having a war going on inside your head. Well, that's what it's like when parents fight. (Andy)

- Teddy bears are good friends. You can tell them secrets and they stay quiet. I told my bear that I was wearing my sister's clothes. I told my bear that I was wearing my sister's makeup. I told my bear that I like 2 boys at the same time. (Camille)

"Right now, would you reread your writing and find a place where you told the truth. Search especially for a place where your writing is so truthful that it makes you realize something you didn't even know you knew. If you don't find a place where you wrote the truth in such a way that your writing comes to life, find a place where you used hackneyed, trite words and rewrite that section, this time telling the truth."

main idea?" he realized that none of the next details—that he got ready, woke up, and traveled to the field—advanced his main idea. I taught him that he had choices. He could include the fact that he washed up *if* (and only if) he could find a way to integrate his father teaching him baseball into washing up. (This might seem like a ridiculous suggestion, but of course all Estefan would need to do is to scrub his face, thinking as he did so about the upcoming game.) Alternatively, Estefan could fast-forward his story, skipping past events that didn't relate to his main idea, which is what he in fact decided to do.

My larger point is that we need to read our children's entries with care, expecting that they'll struggle with aspects of this work. Be prepared to compliment them on what works, to teach skills they need to know—and to learn volumes in the process.

SHARE

Revising Claims to Fit Stories

Tell students that writers have to guard against using stories that don't support their claims.

"Writers, I've watched you holding yourselves accountable to writing the precise truth; by trying to be precisely honest, some of you have actually had brand-new ideas come out of the tips of your pens! This is incredibly important."

"Now I want to show you another powerful way to discipline your mind as you write. Just as it is easy to be a careless thinker and to write 'snow is white' rather than telling the precise truth, it is also easy to be a careless thinker and say that story supports your claim, even though it doesn't. That means that we have to check to make sure every story in each folder supports the claim on that folder."

Tell the story of a child who checked to see if her story supported her claim and found that it didn't.

"For example, Camille has a folder with the claim on it, 'Teddy bears are like friends that stay quiet, but deep down you hear them talking to you.' Camille started to add this entry to the file, but first she asked herself, 'Does this support my claim?' See what you think." [Fig. XII-1]

> Teddy bears are like friends that stay quiet, but deep down you hear them talking to you.
>
> Teddy bears are good friends because when you are sad teddy bears cheer up. They cheer you up because one time I came from school and a boy said a nasty thing to me so I went home and I talked to my teddy bear. She made me feel good.

"Camille realized that her information didn't show anything about teddy bears 'talking' deep down. Instead, her information was all about how she—Camille—talks freely to her bear, sharing secrets."

"Things became even more complicated because Camille had another file titled 'Teddy bears are good friends because you can share your secrets with them,' and that file was bulging!"

Ideally when children write essays, they develop their ideas through the process of writing. The work described in this Share suggests one way in which children use writing an essay as an appointment to think in disciplined, logical ways, and to grow new ideas through the process.

> Teddy Bears
>
> Teddy bears are good friends. I feel this way because when you're sad teddy bears cheer you up. I also feel this way because they are like friends that stay quiet but deep down you hear them talking to you. My third feeling is that you tell your teddy bears all your secrets and you know they won't tell Know one.
> Teddy bears are good friends because when you are sad teddy bears cheer up. They cheer you up because one time I came from school and a boy said a nasty thing to me so I went home and I talk to my teddy bear; she made me feel good. Teddy bears are also good friends because when my friend fell down she was crying and everyone was laghing at her so she talk to her teddy bear and he cheared her up. Teddy bears are good friends because when I fell down my cut really hurt badly so I went to my teddy bear and she cheared me up.

Fig. XII-1 Camille realized her examples didn't support her claim

Point out through the example that writers can revise their claims to match their stories, just as they can revise their stories to match their claims.

"So Camille did something really important. She emptied all her files and then read through all her information. As she did, she asked, 'What are the big ideas here?' And, listen to this, she found the big ideas and then she renamed her files! All of us need to have Camille's courage. Reread the stuff you've collected, and have the strength to see when some of it doesn't go in the file in which you placed it. Let this lead you to revisions! You already know that writers revise stories to support claims, and now you know that writers also revise their claims to fit their stories!"

Expect that this lesson will pertain to half your writers. It's an incredibly important lesson, too, because it teaches people to read with great attentiveness. This is clearly a point that merits emphasis. You may want to give it more attention by writing a minilesson that celebrates the work specific children have done.

● HOMEWORK **Balancing Writing Volume** Writers, before long we'll turn a corner in this unit of study. Instead of continuing to collect materials in folders, we'll begin to combine these into paragraphs. Before you can do that, you need to be certain that you have three or four solid and pertinent entries in each of your folders. Think about your folders and recall which ones need the most attention.

Tonight your homework assignment is to collect two or three entries, amounting to at least a page of writing but written on separate sheets, that you can add to whichever folder is most empty.

If you feel that this will be hard, then chances are you need to rethink the claim on that folder. Consider developing a different bullet and renaming the folder; then gather information for that folder about your new topic sentence, your new claim.

● TAILORING YOUR TEACHING

If your students have experienced writing essays in previous years and they tend to write with honesty already . . . you may want to focus on any one of a host of qualities of good writing. For example, William Zinsser, author of *On Writing Well*, suggests that surprise is important in writing, and I have to agree. Jean Fritz, the author of many history books, seems to agree as well. She writes about the importance of surprising details: "As human beings, we thrive on astonishment. Whatever is unknown quickens us, delivers us from ourselves, impels us to investigate." Fritz includes surprising details in her books. For example, she writes that Paul Revere forgot to bring cloth to muffle his oars for his secret row across the Charles River. This little mostly unknown detail helps the reader feel the urgency and danger of his trip. Instead of just writing that Revere was a silversmith, she lets her readers know that he did unusual jobs, such as whittling false teeth out of hippopotamus tusks. This bit of information is colorful and engaging for readers.

Fritz says, "I dote on small details . . . In researching Ben Franklin, I read in one book after another that Franklin learned ten swimming tricks. What were they?" Her inquisitive nature couldn't let that fact go unexplored. After a long search, Fritz found that one of the ten tricks involved cutting one's toenails under water! (Sutherland, p. 179) Imagine that. What a detail to include in a piece about Ben Franklin!

You could use these examples to suggest to your students that they might consider putting information in their essays to surprise and engage their readers. You might say, "Writers, one of the qualities of powerful writing is that it surprises readers. It makes readers think of things they never thought about before. Essayists hope readers finish their essays and say things like, 'I never thought about it like that!' or 'I never knew that!' or 'Wow. That was full of surprising information.' But you know what? These surprises don't happen by accident. Essayists think about ways they can astound or surprise their readers. As you go through your folders full of supporting stories and supporting evidence for your topic sentences, look for places where you surprise. As you look through your folders, try to answer these questions: 'Of all these pieces, which one will draw my reader in? Which one is most astonishing?'"

You could demonstrate how to do this by going through one of your folders to find a piece of evidence that could surprise readers. You'll also want to model how to ask questions of yourself, like "Which of these is most astonishing?" as you look through your pieces. Finally, you'll want to explain the rationale for why you chose a particular piece as the one that offers a surprise to your readers.

For the Active Engagement, you have a few options, of course. You might decide to use the whole-class sample essay, which in our case is the one about first-grade reading buddies. You can review the supporting evidence with your students to have them consider which pieces are most surprising. Another way to do this is to have students bring one of their folders to the meeting area and have them read through the pieces inside. Give them a sticky note to attach to the piece that contains the most surprising information.

ASSESSMENT

The minilessons in this unit of study may seem fairly clear cut, but I promise you that children will encounter an unusual number of difficulties. The difficulties arise especially because this unit invites children into logical, analytical thought, and this will push them in ways that are new for them—and perhaps new for you as well. You will definitely want to spend time outside of class looking through the files your children collect, trying to assess their understandings of this teaching.

I sometimes find that when I read children's non-narrative writing, sections of it seem to reflect breakdowns in logic. My first reaction is to push their confused, chaotic writing out of sight, saying, "This makes no sense." But, as I've written throughout this series, we need instead to scrutinize the chaotic writing, asking, "What is the source of trouble here? What can I teach that might help?" Resist the urge to ignore the entry, and instead be fascinated by it. Look at it all the more closely to determine what sort of trouble it reveals. You may find several types of problems.

The child may be repeating herself, almost as if she is saying something over and over until she finds a way to say it that works. If this is the case, she is doing good work and just needs to delete many of the problematic versions of the thought, leaving only the best draft. It will help children to know that this is exactly what people do when we talk over a complex idea—and what many writers do. Pros, however, know to cut their rejected writing after they've finally gotten their idea out. Peter Elbow has said, "Sometimes the

water needs to run for a while before it runs clear," and the same can be true for thinking and writing.

Another child may have written his idea in a reasonably clear sentence or paragraph, but he seems to think it's too short and so therefore he keeps writing more at the end of his thought, with the new material fulfilling no real function at all. In other words, the text may reveal a clear thought, followed by disjointed rambling. This child may need to learn strategies for planning and then for writing the idea in more detail in the first place. This child, at the very least, needs to see the pattern in his writing and to learn to cut the parts that don't add to his original text.

Yet another child may be trying to convey relationships between ideas, and expressing her thinking requires her to combine sentences or clauses. This level of thinking can push the child toward sentence complexity that she can't yet master. Celebrate her risk taking and the approximations in thought and sentence complexity you see in her writing just as you would celebrate a youngster's brave, inventive spellings. Teach her how to take the next step from where she is now toward where she wants to be to express herself.

Your colleagues can help you read through some of your students' work. Talk about everything you notice! Do you notice common characteristics? Are these characteristics typical of students in your grade level? Talk with your colleagues about the steps to take with each child, and steps to take with your classes in general, based on the writing you've analyzed.

IN THIS SESSION, YOU WILL TEACH CHILDREN THAT WRITERS GATHER A VARIETY OF INFORMATION TO SUPPORT THEIR CLAIMS. YOU'LL DEMONSTRATE STRATEGIES WRITERS USE FOR COLLECTING AND WRITING WITH THAT INFORMATION.

GETTING READY

- Your own essay demonstrating how observation and statistics can support a topic sentence
- Class thesis and topic sentences
- Samples of student writing where a variety of types of evidence are used to support topic sentences
- See CD-ROM for resources

GATHERING A VARIETY OF INFORMATION

When teaching narrative or poetry, *many of us feel confident teaching lessons on the qualities of good writing. We demonstrate and point to exemplar texts so that our children learn to show, not tell, and to make characters talk. It is just as important to continue teaching the qualities and strategies of good writing once we're in a unit on essay writing! As Don Murray has said, "Writing may appear magic, but it is our responsibility to take our students backstage to watch the pigeons being tucked up the magician's sleeve. The process of writing can be studied and understood. We can recreate most of what a student or professional writer does to produce effective writing."*

Writers don't write with words. Writers write with information. Interestingly, children are much more accustomed to relying on concrete information when they write in narratives than when they write essays. When retelling an event, children keep their eyes on the subject and their writing involves chronicling what happened. When children write about ideas, however, there's no chronology to guide the unfolding of the writing; there's no one image in the mind's eye to trace on paper. The child begins with a topic sentence: My dog is like a brother to me. The child is then apt to just pick up a pen and start holding forth on this topic, writing in circuitous, general, repetitive sentences.

This session seeks to remedy this tendency by highlighting that writers always write with specific, concrete information. Writers need to be researchers, collecting the hard data needed to build paragraphs and advance ideas: details, quotations, statistics, and observations.

This session is especially important because it acknowledges that even when children are writing structured, thesis-driven essays, it is crucial for them to live writerly lives—collecting, combining, sifting, and selecting bits of their life to become their work.

MINILESSON

Gathering a Variety of Information

CONNECTION
Tell children that artists combine a variety of materials in their writing.

"One way to make works of art powerful is to use a variety of materials so that one offsets another—in some art the variety comes from using different colors, in some it comes from textures, in some from flavors. In essay writing, variety can come from different kinds of information. If our essays are going to be works of art, we need to make sure they have a depth, a richness, that comes from variety."

Name your teaching point. In this case, teach children that essayists, like other artists, collect varied materials to assemble in their work.

"Essayists deliberately collect different kinds of information. That variety helps build your case by suggesting to the reader that evidence to support your thesis can be found in a variety of places in the world, not just in one kind of place. You will want to make sure that your files contain not only stories and lists but also observations, statistics, quotations, citations, and questions. The secret to collecting all these things is that you need to learn to see all the world as related to your topic. When you do this, you find material everywhere."

TEACHING
Illustrate all the varieties of information writers can collect around their theses by showing how you observed, interviewed, and gathered statistics on your topic.

"For example, I've been trying to collect material to go in my folders. My folder labeled 'My father taught me to love writing' is almost empty, so I really want to collect stories, quotes, and questions related to it."

"So I went to my parents' house and I said to myself, 'I'm going to try to use observation as a way to gather a new sort of information. I'll observe and record anything I see related to the idea that my dad teaches me to love writing.' Here's what I collected. Pay attention to the different kinds of information I gathered."

COACHING

It is not necessary to introduce a new metaphor in this Connection, but it is important for the children to have a visual image of this process. I try to make sure that my words make a visual image in the mind's eye.

When evaluating an essay, I sometimes ask, "Does this writer use a variety of source material?" In fact, my son is studying for the writing he'll need to produce on the SAT exam, and the test-prep books advise him to develop his idea by drawing on a variety of sources: one bit can come from personal experience, another from literature, still another from politics. This minilesson conveys to children that their essays will be stronger if they draw on a variety of sources. But it does so by turning this quality of good writing into a strategy that yields the quality.

It is tempting to bypass the process and share the products, to cut to the chase and say, "So I collected this, and this, and this," reading aloud the products. Remember that we are trying to show children how to go about doing these kinds of writing, so sharing our products alone won't suffice.

"First, Dad was at his desk. I just took a mental photograph of that scene so I could write about it later. When I wrote, I described the things I saw related to his loving to write."

These days, whenever I arrive at my father's home I usually find him at his desk. He may be writing his memoir, an article, a speech, or architectural sketches and plans for a new sheep house or chicken coop— whatever he's writing, he's always surrounded by piles of papers and books. I get the feeling he's turned his desk into a tree fort, built with walls of books and manuscripts. He's having the time of his life writing.

"I also wanted to collect information by interviewing him, not just by observation, so I talked with him about how he thinks he has taught me to value writing, and I scrawled down his words. He said really powerful things, like, 'When I'm gone, my memoir and my articles will still be there. I'm going into the hospital for a minor operation next week, and you never know. So I'm trying to finish this writing project before I go in.' I copied down his exact words."

"I observed and interviewed, but I also wanted to see if I could collect any statistics. Dad's been duplicating his drafts, and he showed me the bill. He's done $172 of duplicating in the last two months—that statistic conveyed something, so I recorded it too."

Debrief, accentuating all the sources of information you drew upon as you gathered information on your essay topic.

"Did you notice, writers, that just during one little visit home I observed and recorded what I saw (I touched one finger to accentuate that I was making a list of resources), I interviewed to gather quotes (I touched a second finger), and third, I found a statistic that can help me make my case!"

I could have paused at this point to ask children to list across their fingers the different kinds of material I collected: images, quotes, and statistics.

Notice, once again, the use of the graphic organizer: my fingers.

ACTIVE ENGAGEMENT
Ask children to collect observations to support the whole-class essay.

"Now, essay writers, let's try collecting a variety of kinds of information about an essay topic. Let's practice this with our topic, 'Working with our first-grade reading buddies is fun.'" I gestured to the list on chart paper.

> **Working with our first-grade reading buddies is fun.**
>
> • One reason that working with reading buddies is fun is that you get to teach them to read.
>
> • Another reason that working with reading buddies is fun is that you get to read really cool books.
>
> • And, finally, working with reading buddies is fun because they look up to us.

"We met with our reading buddies just yesterday, so the material we need to gather is fresh in our minds! If we were writing an essay on this, while sitting at our desks today we could mentally go back to reading buddies time, and recreate it in our mind's eye. Then we could zoom in on a moment that captures the fun of reading buddies, and describe that moment. I'm thinking, for example, of the moment when we arrived in the first grade and the kids all started saying, 'Hurrah' and greeting us. Partner 1, can you write an entry in the air in which you do an observation of that moment? Remember, it is best to observe people in the midst of actions. And remember that you won't just retell the moment, you'll angle your retelling to show that working with reading buddies is fun." They did this.

Remind the class that they could also collect other kinds of information: questions, quotations, and statistics.

"Class, you might decide that you want to collect not only *observations* but also *questions*. Partner 2, would you tell partner 1 some questions you might write? Remember, these need to relate to our topic that reading buddies are fun."

"It is not easy to think about what statistics we could collect that relate to this thesis. But would you and your partner *see* if you could help us think of statistics we could collect to support our thesis? Partner 1, tell partner 2 some statistics you could gather."

"Now, partners, tell each other how you could gather some quotations to support our claim."

It probably would have been just as helpful for me to ask children to call one of their topic sentences to mind, and then to ask themselves, "What could I possibly observe so as to gather information to support this idea?" After they signaled with a thumbs up when they had an answer, I could move on and ask, "Who could you possibly interview so that you could collect a quote to support this idea?" Again, I'd wait for a thumbs up.

During this Active Engagement, I try to remove distracting difficulties so that the one challenge children deal with is the one that relates to today's lesson. In this instance, I first suggest that children relive a particular moment, observing it in their mind's eyes. I choose the moment and begin conjuring up the mental image. Having gotten them off to a running start, I can say, "Tell your partner what you'd record if you were going to include an observation in your data." I know they can do this in short order. If your children look at you blankly when you ask them to do something during the Active Engagement section of a minilesson, then you know you haven't provided a clear and supportive scaffold.

LINK

Rename the teaching point. Remind children they can use this strategy anytime, not just today.

"Writers, I hope that from this day on, you remember that writers, like many kinds of artists, gather information wherever they go. Carry your writer's notebooks with you at all times, and if you have a thought, an observation, a question, or some statistics that relate to your essay topic, jot them down. Right now, from your seat on the rug, look around the classroom and see if you can find something that relates to your topic—any little thing at all. If you don't notice something in the classroom that sparks a thought related to your topic, remember, you can look all the time, not just in school. You might see something on television at home that supports your claim, or you might hear something in the library— essayists are always on the lookout for information for their work!"

Watch, in this Link, how I circle back to the Connection, picking up terms and images from that section of the minilesson. Also notice that in a minilesson, I'm often teaching a concept and specifics. I think of this as a hand and fingers. I know specifics will be more memorable if they are integrated into a larger concept, so I usually situate details into the larger concept. In this instance, the larger concept is that writers, like artists, collect stuff. Specifically, writers collect observations, statistics, questions, and so on.

WRITING AND CONFERRING

Gathering Enough Material for Effective Essays

Within a day or two, you'll show children how to take the contents of their folders and begin the selecting, ordering, combining, and rewriting work of making an actual essay. Before you can round that bend in the unit, however, you want to be sure that all of your children have gathered enough material to be able to produce effective essays.

You may need to convene the children who simply do not have enough done, and help them make plans for how they will use today to be extra productive. Don't hesitate to make decisions for them based on what you see (or don't see) in their folders; send them off with a clear sense of direction and a lot of urgency! If children really buckle down, they can produce a lot of writing in a single day, but they often need us to add some pressure, raising their productivity a few notches. Sometimes it helps if these children all work alongside each other at a table reserved for the "we're racing to get a lot done" kids. Or it might help to give each of these kids a "private office"—a desk, set far away from the maddening crowd. You decide.

Some children will not have an idea how they can gather information right now, in class, about their topics. Help them realize they can interview *each other*. For example, the child who is writing, "I don't want to let my grandma down," will probably think that no one in the class knows his grandma, so how could he interview a classmate? Show him that he could interview kids to learn the things *they* do to help *their* grandmothers. The writer could then cite what a friend does, using this to set off his own information. In his essay, he could perhaps end up writing something like, "Other children in Mrs. Gammet's fourth-grade class don't *expect* to help their grandmothers. For example, Jeremy says, 'My grandma does things for me, not the other way around. She fixes my clothes and helps with my schoolwork.' But it is different for me. When I visit my grandma, I try to help her. I . . . " The child could also ask someone else to interview him about his own grandma, to help him realize what he knows and what he has to say.

> **MID-WORKSHOP TEACHING POINT** *Using Evidence from Books* "Writers, at the beginning of the workshop today Zora and I talked about the 'scraps' she has gathered for her essay. Zora showed me a piece that she had written long ago in her notebook that she thought could be filed into one of her folders. 'Lucy,' she said, 'Do you think this bit about Rob from *Tiger Rising* could support my thesis?' The example fit exactly! So Zora and I decided we should tell all of you that you can definitely use books you have read to support our ideas. Listen to how Zora did this," I said, and Zora read her entry aloud.
>
> > Sometimes bullies close themselves up and never express their feelings. They think of it as a way to protect themselves. I remember a friend who was poor and embarrassed to be poor, so he put this feeling in his suitcase and shut it just like Rob did in the book <u>The Tiger Rising</u> by Kate DiCamillo. Rob was a boy who kept his feelings inside like my friend did. I could see my friend and Rob both hurting, telling people to stay out of it.
>
> "If any of you are like Zora and can imagine how a book you know well could support your main idea, try writing an entry about this. Add it to your folders."

You may want to do some small-group or one-to-one conferring today to set children up for the thinking they'll soon be asked to do. In the next session, you will teach children to look through their folders, checking whether the material in them actually belongs in that folder. You may want to preteach this by helping children think through the concept of main idea and supporting details, (that is, of boxes and bullets.) You could give a small group of children photocopies of very clearly structured expository texts. "For each paragraph, would you underline the main idea," you could say. Tell children that if the author hasn't come right out and *said* the main idea, they can still infer the main idea, writing it in the margins. Children could then write little numbers (1, 2, 3) beside each new bit of supporting information as they study the way other writers set bits against each other in finished essays.

You could also show children that writers need to be able to look at a pile of information and sort it according to category. To do this work, writers need to keep in mind that some statements are subordinate and others are overarching. You could say to a small group of children, "Let's pretend you had these bits in your file. Would you sort these into two piles? Do all these items go into the same one file? Might one of these items be the topic sentence on the folder itself? Does everything go into one pile or another pile?" The items could be as brief and as obvious as these:

- People should take care of their silverware.

- Sharp knives help you slice through meat.

- Small spoons allow you to eat grapefruit.

- Silverware has different uses.

- Forks help you "fork in" the food.

- It helps to keep forks and knives separate.

- It's easy to let a spoon slip down the drain of the sink.

- We have a new kitchen.

Afterwards you'd want to explain why you asked children to sort through these bits of information. "The work you just did with these sentences is exactly the work that writers do as we reread and reconsider our collections. Sometimes you'll find that the stuff you've collected doesn't go in any folder, in which case you need to set it aside. Other times you'll decide the stuff you've collected doesn't go under a big idea—but that you like the stuff you've collected more than you like the overarching idea, and so you alter the idea! All of this work teaches us not only to write well but also to think well."

SHARE

Gathering a Variety of Information

Create a chart of writing examples from students who have used different types of information. Ask students to talk over the kinds of information they've included and still could include in their essays.

"Writers, I love the fact that you've been collecting a wonderful variety of information. Kayla's claim is that kids can help homeless people, and she's found two ways to include data. She's included figures on the number of homeless people in New York City and she's also written that last year her school collected pennies—worth $4,400! Her statistics say a lot."

"Becca also used statistics to build her case. Here's what she wrote."

> If you've one of the people who won't back away, you are not alone. 15 out of 26 people in Ms. Chiarella's 4th grade class said they have done something they don't want to do just to fit in.

> Nearly 60% of 4th grade kids in this class said they have done something they don't want to do just to fit in. Imagine all those people have done things they don't want to do, and they weren't even forced to do it.

"Sasha has been conducting a survey to illustrate her claim that people shouldn't brag. She asked everyone in the class whether they thought it was okay to brag. She figured everyone would concur with her, but of those she surveyed, almost half surprised her by responding that sometimes it was okay to brag. Now she's trying to figure out how to keep that statistic from derailing her argument."

"Mike is writing about why he doesn't like having a brother. Mike wanted some statistics for his essay, so he set up an experiment. He sat in his room for two and a half hours and counted how many times his brother bothered him. He found out that his brother came into his room eight times!"

"Would each of you tell your partner about the variety of data you've collected to substantiate your claims? Use our chart of possible data and for each item on it, think, 'Have I collected *this* kind of data?' If the answer is no, talk together about how you *could* find that sort of data pertaining to your idea."

The truth is that your kids will only be able to collect a variety of evidence, as in these examples, if you give them more than a day to do this work. You'll still want to teach a minilesson in which you highlight that essayists value drawing from a variety of sources, but you need to decide whether to make this a priority and, if so, you'll probably need to give children a bit more time for the research involved.

It is not necessary for an essayist to include all of this support material. However, it is helpful for children to realize that when writers want to support a topic sentence, we don't write with words alone. We write with stories, lists, statistics, and observation.

HOMEWORK *Getting Ready to Draft* Writers, we have been talking over the last few days about collecting materials for our essay. I have shown you the different kinds of data that writers can collect. Starting tomorrow, you are going to need all your materials in one place because tomorrow you'll learn how writers begin to assemble their material into essays. This means that some of you need to put on your hard hats and work overtime tonight. If you're not ready to write an essay tomorrow, then you'll need to collect more support material tonight.

Meanwhile, keep in mind that the best place to gather a variety of support information on your topic is your home. Consider interviewing a family member, doing a small observation, or finding words from a song or a book that will help you build your case. By all means use your family members to help you—writing is usually a family affair!

Once you've collected lots of good material in each folder, take some time tonight to reread mentor essays that you were given earlier in this unit, putting sticky note tags when you notice something the writer has done that you admire.

TAILORING YOUR TEACHING

If your children have worked through this unit in a previous year and you'd like to vary this minilesson . . . remember that you can add your own stories and metaphors to any session. You might vary this minilesson a bit by changing the metaphor. You could say, "Gathering information for your essay topic is much like gathering information in science class. Think about how we have used our magnifying glasses to look very closely at beetles in our tanks, counting their legs and noting the color and pattern of their shells. Many of us have also collected observations about the color and texture of the leaves in our plants, the patterns in their veins, the plants' growth, and their smells. As scientists, we've gathered and recorded the tiny details of whatever it is we're studying. We have asked questions, taken measurements, run experiments, and recorded observations. You can do all of these things as writers, too, researching the topics that will be the subjects of your essays."

If your children don't see possible ways to collect information related to their topic sentences . . . show children that researchers find valuable data everywhere. If your thesis was "Children love to read," you could find evidence by opening up a child's desk, by noticing the circulation of a book or a library card, by interviewing a child . . . Help children be inventive and resourceful as data gatherers.

MECHANICS

Every new unit of study provides special opportunities for work with punctuation. When children wrote narratives, for example, they needed to learn the punctuation required to show when characters were speaking, and to shift between speaking, thinking, and acting. Now that children are writing essays, they'll need to learn to add support information into a sentence. If Zora wants readers to know that Matthew was regarded as the toughest bully in her former school, she needs to be able to tuck this information into a sentence. She doesn't need to name participial phrases or predicate nominatives, but she will benefit from knowing that she can put more information into a sentence by using parentheses or commas:

> Matthew (the toughest bully in the school) had a soft heart.
> Matthew, the toughest bully in the school, had a soft heart.

Dashes can be used to accomplish a similar task. In this sentence from the foreword of Milton Meltzer's *The American Revolutionaries*, notice the way a dash allows him to insert facts into his sentence:

> It took a long time to people the land. In 1650 there were only 50,000 settlers—about as many as live in Pittsfield, Massachusetts, today—huddled mostly in Massachusetts and Virginia. A hundred years later the number had grown to . . . (1993, p. 2)

Becca could use a dash similarly in order to insert facts into her sentence:

> People who compromise to make yourself popular aren't alone—15 out of the 26 kids in Ms. Chiarella's class have done this—but this doesn't mean it's a wise thing to do.

Similarly, essayists often write with lists, and nothing helps a list more than a colon. Children can learn that essayists use a colon in order to make the transition from a generalization to a list of specifics. An essayist who also loves dogs might write, 'I love all kinds of dogs: flat-coated retrievers, English cockers, standard poodles.'

In all of these instances, essayists use punctuation to fill their writing with more precise, specific information.

IN THIS SESSION, YOU WILL
TEACH CHILDREN THAT WRITERS
TAKE THEIR COLLECTED FILES OF
WRITING AND TRANSFORM THEM
INTO DRAFTS BY ORGANIZING AND
PIECING THEM TOGETHER.

GETTING READY

- Your own essay, with supporting evidence collected in colored and manila folders

- Copies of a story from one of your folders that doesn't support your claim, written on chart paper

- Several student essays, with supporting evidence collected in colored and manila folders

- Questions to Ask of Writing Before We Draft chart

- See CD-ROM for resources

ORGANIZING FOR DRAFTING

When this country was young, barn raisings were a common occurrence. When I close my eyes I can imagine the people gathering. They bring all types of supplies: hammers and saws, lumber and nails, watermelon and pies. I can see the whole neighborhood gathered, hauling ropes, lifting first one of the barn walls into place, then another. Those barn raisings were spectacular events. People had worked for weeks preparing the walls, aligning the structures of each, gathering all the materials in place; as a result, within a single day the smaller pieces could come together quickly, into a whole. Presto—suddenly, where once a flat field lay, now a barn stands tall, its completed form outlined against the sky.

The time has come in this unit for an "essay raising." After weeks of collecting, researching, writing, and planning the structure of the piece, after the long sessions of making sure the supports are in place, it's time to pull together the full form of the essay! Today you will ask children to take all of their folders and all the information they've collected within each folder and make sure it does the job it was intended to do. Does each folder have the material needed to support the thesis and the topic sentence? Are all the pieces ready for the final essay? You'll offer children a small set of questions to ask of the writing in each folder, questions that can guide their thinking today and whenever they are in this phase of essay writing.

Then, in the mid-workshop teaching point and again in the next session, you'll ask children to nail together the pieces of writing into paragraphs. You'll offer them suggestions for making sensible arrangements and for organizing each little bit of information so that all the pieces fit together neatly to support the essay's claim.

MINILESSON

Organizing for Drafting

CONNECTION

Use a metaphor to infuse your students with a sense of celebration and anticipation—in short order, they'll each have written an essay.

"Once, long ago, some friends and I built a very small house—a cabin, really—on an island. I remember that it took us forever to gather the materials, to creosote the beams, to pour the cement and build the foundation, to frame out the walls, and to hammer planks onto those frames. Then one day we tied ropes to the two upper corners of a wall that we'd built flat on the ground, and dragged on the rope until that wall stood upright. Within another hour, we'd done the same with a second wall. Almost magically, the components that'd we'd labored over in isolation rose into place and suddenly, presto! We could see that we had built ourselves a house!"

Name your teaching point. In this case, teach your children that writers have a process they use to go from folders full of entries to a draft in a day.

"I'm telling you this because today I want to teach you that after writers plan and collect for our essays (as you have done), the day comes to put everything together. Once a writer has planned and collected, then presto! The pieces of the essay can rise into place. It won't be finished—writers revise essays just like we revise any other kind of writing. But in the space of a single day, you can go from a bunch of entries in some folders to a rough draft of an essay. Today I will teach you how to do that."

TEACHING

Extend the metaphor to help explain to children how drafting happens.

"If we want to build a building—or an essay—and the day to raise it is upon us, we need to make sure we actually have the materials we need to proceed. Now is the last

COACHING

It's important to recognize that any phase of this entire process can be as complex or as simple as you decide it should be. You'll see that I approach the prospect of drafting the essay in a breezy, no-nonsense fashion, conveying the impression that a writer will find it no big deal to combine his or her entries into paragraphs, paragraphs into an essay. As a writer, I also know this work can be infinitely complex. But for a child's first journey through this process, I think we need to simplify and condense the steps so that the writer can get into the swing of this kind of writing. During a second, third, or fourth cycle of essay writing, a teacher can help writers realize that nothing is as simple as it may seem.

I try to use stories from my life to teach. It gives my students a chance to get to know me better and it allows me to use a story to teach an idea.

I want to make today feel like a celebration, while at the same time pushing kids' stamina. There is still more work to be done. Like our cabin, their essays will have all the necessary parts, but now they will need the trim, paint, and final details.

If you are a discerning critic of minilessons, you may notice that my teaching point was vaguer than usual. I essentially said, "Today I'll teach you how to go from folders to a draft," and yet until the Teaching component of this minilesson I didn't zoom in and name the specific strategy I'd teach. In this minilesson, I think I'm covering so much ground that this works fairly well, but I'm aware that the teaching point was undefined and as a result the teaching doesn't exactly align with it.

chance to alter those plans before it's begun! We don't want to be stuck with a half-finished house—a half-finished essay! Before I write a lead saying there are three reasons why my father has been one of my most important teachers, I look over the material I've collected to make sure I have enough evidence to support all three of those reasons."

"Usually what I do is I take one folder at a time—one pile of materials—and I lay whatever I've collected out on the table and then I look over my materials. I ask a couple of questions." I pointed to chart paper on which I'd written these questions:

> ## Questions to Ask of Writing Before We Draft
>
> - Does each bit of material develop the idea?
> - Is each bit based on different information?
> - Does the material, in total, provide the right amount and right kind of support?

"After I ask each of these questions of the writing in each folder, then I decide whether these are, in fact, the topic sentences I will use, or whether I need to revise the topic sentences to match my material."

"So let me start with this folder, this idea: 'My father taught me what it means to regard a job as a hobby.' Remember that I collected a story about him taking the waffle iron into the hospital on Christmas mornings? Watch how I reread that story, asking, 'Does this really go with the idea that my dad (it will need to include that *subject*) showed me what it means to think of one's job as a hobby (it will need to show that *point*)?'" Muttering to myself, I said, "I'll reread the story I collected in this folder, and when I find sections that go with my point I'll underline them." Then I read this:

> I remember on Christmas mornings after the presents had been opened, my dad always went into the kitchen and began doing the <u>one bit of cooking that he did all year.</u> He stirred Bisquick and eggs in a huge bowl and set off for the hospital, <u>leaving us to finish Christmas celebrations without him.</u> For Dad, Christmas mornings were <u>not just a time to be with family, they were also a</u>

As I teach this I want to convey that the construction of the essay does follow a set plan. The frame needs to be just right before the materials can be added in. Double-checking now that the topic sentences match the supporting evidence prevents instability in the final essay. Fixing the structure now is much, much easier than trying to revise a nearly complete draft.

When I teach students to ask themselves a series of questions, I usually make sure that I have written the questions where students can refer to and remember them after the lesson. Whenever you are preparing a set of questions you hope students remember, try to make them short and sweet. Otherwise, there's little chance they can stick in anyone's mind easily.

time to serve hot waffles to the medical residents and patients. When I asked him once why he didn't send someone else with the waffles, he told me he loved being at the hospital on Christmas mornings. "It's my hobby," he said.

"So I think the answer is yes, this does support the idea that my father showed me what it is like to have one's job feel like a hobby. And I think the story is pretty persuasive. Let me continue looking through the folder."

ACTIVE ENGAGEMENT
Ask children to practice this work on another example from your folder.

"I also have another Christmas day story in my folder, and I've made copies for you! It's the one from earlier in the year and it tells that my father got a cut on his head and used a bag of frozen peas as an ice pack. Would you and your partner reread this story and ask those same three questions?" I gestured toward the list of questions on the chart and pulled in to listen as children reread and rethought this entry:

> On Christmas Day, my dad went to move a log in the fireplace and gouged his head on one of the nails from which the Christmas stockings hung. To stop the ferocious bleeding, he held a bag of frozen peas on the top of his bald head. Guests arrived for our Christmas party and he greeted them with the bag of frozen peas draped over his forehead. The guests weren't surprised to see Dad's odd ice pack because he's always done what he pleases without much concern for fitting into social norms. It isn't important to him to dress "right." He wears his red plaid hunting cap everywhere. When I was a teenager and he wore that hunting cap to my school events, I was often embarrassed by him.

After children talked among themselves, I called on Sophie, who said, "It is a good story but I don't think it really goes in this folder 'cause it doesn't show anything about his job, it only shows about his *ways*."

Notice that during my demonstration I was thinking aloud and going through a process in front of my students. Especially when I am teaching something that has multiple steps, I want to make sure that I convey the different parts by slowing down my teaching. One technique I often use is to pause after each step.

Questions to Ask of Writing Before We Draft

- Does each bit of material develop the idea?
- Is each bit based on different information?
- Does the material, in total, provide the right amount and right kind of support?

Of course, I deliberately show children how to do this by using a text that does not support my claim!

Another time, I could certainly teach a minilesson to show children how the same bit of information could be angled differently to fit into different folders (and thus to advance different ideas).

"Oh dear," I said. "You mean I can't use this? Could it go in another one of my folders?" I reread the topic sentences:

> My father has been my most important teacher.
>
> • My father taught me what it means to regard a job as a hobby.
> • My father taught me to love writing.
> • My father taught me to believe that one person can make a difference.

"Writers," I said. "This is probably going to happen to you. You'll find that you have a great entry that doesn't really fit with the essay you'd planned to write. And if that happens, you have three choices. You could tweak the story so that it does align with one of your topic sentences. You could save the story for another time—another essay or another narrative. Or you could do what I want to do right now, and that is to rewrite your topic sentence. What about if I added a new folder so now my essay shows four ways, not three, in which my father was my most important teacher? I am thinking that I could add a folder that says, 'My dad taught me that it is okay to be myself and not worry about fitting in.' I've got other information that could go in that folder too, and I'm willing to work hard to fill the folder!"

LINK
Restate the teaching point. In this case, remind children to check and organize their materials before they draft.

"So writers, like I just demonstrated, you need to go through your files. You will find that some of the material in a file doesn't really belong in that file, and so you'll either need to tweak the story so it fits, save it for another time, or do as I've done and revise your bulleted sentence to better match the information you've composed and collected. Once you have checked your material, you'll need to organize it—line it up on the floor or make a stack on your table spot with each bit of writing resting in the order you'll put it in your essay. That's what writers do—they organize their writing into a rough draft!"

Notice how I set my students up by giving them an example that didn't fit. Sometimes highlighting what doesn't work makes the teaching point more vivid. Now we will collaborate on a solution.

This is complex work. If you feel your kids would do better with a condensed version, where you simply take away the story that doesn't fit, saving it for another day, then by all means do so!

I want children to see that although essayists do develop a plan for what we'll say and we search for material that can support the ideas we plan to advance, we also know that the material we collect will often lead us to revise our original plan.

You'll have to modify this Link to describe to children the physical places they can use in the classroom to organize their writing. Can they use the hallway? The top of a bookshelf? The library? Some children will find it much easier to envision their draft if the writing is visible in a row rather than lying hidden in a stack.

WRITING AND CONFERRING

Checking Material

Lots of children will need a similar kind of help today, so you'll probably want to go from table to table, convening all the children at that table to watch as you work with one child, using her as a case-in-point. For example, I drew a chair alongside Brianna, asking others at her table to pause and watch and learn.

"Okay, Brianna, what have you done so far? Have you chosen one folder, laid it out, and asked the questions?" I asked, pointing to the list. "Or were you just about to do that?"

"I was gonna," Brianna said.

Questions to Ask of Writing Before We Draft

- Does each bit of material develop the idea?
- Is each bit based on different information?
- Does the material, in total, provide the right amount and right kind of support?

"Will you get started while all of us are here to help?" I said, my eyes circling the cluster of children at the table. "Pick any entry pertaining to your folder, 'I love amusement parks because I love games.' Then ask [I gestured again toward the questions], 'Does this bit of material develop the idea?'" Gesturing to Brianna's entries, I said, "Read aloud so we can hear, okay?" Brianna read this tight list:

> When I play "get to the top," I get very competitive. I might try to hit the water gun out of your hand. When I play "hit the target," I get nervous, my palms get sweaty. When I play bumper cars, I get mean. I will bump you into a corner and keep you there.

MID-WORKSHOP TEACHING POINT *Organizing Writing for Body Paragraphs* "Writers, can I have your eyes and your attention?" I said. "Takuma just came to me with a concern, and I bet it will be a concern for many of you. He's worried that the folder he's been working on is so full of great stuff that he can't imagine how he'll be able to hammer and nail all the contents of the folder together into a single paragraph. Would you give me a thumbs up if any of you have worried about the same thing?" Many children indicated they had.

"Your worry is a wise one, and what I want to tell you is that in your final essay, a file of material will probably be turned into more than a single paragraph.

continued on next page

When she finished reading, Brianna looked up at me as if to ask, "What next?" I turned to the observing group and said, "What is the question Brianna needs to ask of this entry?" The group decided that Brianna needed to ask whether this entry goes with her claim that she loves amusement parks because of the games.

Brianna said, "Yes? 'Cause it's about the games?"

I looked at the listening children, as if asking whether they concurred, and mulled over Brianna's topic sentence and her list, thinking aloud about whether I concurred. She claimed she loves amusement parks because of the games, and had certainly listed the games—but had she made her point? "Remember, Brianna, you'll answer yes if your entry is about the same subject (the games at the amusement park) *and* if it makes the same point (that the games are great, and they are the reason you love the amusement park)." Turning to all the children, I said, "Ask yourselves, does Brianna's entry talk about the *subject* of her claim? Does it match the *point* she wants to make?"

Once everyone had agreed that no, this entry didn't show that Brianna loves the amusement park because of the games, we helped Brianna decide whether to revise her entry to support her claim or to move on to examine another bit of data. She did the latter.

> *continued from previous page*
>
> Your entire essay will have two or three major 'body paragraphs,' they're called, but really they make up a 'body section.' Readers will be able to see when a new important section begins because they'll see the stem of your thesis reoccur. But within that section there will probably be several paragraphs."
>
> "So, Takuma, yes, as you select material to include in your essay, you can include a story that may be a page long, then a list that may be half a page. For now, just seat these beside each other."

SHARE

Teaching Our Topics

Remind students that talking through essay drafts can help writers organize their thoughts. Ask them to tell the first folder contents—the first paragraphs—of their essay to a small group.

"Writers, you'll remember that earlier this year, before we wrote our stories, we told versions of them to ourselves, to each other, to anyone who'd listen. And earlier in this unit we taught each other about our topics. But that was before we'd lived with our topics, collecting lots of information and ideas. Now that we've moved from collecting to drafting, and each of you has not only gathered a lot of material but also thought through how you might order that material, it's time to again teach each other about our topics. And we're just going to teach each other one claim—the one folder that you've worked on. Take a few minutes right now to reread your material, wrap your brain around it, and get ready to act as a professor lecturing to a whole group of people on your topic."

After a few minutes, I stationed five children in different areas of the classroom, and set each child up to sit before a small audience. In each circle, one child—the professor—sat on a chair, with other children grouped around. Then I asked the one child to teach a small class on his or her topic. When that child was done, the child selected someone to follow.

Debrief. Highlight what you hope students heard and did in their small groups.

"Writers," I said, "I just attended some lectures that were much more interesting than those I attend at the university! You are speaking with voices of authority, with clarity, and with precise, specific information—and that makes for some fabulous instruction. LaKeya's lecture went like this:" [Fig. XIV-1]

> Being a girl is hard because we go through a lot of changes, and have mixed/sensative feelings. I can be happy but in a moment I can be mad. I can not care how I look and then in a moment I can look in the mirror every minute. I can feel thin and then all of a sudden my rear end is getting bigger. I can smell good one moment and the next moment my armpits stink.

Notice that again I am asking students to rehearse their writing orally. Once they practice speaking about a section in their essay, they can go back to their written work to see if they need to make any revisions.

If children aren't stepping into professional roles, listen for a minute and then say, "Can I interrupt?" and for a minute press the rewind button on the course of study. Give the same lecture, only use your best professional tone, complete with the transition words that are part of this discourse. Then debrief, asking the child you displaced to try a new version of the lecture. The whole point of this is to help children step into the role, the voice, of being a teacher.

> Being a girl is hard because we go through a lot of changes, and have mixed/sensat ive feelings. I can be happy but in a moment I can be mad. I can not care how I look and then in a moment I can look in the mirror every minute. I can feel thin and then all of a sudden my rear end is getting bigger. I can smell good one moment and the next mom ent my armpits stink.

Fig. XIV-1 LaKeya's notebook entry

"As you taught others about your subjects, I have a hunch that some parts of your teaching felt especially vital, especially alive. Remember those sections when you go to draft your essays, because you'll add to these when you write your final draft. On the other hand, some parts of your lecture may have felt hollow or wooden or irrelevant. When you go to write your final draft, you'll want to trust your own intuitions! If some sections of your 'class' didn't work, when you go to write them you'll want to teach them differently. But above all, remember the teaching voice you used today, because when you write an essay you are teaching a course!"

HOMEWORK *Telling Essays*   Earlier this year, I told you that fiction writer Robert Munsch says he tells a story a hundred times before he ever writes a draft. Today I want to teach you that essayists seize every opportunity they can to teach people about their subjects. So tonight, find two different people and teach each one of them, just as some of you just taught your classmates today. Become accustomed to talking about your information as if you were teaching a class, because writing essays has a lot in common with teaching. Then tomorrow we'll all draft our essays. Come to school tomorrow ready to write with authority, clarity, and precise information!

TAILORING YOUR TEACHING

If your students seem overwhelmed with the task of organizing the writing in their folders into a rough draft . . . you'll want to offer a couple of solutions, depending on the origins of the problem. For some students, the volume of material they've collected could be at the root of the problem. Perhaps these students have gone through their folders a few times already to make sure the entries match the idea of the topic sentence, but they are still left with lots of relevant material. You'll want to support these students as they cull through the entries yet again, this time selecting a few that "best" support the topic sentence. You'll want to teach them to pick what they consider the very best evidence they have that supports their claim. You can also suggest that sometimes our favorite entry may not be the best evidence, so we need to reexamine our entries with essayists' eyes and minds.

Another reason your students might be overwhelmed is that they are imagining using every bit of every piece of writing they have collected. If this is the case for some of your students, remind them that as they draft they'll include only that part of their writing that is directly helpful to them in supporting their claim. The rest will be left out. For example, they may not need to include details about the setting in an anecdote they are using to support their claim. They can cross those details right out.

If your children are working through this unit for a second year and they are writing essays intended to persuade . . . then you may want to teach the particulars of persuasion. "I love my mother" is not a thesis that can be disputed, whereas the thesis "Homelessness affects all of us" is intended to persuade. One strategy you can teach children is that when writing to influence others, writers acknowledge the dissenting opinion in order to argue against it more effectively. Instead of pretending that our view is the only view, we acknowledge the other side and then make sure that our essay gives convincing reasons to support our side, or refute theirs. For more ideas on strategies writers use to persuade their readers, you could read Heather Lattimer's *Thinking Through Genre: Units of Study in Reading and Writing Workshops 4–12*.

ASSESSMENT

One beautiful spring day a few years ago, I brought my sons to visit Harvard Square in Cambridge, Massachusetts. The day glistened in sunshine, and so I bought a Frisbee and we played catch in the quad outside Harvard's library. Then I got the bright idea to rent roller skates and skate along the Charles River. I think I imagined that my sons and I would weave our way among the walkers, skating in those long, effortless gliding strokes that I'd seen others make. From the moment I strapped on the skates, it was clear to me I was in for trouble. I stood, and whomp! I was sprawled on my backside. I gingerly got to my feet and my skates took off, with me riding shakily above them. We—the skates and I—rattled down the sidewalk. (I'd completely forgotten my sons, who were engrossed in their own life-and-death travails.) A cross street approached: how to stop? I careened into the people who were waiting on the curb, knocking a few of them down. Soon I was mopping blood off my knees and elbows, reexperiencing road burns I hadn't felt since my childhood.

Whenever any of us try something new, we mess up. Until we get the hang of the new enterprise, we flail about. This is absolutely true for roller-skating, but it is also true for essay writing.

When children begin to draft essays, their drafts will be full of mechanical problems. As teachers, it's easy to feel overwhelmed by all the errors we see in our children's drafts. It's important to understand that once they get the hang of this new enterprise, many of those errors will go away.

Jumping on every error will not instill confidence; however, there are a few mechanical errors you're sure to spot that do deserve speedy intervention. As I've mentioned before, you may find many drafts are mired in pronouns with unclear antecedents—as in this example from Becca.

> My sister is spoiled by my mother because she is going
> through the process of being adopted. She was close
> to her old foster mother and she was very nice.

When we read a passage and come to a pronoun (in this example, *she*), we need to be able to substitute the name of the person or thing referenced. In this passage, it is not clear just who is going through the process of being

adopted—the sister or the mother. That is, in the first sentence there is no clear antecedent for the pronoun *she*.

I recommend teaching writers to control pronouns by asking either the whole class or the children who need help with this to work together on some shared reading of a published text. I'd ask them to insert parenthetical antecedents for each of the pronouns. For example, the class could read aloud *Gorilla* by Anthony Browne, and the lead of the book would sound like this:

> Hannah loved gorillas. She (Hannah) read books about gorillas, she (Hannah) watched gorillas on television, and she (Hannah) drew pictures of gorillas. But she (Hannah) had never seen a real one (gorilla).
>
> Her (Hannah's) father didn't have time to take her (Hannah) to see one at the zoo. He (Hannah's father) didn't have time for anything.

Then children could try to read each other's drafts in a similar fashion. If one reader found that a pronoun reference wasn't clear, the writer could either substitute a name for the pronoun or add a more specific reference.

Language will be less redundant if the writer introduces a person using more than one identifying term. For example, Becca revised her draft like this:

> My sister, Star, is spoiled by my mother because Star
> is going through the process of being adopted. My
> sister was close to her old foster mother, Mrs. Luke,
> and Mrs. Luke was very nice.

But despite your work with pronouns, you'll probably see that children's essays are either repetitive or they sprawl all over the place. If you have a chance to show children how to eliminate redundancy in an essay, by all means point this out. But you probably won't get to all children, and it really is totally okay that their final essays are not what you would have written. After all, these children are eight, nine, ten years old! They're all roller-skating for the very first time! Let them career about a bit, and hope the experience is more rewarding for them than my Harvard Square experience was for me!

GETTING READY

- One folder from your own sample essay, with entries organized into categories (extended list, tight list, quotes, and story) and written on chart paper
- List of transitional words, written on chart paper
- Second example from your essay, illustrating transition words and another way to organize the material
- See CD-ROM for resources

BUILDING A COHESIVE DRAFT

You've taught children that essay writers combine different materials to lend more power to their claims and more artistry to their writing. In one essay, then, a writer may piece together an anecdote, a list, a statistic, an observation, a generalization—and a variety of other forms of writing as well! It's no surprise, then, that one of the challenges a writer faces when building a draft is the need to arrange these diverse materials into a single, cohesive whole. Ideas do not in themselves take a form in space or time; they do not lay themselves flat or set themselves up in three dimensions. The forms they take in words and on paper are completely up to the writer. Of course, many, many writers and essayists have taken up this challenge, and we can learn from the ways of communicating ideas that they have created.

In this session you'll teach children a couple of ways essay writers often organize their ideas and create unity in their assemblage of pieces of writing. To get started, you'll also teach them to use special transition words that indicate certain types of relationships between ideas. Also, you will explain that essayists often repeat crucial words from their thesis in each supporting paragraph so the reader hears the message again and again and knows those words are the key to understanding the essay. These repeated words become a unifying refrain that creates cohesion in the writing. All three of these suggestions, combined, should help students get off to a strong start, turning the collections of writing in their folders into whole, unified, cohesive drafts.

MINILESSON

Building a Cohesive Draft

CONNECTION

Restate the building metaphor to help students imagine their essays as materials arranged in a structure. Tell students that today they'll learn to assemble these materials together.

"Writers, earlier I told you that to write an essay, essayists collect folders full of diverse material. Your folders are bulging with stories, lists, quotations, statistics, observations, and citations. Yesterday you began to sort through these materials, just as a builder might double-check her materials, thinking, "Is it all here? How will it look in the end?'"

"Today I want to remind you that once a builder has selected the materials she plans to use, she still needs to assemble them. Similarly, once you've selected the anecdotes, lists, statistics, or observations you'll use in a paragraph, you, too, will need to put these together."

Name the teaching point. Specifically, tell children that they'll put their materials together by selecting a system for arranging the data, by using transitional words, and by repeating key words.

"Today I'm going to teach you that writers put materials together by using a couple of techniques. First we arrange the writing pieces in an order that we choose for a reason. And second we use transitional words and key words from our thesis or our topic sentence like cement between bricks, holding one bit of material onto the next."

TEACHING

Demonstrate that you choose a logical way to sequence materials within a single category.

"You'll recall that I've collected lots of materials to support the broad thesis, 'My father has been my most important teacher,'" I said, gesturing to my outer folder. Turning to one of the inner folders, I said, "Let's look at this particular folder," and I read the sentence on the outside of the folder: "My father taught me that one person can make a difference."

Spreading out the folder's contents, I muttered, "I already took out the material that didn't make my case." I picked up two separate pieces of paper and, in a parenthetical comment, said to the children around me, "Watch closely, because this is intellectually demanding work. I actually copied these bits onto chart paper so you can watch more closely."

COACHING

You actually didn't spend much time teaching children the principles they can draw upon as they sequence their materials. You could, another time or in small groups, show children that some people organize topically, some chronologically, and others strategically, placing their strongest material at the beginning and at the end.

This information can be said quickly, but it is complicated, provocative, and important. Whenever my teaching point is especially important, I try to speak clearly and slowly to show that the words are carrying a heavy cargo of meaning. I find that if I consciously think about the significance of my words as I speak, my tone helps children to listen carefully.

Notice the way that the concrete visual materials help to accentuate the structure of my essay. The thesis is written on a colored file, and the topic sentences are written on manila files that are contained within the thesis file. Incorporating the color-coded files into my demonstration teaching serves as a way to subtly remind children of the text structures that I'm assuming they recall.

Then turning back to the work, I muttered to myself, "I have these bits, among others, in the folder. As I read through them, I'm going to think, 'What order makes sense to put these in?'" I read aloud, as if to myself, a few pieces of material from the folder that would become the paragraph supporting this sentence: "My father taught me that one person can make a difference." Children, meanwhile, followed along on a chart-sized version of the material.

My father taught me that one person can make a difference.

A List
When patients wanted to squeeze into my father's full schedule, he always said yes. When organizations wrote to my father for support, he always said yes. And although he and my mother have nine children of their own, when a local couple died in a car accident and someone needed to take in the their children, he said yes.

Quotes
My father often quoted Rockefeller to me: "To whom much is given, much shall be asked."

Extended List
My father got arrested for participation in a political protest. He volunteered at our church, at the local soup kitchen.

Story
My father once told me a story that made a big impression on me—it was of how he decided to be a doctor. As a teenager, he went to Camp Merryweather. One day, after lunch, the wife of the camp director read aloud from <u>The Microbe Hunters</u>, sharing stories of Marie Curie's and Louis Pasteur's research. Lying in his cot with a green army blanket over him, my father thought to himself, "That research is their job!" His father was a banker and it had never, until that moment, occurred to him that a person's job could be their hobby, their passion. The fact that my father told me his story and shared his insight has changed my life.

The use of "parenthetical" comments, or asides, in the midst of a demonstration is important. This is how I keep two tracks going. On the one side, I am being a writer, working publicly. On the other side, I am being a teacher, explicitly explaining to children what the writer under scrutiny (also me) is doing. I encourage teachers to use parenthetical comments when working with small groups, too, because these comments allow us to explicitly name the transferable processes one child is learning that every child can use.

Demonstrate to show that you reread one bit of data, trying to figure out what exactly it is about so you can decide where it belongs.

"Hmm . . . I'm thinking that this one is about my father getting arrested when he was trying to make a difference, and this one is about him volunteering to make a difference. They aren't really about the same thing! I could make one pile for 'getting in trouble' and one for 'helping,'" I said, starting to make two piles. Pulling back and looking over the nascent organization system represented by those two piles, I muttered to myself, "But I am thinking that I won't have much in the 'getting in trouble' file." Turning to the children, I said, "Once I've decided that the pieces of information support my claim, my job is to find out what kind of order makes the most sense to say it in."

Picking up the two bits I questioned, I muttered, "Maybe I could arrange these according to the order in which they happened—chronologically!" Getting excited, I added, "I think this would work! I could start with the story of my dad telling me how he chose to be a doctor, because he told me that story when I was just a little girl. Then I could tell the parts about other children living with us because that happened when I was in grade school. Then I could tell about all the times he quoted Rockefeller because that happened even when I was older and he wanted to steer my direction. I think this will work well! This organization shows that throughout my whole life my dad has taught me how one person can make a difference."

ACTIVE ENGAGEMENT
Debrief. In this case, name again the steps you took in choosing how to line up the writing material from one of your folders.

"Now you've seen how I thought about how to order the information in one of my folders. I laid it all out, reread it, and thought about how the bits related to each other, and about the impression I want to give my reader. In the end, I decided the order for the material in that folder will be chronological. I'll have to decide on an order for each of my other folders as well, won't I? They might all be chronological, or I might figure out another way to do it. Essayists sometimes decide to put the strongest evidence for the claim first, to hook the reader in, and then last, to leave a strong memory. Essayists might decide to make categories with their information—maybe the first few bits of material are related to writing and the second few bits are related to reading, for example."

My actions support the words I say here. The truth is that in every minilesson we need to use gestures and materials to accentuate our content. I am being more explicit about the use of gestures in this particular case because I know the minilesson's content is complex. I would not have dreamt of making minilessons this dense earlier in the year or in the unit, and as I talk now, I am aware that some children will need to hear this again in small groups or in another minilesson tomorrow.

I know that some people read children's "five-paragraph essays" (as some people disdainfully say) and claim that the writing is mind-deadening. I agree that the products that result from all this work are always not the most spectacular pieces of writing in the world—but I invite any critic to come backstage and watch children as they begin to grasp the complexities of composing these essays. Then I'd like those critics to tell me if they still believe this work is mind-deadening. When I am in the company of teachers and children who are struggling in their first forays through expository writing, I am watching minds challenged and growing!

Many of your students will no doubt choose chronological order for the information in their own folders, since that was your example. Finding a chronological order isn't easy in every set of materials, however—these materials are ideas, not necessarily events that happen in a fixed time. One way to make sure that every set of materials has a chronological order is to think of when the writer experienced each bit of information. In that frame of mind, there is an order to the information, set in time. It would be marked by phrases such as I used to think; Then I learned; The next day a friend told me; Thinking about all this, I finally figured out . . . . This frame can be a helpful one to teach students, as it will always be possible (though it may not always be the best choice).

Ask students to talk with their partners about what order they will use for the information in one of their folders.

"Now take one of your own folders and talk to your partner about the material you have and the order you might choose to present it in. Partner 1 go first, and I'll let you know when it's your turn, partner 2."

LINK
Remind students that every time they want to build a draft of an essay, they need to figure out a structure, an order, for the materials they've collected.

"Wow, guys, I've heard some wonderful ideas for ordering the information in your folders sensibly! Ho said he'll put the funny parts together in one paragraph that supports his claim, and the serious parts together in a second paragraph that supports his claim. He said he'll start the second paragraph with a sentence that goes 'In some ways, the reasons are funny, but in other ways, it is no laughing matter.' Isn't that a great idea? A lot of you had strong logical reasons for putting your materials in a certain order. Congratulations! That's a step every essay writer needs to take every time he or she writes an essay."

"Remember not to waste time copying a part into your draft that is just the same as what is in your folder—simply staple it to the page where you want it to go! You will probably also need scissors and tape so that you can piece your draft together efficiently."

Time is short, so I'm suggesting children use every moment to accomplish the job. You may decide that this Active Engagement is too messy to take place on the meeting area, in which case you could bypass it altogether.

WRITING AND CONFERRING

Recognizing Sources of Supporting Material

When you confer with children, you will certainly find that some of them have a couple of folders that are almost empty. It's tremendously gratifying to them if you help them see that they have more material than they may have realized. Suggest they read through their notebooks, looking for any entry that in any way fits with one of their topic sentences, including entries they wrote earlier in this unit. For example, at the beginning of the unit, when you taught children to consider possible stories that could support a bullet point, many children made lists that could, in fact, be pieced into their essays. You can help children see that their lists could probably be spiffed up and become part of a paragraph.

This was my earlier list:

> My father taught me what it means to regard a job as a hobby.
>
> My father confided that he couldn't wait to get back to his job after summer vacation.
>
> My father made waffles for doctors and patients at work on Christmas morning.
>
> My father realized Louis Pasteur's job was his hobby.

My list could become an entry like this:

> My dad taught me what it means to see a job as a hobby. For example, on the last day of summer vacation, my dad and I sailed together and he confided that he couldn't wait for vacation to be over so he could get back to his job. Another example occurred on most Christmas mornings. My father went to the hospital carrying a waffle iron, ready to make waffles for the doctors and patients. I asked why he didn't send someone else and he admitted that he liked going to work. "It's my hobby," he said. Once Dad told me that when he was a kid, the wife of the camp director read a book aloud about Louis Pasteur. Dad said to me, "Listening to that read aloud, I thought, 'That research is his job.'" He explained that at the time, this was a whole new idea to him!

With this as an example, some children should be able take some of the barely developed entries in their notebooks and make them into useful material for their sparsely populated folders.

M I D - W O R K S H O P   *Lining Up Materials According to Importance* "Writers,
TEACHING POINT   I want to tell you another way that essayists sometimes organize their materials. Sometimes, we look at all the material and rank it according to importance, least important bit first and most important bit last. To do that, we use transition words to introduce each part, like *first, building on that point, more important,* and *most important.*"

"Can you see how that would help you line up your material into a big finale? You can try that organizational structure and those words for one of your folders if you think it could fit well with what you have to say and would help support your claim. Listen to how Takuma has used a few words to tie sections of his essay together": *[Figs XV-1 and XV-2]*

> Not only do my grandparents play games with me but when I'm with them I feel safe and comfortable.
> I feel safe and comfortable with them when I'm lost.
> I feel safe and comfortable with them when I'm sick.
> I feel safe and comfortable with them when I woke up at the middle of the night.
> An example of when I felt safe is when I was going to a haunted house with my grandma and grandpa. I felt scared and didn't want to go.
> My grandma and grandpa said, "Just try once." So I tried to be not scared. I went in the haunted house squeezing my grandma's and grandpa's hand.
> "Don't let go of my hand I said in a worried voice.
> "I won't," my grandparents said.
> "ok" I said. "I belive you." I squeezed even harder on my grandma and grandpa's hand.

Fig. XV-1 Takuma's essay

> "I'm scared," I said. I stuck right behind my grandma and closed my eyes. And through the hounted house I felt safe.
> It feels so good to have someone to comfort you and also make you feel safe. And this makes my grandparents precious to me.

Fig. XV-2 Takuma, page 2

SHARE

Selecting Words to Make the Organization Strong

Share with your students that once they've chosen an order for their material, writers cement it together using transition words that match the organizational plan. Tell them that writers repeat parts of their thesis and supporting sentences to help readers understand the most important parts of the essay.

"Writers, you've done a great job deciding on your organizational structures. How many of you think that you'll organize the content of this first folder into logical categories—thumbs up? How many of you think you'll organize your material in a line that has some order, perhaps chronological order—thumbs up?"

"The next thing I want to teach you is this. When you actually recopy and combine your material, we need to cement it together. One way we do this is by repeating the key words from our topic sentence or our thesis sentence often. So I will be repeating 'one person can make a difference' and, from the larger thesis, 'my most important teacher.'"

"The other way to link material together is by using the cement we call *transition words*. Transition words tell you how one thing you say relates to the other things you say in your essay. We choose transition words that go with our organizational plan. If I'm going to organize my bits by time, then I'll want to use transition words that show first one thing happened, then the next, then later something else, and so on. If I'm ordering my bits by degree of importance, I use different transitions."

Share some examples of transition words by themselves and then in the context of an essay.

"Here are some examples of transition words you could use if you choose a chronological order for your information." I read aloud the list I had prepared on chart paper.

- When I [he, she, it] was young
- This began when
- At first
- After awhile
- Later or Still later
- Finally
- Recently
- Now

The children will be working with a great deal of material. Encourage them to literally staple or tape bits that they have collected so they adjoin each other, adding sticky notes or inserted sheets of paper with transition words and phrases. Then you'll need to decide whether you want their final drafts to be more correct than the children can make them when working with independence, in which case you'll need to edit these drafts. Finally, your children will make one final copy. Don't expect them to be able to write a sequence of drafts— each essay will be several pages long.

This is a trimmed-down, simple list. When children progress through this unit a second or third time, you can certainly add to the list or show them other lists. Children can help you do this by studying mentor texts and compiling other ways of using transitional words. Help them to notice that usually writers choose sets of transition words. For example, your children may notice that writers find ways to compare one example to another, using words such as similarly, along the same lines, in a similar way, *or* likewise. *Writers also use transitional words to highlight significance. They may use terms such as* notice that, it is important to note that, significantly, *or* most importantly.

"Remember I decided to organize my material about my dad chronologically. This means I can use those words to cement my material together. But here is another way I could, on the other hand, decide to organize the same material differently. For example, I could organize my information from this folder into two categories. I could put all the materials about my father's life of service in one category, one part of my essay. Then in the next category I could put all the materials about people who taught him how one person can make a difference. You'll hear my order, because I use transition words to tell about those two groups so my readers will know how to listen. Notice that I also repeat key words from the thesis and topic sentence to remind readers what my claim is. I'll write in the air, saying exactly what I'm going to write."

My father, my most important teacher, taught me that one person can make a difference. One way that he taught me that one person can make a difference is that he lives a life of service. For example, when I was a child, my father got arrested for participation in a political protest. Requests for donations used to flood our mailbox and I knew he always said yes. We often had other people's children living with us: three orphans for one year, a couple of international exchange students for another year. Another way that my father lives a life of service is that he volunteers. For example, he teaches Sunday school, he helps his professional organizations, he works at the soup kitchen.

Another way that my father taught me one person can make a difference is that he often told me stories about people who taught him this. For example, he often quotes Rockefeller, who says, "To whom much is given, much shall be asked." Another example is that my father once told me the story of how he decided to be a doctor. As a teenager, he went to Camp Merryweather. One day, after lunch, the wife of the camp director read aloud from The Microbe Hunters, sharing stories of Marie Curie's and Louis Pasteur's research. Lying in his cot with a green army blanket over him, my father thought to himself, "That research is their jobs!" His own father had been a banker and it had never, until that moment, occurred to my father that a person's job could be their hobby, their life project. Right then, he vowed that he wanted his job to make a difference.

This is way too long to write onto chart paper. I'd just ad lib the passage, writing-in-the-air. I probably wouldn't make it so complete.

"Did you hear the organization—in other words, did you hear the transition words?" I quickly reread the transition words to the class. "Did you hear how I echoed my thesis and supporting sentence?" I reread those parts to the class.

Ask writers to share the organizational structure and transition words from their own work with their partner. Also ask them to share where and how they've used key words from the thesis and supporting sentences.

"Writers, take this time to share with your partners the organization you chose for one of your folders. Ask your partner whether the transition words you used clearly show the reader how you are organizing the materials. You can then talk about the key words from your thesis and supporting sentences that also need to be in your paragraphs. Are they there? Where could you put them if they aren't there yet? Okay, go ahead."

HOMEWORK *Lining Up Materials for Supporting Paragraphs* Writers, today you've done extraordinary work. You thought through the way in which you'd sequence your material for one folder, organizing it as a paragraph, and realized which transitional words would most help you link your pieces together. You said your draft aloud in your head or to each other, then drafted one paragraph. Some of you found that your paragraph was too long to be a single paragraph, so you divided it into two.

Tonight do this same work again for your next section. I know you are so excited to finish this part so we can put the essays all together! Our celebration is coming soon and we can't waste a minute!

TAILORING YOUR TEACHING

If your students seem to be getting tangled up as they organize their piles of supporting evidence . . . you may decide to devote more time to teaching students how to organize evidence chronologically (if you think that will help a majority of your writers) or how to organize according to importance (if many of your writers would benefit from more instruction on this method). For either or both of these lessons, you could use a published essay to illustrate the organizing structure you're teaching, and then for Active Engagement, you could have your students look through their topic sentence folders to see if any of them would be appropriate to organize either chronologically or according to importance. They can turn and tell a partner how they will organize and then go off to work to try it.

If your students have worked though this unit in a previous year and you'd like to vary this minilesson . . . you might offer students several mentor essays from published authors, from other students, or from the students in this unit to study. By analyzing the ways that other authors have arranged information, writers get ideas to try in their own writing. Here are two samples students could study in partnerships, noting their observations in their notebooks. Remember—students can learn from the mentor texts, weaknesses as well as strengths!

COLLABORATING WITH COLLEAGUES

It is important for teachers at different grade levels to meet and talk about ways in which children's work becomes more complex as they grow older and more experienced. As you try to articulate lines along which you expect children in the upper elementary grades to grow as writers, you'll also want to consider ways in which you foster children to do this increasingly complex thinking and writing.

The easiest way for a child to elaborate upon an idea is to provide one example, then another, then another. The logic is associative. For example, Ayana writes, "It is wonderful having kind friends. It is wonderful because your friends don't laugh at you if you get something wrong, your friends help you if you need help, and they never break their friendship." Then each paragraph states one claim ("It is wonderful having kind friends because your friends don't laugh if you get something wrong") and cites one example ("One day when I was in third grade . . . ") followed by another example ("Another time I was outside playing a game called 'Math Quiz' and I got an answer wrong").

> It is wonderful having kind friends. It is wonderful because your friends don't laugh at you if you get something wrong, your friends help you if you need help, and they never break their friendship. One day when I was in third grade and my friend sat next to me and my teacher asked me a math question and I got the answer wrong, everyone laughed except for my best friend. Another time I was outside playing a game called "Math Quiz" and I got an answer wrong and 2 girls laughed, but my best friend didn't laugh at me.
>
> It is wonderful having kind friends because your friends help you if you need help. One time I left my calculator at home and my friend let me use hers until I got mine. Another time I was doing my homework and I needed help with my homework and my friend helped me.

It is more challenging for children to elaborate on an idea by elucidating causes. In the preceding example, Ayana could have explored causes had she written about why kind (as opposed to unkind) friends don't laugh at each other, and why friends don't abandon each other when they need help or break friendships. Such an essay could have been interesting because of course people do sometimes have friendships with people who tend to be unkind, and those friendships probably do get strained.

When teachers scrutinize student work, asking, "What kind of thinking has this writer done?" it sometimes becomes clear that a child had nearly called on a more challenging level of thinking but settled on easier ways to elaborate. For example, although in the end Rebecca's essay about her sister is a straightforward list of all the times her sister acts in annoying ways, in one of Rebecca's earlier entries she'd explored causes for Star's behavior. *[Fig. XV-3]*

> My sister is spoiled by my mother because she is going through the process of being adopted. She was close to her old foster mother and never knew her biological mother. She cries a lot and says that she misses her foster brother, Ronny. I feel really bad for her and I would have acted just like her, however she gets me really irritated. All the time before I get in bed at night Star climbs into my bed, pulls the covers over her head and waits for me to go to my bed. That also gets me extremly annoyed.
> Star can be annoying but yet, sometimes she can be cute, funny and nice. It makes me really happy to see her happy

Fig. XV-3 Rebecca's notebook entry

My sister is spoiled by my mother because she is going through the process of being adopted. She was close to her old foster mother and never knew her biological mother. She cries a lot and says that she misses her foster brother, Ronny. I feel really bad for her and I would have acted just like her; however she gets me really irritated.

In this instance, if Rebecca's teacher had decided to help her explore causes and effects and make comparisons as she developed this piece, Rebecca's essay might have focused on causes for her sister's behavior instead of becoming the more simple list of times when Rebecca is irritated by her.

GETTING READY

- List of common ways to begin an essay on chart
- List of common ways to conclude an essay on chart
- Possible introductions and conclusions for your own essay on chart
- Sample student essays, with drafts of several introductions and conclusions
- See CD-ROM for resources

WRITING INTRODUCTIONS AND CONCLUSIONS

When children write stories, we hand story language over to them that can cast magical spells over their narrative accounts, turning plain-Jane recounts into stories that pull listeners close, giving them goose bumps. We do not hesitate to suggest to a child that he or she start a story with phrases like "On a dark and stormy night" or "Once, long, long ago, I . . . "

It is just as important that we also hand over language that essayists use, allowing youngsters to feel the persuasive power that special sets of words can have on listeners. In this session, I am direct. "Try these phrases on for size," I say, and hand over some of the language that I know will work for these youngsters' essays.

The results are once again magical. Try this with your own writing. Use these phrases when you address your children's parents in open-house meetings. Notice how the words work, just as the start of a story works, to cast a spell, to set the stage, to invite listeners to draw close, to lean in. Notice also how the words work on us, not just our listeners. As we say the words, essay-like language and structure flow from us more easily, evoked by tone and expectations we associate with those "expository" phrases.

I used to think each writer always needed to use brand-new words—words written for the occasion that come from the heart. But I've come to realize that for generations, people have begun stories, "Once upon a time, long, long ago" and not felt abashed to do so. Why not, in a similar way, borrow from the language of essayists and orators? I've done so in this paragraph, in fact, using borrowed phrases to frame my sentences— try doing the same! Some people begin their speeches awkwardly, hemming and hawing, but if you draw from great orators or writers, you will have words that you can rely on whenever you want to teach listeners something important.

MINILESSON

Writing Introductions and Conclusions

CONNECTION

Remind writers of the work they've done so far in this unit—the process that essayists use.

"Writers, you've done so much great work in this unit so far! Let's think again about what you've done, about how a person goes about writing essays." I held up my hand and touched my first finger, "At the start of our unit, you learned that when we want to write essays, we *first* live wide-awake lives, paying attention to things in our lives that are provocative, that make us think. We discussed a bunch of ways to gather essay entries— collecting observations and then writing off from them and from our earlier writing." I touched my second finger as I said, "Then we used thought prompts to push ourselves to extend our first thoughts."

Touching my third finger I said, "You learned that writers form a picture, an image, of the sort of thing we want to write. We do this by studying writing others have done, texts that resemble those we want to write." I held up three more fingers to go with the next three steps and said, "Then you learned to choose a seed idea, to write it as a clear and strong thesis, and to plan or frame the main sections of your essay. Next you sorted through your entries, selecting and sequencing them. And, finally, you began drafting!"

Name the teaching point. In this case, writers use several phrases to help us create introductions and conclusions for our essays.

"Today I know you'll continue to cement your selected material into paragraphs, but I know you will also want to learn a bit about how essayists write introductions and closings for our essays. Specifically, I want to teach you that essay writers often use the beginning of an essay as a place to convey to readers that the ideas in the essay are important. The lead briefly places the essay into a context."

COACHING

It helps to organize and consolidate the processes and strategies that we've taught thus far so children can draw on them as they cycle through the stages of the writing process with independence, at whatever speed works for them. Although in this unit we are inching through some detailed steps in the writing process, I pause at crucial junctures to give children an aerial view of what they are experiencing. I want them to grasp the main contours of the process. The good news is they'll come to know the process better across the year because they will have chances to reexperience it.

TEACHING

Tell writers that at the beginning and end of essays, essayists often rely on some common ways to say, "This is important!"

"I think you know by now that when we want to do a new kind of writing, we often get ready for this by reading texts that resemble those we want to write. We could go on a search, collecting ways that writers usually introduce and close their essays. But this time I'll simply tell you what I've already found from studying people's essays."

"What I've found is that often essayists want both their introduction and the closing paragraphs to say to readers, 'This essay is *really important*. Listen up!' Essayists don't usually use those exact words, however. But essayists sometimes convey that the content is important because it answers people's questions or helps with their needs or changes their mind." I revealed a chart on which I had written a few common phrases for introductions and conclusions of essays. "I might, therefore, start in one of these ways."

You'll recall that in order to teach children to write leads and endings to narratives, I invited them to pore over texts by authors they love. I invited them to find patterns in those leads and endings. As you realize by now, the truth is that I do not have a vast storehouse of exemplar essays that are simple enough for children to study and emulate. That explains why I've been the one to do this research and extrapolate these patterns, rather than sending children off to search through the essays they love, noticing how authors began and ended those essays. If you discover enough texts, you could structure a minilesson in which children extract for themselves a host of ways to start and finish an essay.

Ways to Start an Essay

- Tell a story about one person needing the information this essay will convey. What (that person) and others need to know is that . . .

- Many people (don't know, don't think, don't realize) but I've (come to know, think it's important) . . .

- Have you ever (wondered/wanted to know) . . . ? I have found . . .

- Raise a question that people ask . . . and show that this essay will answer it.

"At the end of my essay, I want to say to my readers that now that I know something, I will act differently, or other people should act differently. So I might fit what I want to say into phrases like these."

Ways to End an Essay

- (My thesis) is true. Because this is true, isn't it also true that . . .
- I realize that . . .
- This makes me think . . .
- I realize that when I . . . , I feel . . .
- Other people should care about this because . . .
- This is important because . . .

"So let me show you how I take these phrases and see if they might work for my essay. You'll notice that some do, some don't. They never work exactly, so I change the wording around a bit to fit what I want to say. And I often write beginnings and endings that don't use these templates. I usually list a couple of possible introductions and then choose one that will especially work for my essay."

"Here's how I might try these phrases with my essay that has the thesis 'My father's been my most important teacher.' First I'll reread these suggestions, trying each one to see if it helps my essay get started well."

Looking at the list, I read the first item aloud. "'A story about one person needing the information this essay will convey . . .' Hmm . . . Who'll *need* to know that my father is my most important teacher? That's a big question, now that I think about it. Who *will* want to read this essay? Maybe my father? Or people who want to know him? Or parents who need to realize they could be the important teachers for their children? Let me keep that last audience in mind, and I'll try telling a story about one person who needs to know that."

> A friend of mine is expecting her first child soon, and she is already worrying about the schools that her child will attend. I tell her not to worry; what she needs to know is that she and her husband will be her child's most important teachers.

Notice that I have given my students many different phrases to choose from. You may decide to use fewer examples. I want to make sure that my students choose a phrase based on what they are trying to say to their readers. Also notice that any of these phrases could be used in an introduction or a conclusion.

These lead sentence templates can have a dramatic effect on children's essays. Just as starting with "Once upon a time" can lift the level of a story, these leads can wrap children's rather pedestrian paragraphs in an aura of drama. Be sure to emphasize that writers need to try them on for size, to revise the set phrases a bit so they fit exactly with each essay.

"I have to get to my thesis now," I said, so next I said:

> My father has been my most important teacher, teaching me to
> regard my job as a hobby, to love writing, and to believe that one
> person can make a difference.

"Let me go back to the list. I'll see if this next one could work: 'I used to think . . . but now I realize . . .' Let's see. I don't want to say, 'I used to think my father wasn't a good teacher' because that's not true. How about this:"

> I used to think that the teachers my children have in school would
> make or break them. I'd worry frantically if one of them had a
> teacher who wasn't superb. But I've come to realize that the teachers
> who matter most aren't always the official ones we have in school. In
> my life, my father was my most important teacher. He taught me . . .

"That one works too, doesn't it? It's totally different, but it still sets up my essay for my audience."

ACTIVE ENGAGEMENT
Ask students to try some of the introductory phrases to frame their own essays.

"Right now, would you work with your partner to see if one of these starting phrases might work for your essay? Partner 1, would you talk with partner 2 first? Does partner 1 want to use a lead that shows that this essay is the answer to someone's concerns? If so, try the first lead idea. Talk about who the reader is and how this essay could fit with the reader's questions and concerns. It might be that partner 1 wants to emphasize that this thesis is surprising, in which case both of you could talk about what the surprising aspect of it is and draw from the second batch of lead ideas."

LINK
Restate the teaching point. Remind students that writers use introductions and conclusions to help readers grasp the importance of the essay's thesis.

"So writers, I know that today many of you will be sifting through your folders, lining up the materials, taping them in or revising them as needed to finalize your supporting paragraphs, and then connecting those materials into one draft. Once you have done that (today and whenever you write an essay), write a few possible introductions and a few possible conclusions. Then choose the ones that best make your case that your thesis is important and should be listened to."

As you can see, the metaphor I mentioned in passing about "trying these on for size" is an apt one. That is exactly what this process feels like to me. You could decide to highlight this trying-on aspect at greater length.

I don't try out every single possible way to start an essay, because by now children should grasp my point—and be eager to try this themselves.

You could instead ask kids to take the third option on the chart and try it on for size, using my essay as the exercise text. "Would you and your partner help me consider whether the third suggestion on our chart might work for my essay," you could say. Instead, I ask children to try these leads out with their own essays. I know the latter is more supportive of children's work on this day; the former makes it more likely that children will learn from today's lesson in ways they can transfer to other texts and use with independence. For this class at this time, I am focused more on being sure all of them can get the job done in a timely manner and less on making sure they take these lessons home for use throughout their lives. Thus, my choice.

Whenever I link the minilesson, I try to make sure that the students understand that their work for the day is not just the work of the minilesson. Notice that I said they are drafting and trying out introductions and conclusions. If the minilesson alone is the work for the day, then this session becomes an activity instead of a workshop. Workshop teaching means that there is always something to work on.

WRITING AND CONFERRING

Turning Scraps of Paper into an Outline

You will probably find a small group of writers who are having trouble turning their materials into a draft, even when those materials are already lined up, revised, and ready to go, and even though you've coached them through this process before. When I encountered this situation I handled it like this: "Writers, would all of you gather in a circle around Diego and me because I'm going to show you how Diego goes from having all these bits and pieces to having a whole rough draft of an essay."

"You'll notice that Diego has a stack of blank notebook paper and scissors and tape. Now watch." Turning to Diego, I said, "I'll coach you, telling you what I'd probably do to make an essay, and then you do it while all of us watch and learn, okay?"

"First, Diego, I'd look over your folders, your topic sentences, and the way you plan to organize the material for each one, and decide whether each folder will be one long paragraph or several different ones. If you are organizing it by saying one group first and one group second, you will probably need two paragraphs, right?" Diego had organized the information inside each folder, and showed which bits were going to be one paragraph and which the second.

"Next, I'd decide the sequence of your topic sentences. Does one somehow seem like it belongs earlier or later? If you have no other way to sequence them, put your most convincing argument last," I said, and Diego shuffled through his folders, rearranging them so his most important idea was last.

"Now take your first folder and your first sheet of notebook paper. Copy your topic sentence onto the first line of the notebook paper. It will be the start of a paragraph, so indent." Diego did this, copying "Friendship dies when there's new friends" onto the top of his paper.

> **MID-WORKSHOP TEACHING POINT**   *Revising Introductions*   "Writers, listen to the three different drafts Mimi has written of her introduction. You'll see she's taken ideas from our chart but switched them around so they work for her thesis, which is 'School is important because you learn to work with people who are different from you, you make friends who help you feel less alone, and you learn skills that will be important for life.'"
>
> "These are her first drafts of an introduction."
>
> 1. Recently I have known people to think that school is just not important and a waste of time. But I think differently. I think that school is as valuable as gold.
>
> 2. Other people have a theory that school isn't important. But lately, I couldn't disagree more. I think school is important.
>
> 3. When people talk about wishing to miss school, I just don't understand it. I think it is wrong. They should find school extremely important.
>
> "I hope hearing what Mimi has done helps you with the work you are doing with your introduction. You can try making a list of possibilities like she did!"

"Now you need to place the bits you'll use in the order you decided. So spread the contents of this folder out in front of you, and move the bits around until they are lined up the way you've planned for them to go. I see you put numbers, right? That's a great idea." Diego did this. "Now, tell us which kind of order you have planned for this, Diego. Okay, chronological, great. So now, Diego, talk us through how this essay will go, and look at your bits as you talk to us, saying the words you will actually write. You'll be using the transition words that go with chronological essays, right? Like first and then and next? Okay, talk it through for us." *[Fig. XVI-1]*

> Friendship dies when there's new friends. When I was a friend with James when I was in first grade, but when new people came we started giving up our friendship for others. Two months passsed and before you knew it, he and I didn't say a word to each other and played more with others.

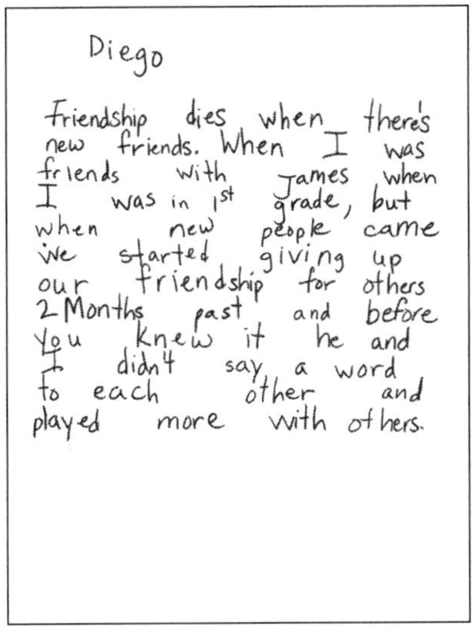
Diego

Friendship dies when there's new friends. When I was friends with James when I was in 1st grade, but when new people came we started giving up our friendship for others 2 Months past and before You knew it he and I didn't say a word to each other and played more with others.

Fig. XVI-1 Diego's entry

"Wow, you can put that down on paper just the way you told it, can't you? If you like the way you've written your entries, you can tape them in sequence onto your notebook paper with your transition words written in between. If you don't like the way you've written them, you can revise them, writing them better."

"I bet you can figure out how to keep going from here," I said, and Diego nodded and set to work with tape and scissors. Turning to the rest of the group, I said, "When you have sorted through your folders, you'll want to assemble a first draft of your essay just like Diego has done, revising as you go to make the pieces fit."

While I was working with that small group, others in the class had relied on the teaching of the minilesson to draft introductions and conclusions. *[Figs. XVI-2, XVI-3, XVI-4, XVI-5,* and *XVI-6]*

Sophie's introductions:

> Times with my great-grandmother Evelyne are special to me!
>
> Times with her are special because I understood her, I could tell her anything and I feel happy when I see her.
>
> Do you have a great-grandma? I do, most people don't , if you do you're really lucky. I know I'm lucky because I have one.
>
> Some people think that your great-grandmother is just another person, but I know that's not true. Having a great-grandmother is very special, this is how!

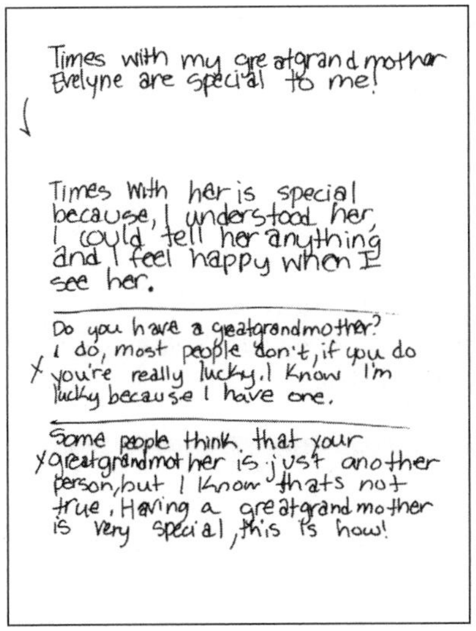
Times with my greatgrandmother Evelyne are special to me!

Times with her is special because, I understood her, I could tell her anything and I feel happy when I see her.

Do you have a greatgrandmother? I do, most people don't, if you do you're really lucky. I Know I'm lucky because I have one.

Some people think that your greatgrandmother is just another person, but I know thats not true, Having a greatgrandmother is very special, this is how!

Fig. XVI-2 Sophie's introductions

Olivia's introductions:

Sometimes I hurt people's feelings

Sometimes I hurt people's feelings to get back at them, to fit in, and when I am having a hard time.

Do you get mad and call somebody names and hurt their feelings? I sometimes hurt people's feelings. I hurt people's feelings to get back at them, fit in, and when I am having a hard time.

Some people think I am always nice to my younger siblings or friends, but really I get mad at my siblings almost every day and sometimes I hurt people's feelings. Sometimes I hurt people's feelings to get back at them, to fit in, and when I am having a hard time.

Some people think it is realistic that friends and siblings and some don't. But I've had experiences where I tease and hurt my friends' and siblings' feelings. Sometimes I hurt people's feelings to get back at them, fit in, and when I am having a hard time.

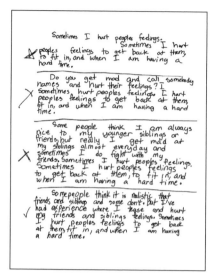

Fig. XVI-3 Olivia's introductions

Olivia's conclusions:

Endings

What I've realized now is when you are mad you say words you don't mean to say. My dad said when you hurt people's feelings you are just hurting your own feelings.

My dad said, "When you hurt people's feelings you are just hurting your own feelings." This made me realize when I was hurting people's feelings I was really hurting my own feelings.

A few nights ago my dad told me "When you hurt people's feelings you are just hurting your own feelings." That made me realize that when I hurt people's feelings I feel hurt too. Also that I don't want to be the person who hurts people's feelings.

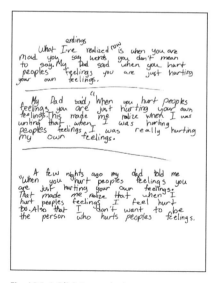

Fig. XVI-4 Olivia's conclusions

Rie's introductions:

Not everyone fears making mistakes. Many famous inventors, authors, statesman, etc. have expressed a positive view toward mistakes. For instance, Henry Kaiser said, "Problems are opportunities in work clothes."

Albert Einstein said, "In the middle of difficulty lies opportunity." Katherine Graham offered a creative view by saying, " A mistake is simply another way of doing things."

And Ralph Waldo Emerson reminded us that "Our greatest glory is not in never failing but in rising up every time we fail."

quotes

Rie's conclusions:

Ending

As I was writing this I realized that making a mistake wasn't a big deal.

I hope to keep on skating even if I fall. I hope that if people are laughing not to hear them.

I hope that if I make a mistake I just shrug my shoulders and I'll just laugh at myself.

Not everyone fears making mistakes. Many famous inventors, authors, statesmen, etc. have expressed a positive view toward mistakes. For instance, Henry Kaiser said "Problems are opportunities in work clothes." Maybe
Albert Einstein said, "The middle of difficulty lies opportunity." Katherine Graham offered a creative view by saying, "A mistake is simply another way of doing things." And Ralph Waldo Emerson reminded us that "Our greatest glory is not in never failing but in rising up every time we fail!" Maybe
quotes

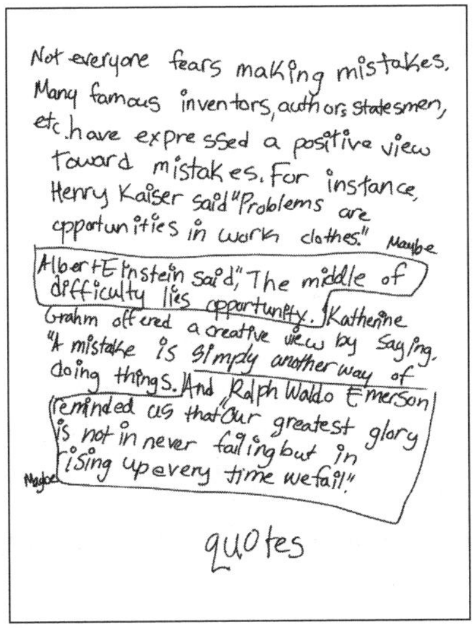

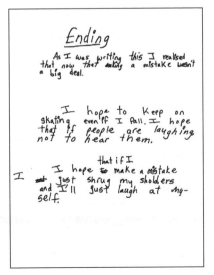

Fig. XVI-5 Rie's introductions

Ending
As I was writing this I realised that now that making a mistake wasn't a big deal.
I hope to keep on skating even if I fall. I hope that if people are laughing not to hear them.
I I hope that if I make a mistake I just shrug my sholders and I'll just laugh at my-self.

Fig. XVI-6 Rie's conclusions

SHARE

Illustrating a Thesis with a Mini-Story

Explain that essayists sometimes use a mini-story to show, not tell, their thesis.

"Writers, many of you worked on using phrases to help you convey your message in the introduction and conclusion of your essay. However, some writers do this differently. Some writers tell a little narrative, a little story to show their thesis in their introduction. It is usually a little snapshot that gives the reader a clue about the thesis for the essay. Two writers we know tried this and I wanted to share with you what they did."

Share the introductions of two students who illustrated their theses with stories.

"Here's Zoe's introduction." [Fig. XVI-7]

> "Get down lower! That's not a side split! You're a yellow belt, you should know better!" My sensei (teacher) was yelling at me again! I was as low as I could get, practically touching the floor, yet he was still demanding perfection. He was going around barking orders. He always finds something wrong with what I am doing. Karate is so demanding!

"Did you notice that Zoe told a little story about karate showing us, her readers, her thesis? From her story we get the idea that karate is a lot of hard work and that much is demanded of her."

"Now listen to Yashoda's introduction."

> When I first came to the orphanage I didn't know anyone there. I was as scared as a mouse running from the cat. When I first saw them they all looked mean. I felt lonely. In a few days things started to change. Vinita and I became friends. Every day we played together. We took turns being a leader of little kids. When we went to sleep Vinita told me stories about her life, and she slept beside me every night. Vinita is such a good friend because she cares for me.

In many ways, using a mini-story in the introduction, using a story to explain and support the thesis, is exactly what children did earlier in their body paragraphs. The only difference is that this mini-story illustrates the overarching topic of the essay, not just one part of the evidence. You'll have to decide if this bit of information would help your students understand this teaching point or if it would confuse them.

> *Zoe*
>
> ✳ "Get down lower! That's not a side split! You're a yellow belt! You should know better!" My sensei (teacher) was yelling at me again! I was as low as I could get practicly touching the floor, yet he still was demanding perfection. He was going around barking orders. My teacher always finds something wrong with what I'm doing that is how Karate is so demanding.

Fig. XVI-7 Zoe's introduction

Ask students to discuss how a story might illustrate the thesis of their essay.

"Can you take a moment right now and think about your thesis? Could your thesis be revealed through a snapshot story? When you are ready, turn and tell your partner a little story that could illustrate your thesis."

"Essayists, can I have your attention please? I want to compliment you on how thoughtful you were about constructing your stories to illustrate your introductions! You are thinking hard and not giving up! You can keep thinking about this in the back of your mind as we go on to other work. Sometimes the best ideas come when we think we are thinking about something else."

HOMEWORK *Reading Essay Drafts Critically* For homework tonight, I'm going to ask you to practice being a reader of essay drafts. I've made copies of the work a student in my class last year wrote. Pretend this is your essay, and ask, "Is this writer's support material really aligned to her claim?" If it isn't, would you see if you could help the writer out by either revising the claim (the idea) the writer is advancing, or by revising the support material (you may need to pretend to be an expert on the topic)?

Shanice's thesis is, "I'm proud of my cat." One of her folders says, "I'm proud of my cat because she just had kittens." Tonight, read this entry and think, "Does this support Shanice's claim?" and fix it if it doesn't.

> For example, one morning I woke up to a screaming noise.
> It was the sound of a baby kitten. I looked under my
> bed. My cat was giving birth. Later on I found out there
> was 4 baby kittens and we were giving them away. We
> were only keeping the mother and a brown kitten.

If your students have already worked through this unit in previous years and you'd like to teach a variation . . . you could teach that another technique writers use to introduce an essay is to quote a published author or a famous person. You can find many examples in this book; I often introduce a new idea by quoting another author. In the Tailor Your Teaching segment for Session XII, I wrote:

> William Zinsser, author of *On Writing Well*, suggests that surprise is important in writing, and I think he is right. Jean Fritz, the author of many history books, seems to agree. She writes about the importance of surprising details: "As human beings, we thrive on astonishment. Whatever is unknown quickens us, delivers us from ourselves, impels us to investigate."

Using the words of these two master writers helped me introduce my idea. This is something that writers do; we find other people to help us describe what we are thinking.

Another way to teach this minilesson would be to ask students to collect introductions and conclusions from published essays or from essays other students have written. Remind them how to study a mentor's writing techniques by asking, "What has this author done that I could try?" Then invite your students to "have a go" and try the technique themselves.

COLLABORATING WITH COLLEAGUES

As you near the end of this first unit focused on expository writing, you and your colleagues may want to get together to discuss and plan how the momentum of this unit can carry you and your students toward related goals.

You might want to consider planning several days in a row to coach kids in how to write a compressed version of an essay for timed testing situations. You and your colleagues can study the past tests used in your region to determine the specifics required of essay answers. How long will children have to write, and precisely how are they expected to structure their answers? Whatever the answers to these questions, the children will undoubtedly be required to have a thesis, topic sentences and supporting paragraphs, and introductions and conclusions to their essays. With practice, children can complete an essay test using an abridged version of the writing process they've experienced in this unit, drawing on all they've learned this month, and create structured, thoughtful essays that offer opinions and provide evidence to support them. You and your colleagues can determine how best to modify the writing process to fit the demands of the tests.

Another unit extension you and your colleagues could plan together could be about listening to and/or taking notes on expository texts. Since children are fresh from creating essays and thinking about their basic components and structures, this is an opportune moment to help them listen for and read for those same structures in the nonfiction texts they encounter in life. Where is the thesis? Where are the subordinate topic sentences? What is the evidence or examples? This mental checklist can help students know which parts of what they see or hear are worth remembering or writing down. We all know that we can't take notes on everything we read, and we can't remember everything we hear. Having a structure gives us a way to make sense of the world and make thoughtful choices about the relative importance of the information we take in. It also gives us a structure on which to hang the information we take in; then, looking at the whole, we can see where the gaps are and where the information is solid. That knowledge of the essay structure gives us, as listeners or readers, a way to judge and critique texts.

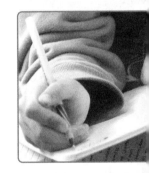

CELEBRATING JOURNEYS OF THOUGHT

IN THIS SESSION, STUDENTS WILL
SHARE THE PERSONAL DISCOVERIES
THEY'VE MADE IN THIS UNIT AS THEY
CELEBRATE WITH FAMILY AND
FRIENDS. THEY WILL NOT ONLY
CELEBRATE THEIR PUBLISHED ESSAYS,
THEY WILL ALSO CELEBRATE THE
WRITING THAT LED TO THEIR ESSAYS
AND THE WAYS THIS WRITING HELPED
THEM DISCOVER IDEAS ABOUT
THEMSELVES AND THE WORLD.

GETTING READY

- Parents or other adults previously invited
- Students' writing neatly organized on tables
- Three students prepared to read during whole-class celebration
- Refreshments
- See CD-ROM for resources

During this celebration, *children (and those who care for them) will celebrate not only the essays that children have written, but also the insights they've developed about themselves, their subjects, and writing itself.*

Each child's work represents that child's journey of discovery, and on this occasion these will all be proudly displayed and mined for significance.

After children participate in the rituals that will by now have become familiar, the class will disperse into corners of the room for small-group sharing. Then parents, other visitors, and half the class will be invited to visit the other half at stations where the children will sit, with their work displayed in front of them. Visitors can browse through the child's notebook, folder, rough draft, and final essay, and they'll find that throughout it the writer will have left sticky notes saying, "Ask me." If the viewer wishes, she can point to one of those notes and say, "Can you tell me about this part?"

By this time in the year, there will be a great deal to celebrate in your class. Children will have used writing to come to new insights about themselves. In this world of ours, where the commercialized culture of marketing and advertising spews out messages like, "You must buy this, own this, eat this, wear this—or your life will be miserable," the writing workshop conveys an entirely different message. The workshop says, "You and I can take the details of our lives and we can make something of them." The writing workshop says, "Significance and meaning aren't bought or even found, they are made, and each one of us has the capacity to take the truth of our lives and to come to new understandings, new levels of thinking about the life that we lead."

Today, we celebrate the fact that writing gives us new eyes to see and understand ourselves. We also celebrate that the youngsters in this community have grown taller as writers. Their texts are longer. Their notebooks are fuller. Their voices are stronger. Their sense of themselves and of each other as writers is more buoyant.

If we, grown-ups, can see our children's growth and help them to see it as well, they'll flourish, sprouting with new inches of power, confidence, sensitivity, zeal. So today teaching will have a lot to do with finding a moment to look a child in the eyes, to help a child feel seen and celebrated.

CELEBRATION

Welcome visitors to the classroom. Explain how the celebration will go. In this case, again, a few children read to the entire class and then everyone disperses to small groups for sharing.

"Welcome to this incredible occasion. Today we want to talk with you about life journeys. When my children were young—in second and fourth grade—we took a trip to a faraway place, where we lived in a little village that was utterly different than our home town. Last summer, just before he headed off to college, my son, Miles, gathered all the photos we'd ever taken and constructed five photo albums that resurrected our life together. We were all amazed to see that there were far more photographs of that one journey than of anything else. "What if we'd never taken that journey—how much we would have lost!" I thought.

"Journeys matter. They create memories… they recreate those of us who are travelers. And the journeys that matter most may not be the ones that take us to far-away places, but instead the ones that take us to new understandings. They are journeys of thought— journeys that help us understand our own lives in a new way."

"I'm telling you this because the writers in this classroom and their teacher and I have all been on a journey together, and we have also taken a journey alone, inside our own notebooks and drafts. Today's celebration is like the class photo album, showcasing turning points from all of our journeys."

Explain that in this celebration the readings will be in a symphony, with one person acting as conductor, using a baton to indicate the child who will read next, next, next. Voices will tumble, one against the next, with no applause or other sound in the interim.

"First, we're going to listen to three writers, as usual, reading to the entire assembly. Our reading today will be what we call a symphony. Teacher Mary Chiarella will be the conductor for these readers who will read to the whole class, then each one of those readers will the conductor for a smaller circle of readers. One reader after another will "play his or her instrument," (you'll see what I mean) and all of us need to be as quiet as if we were at a concert. When every voice has been heard, then each circle needs to talk quietly until the others are done as well."

COACHING

One of the challenges in teaching writing is that there are many ways in which this is a cyclical curriculum. This is your third celebration, and there will be many others. So it is a challenge to find ways to keep each celebration a little bit new. There is nothing sacrosanct about the metaphor of a journey. Find your own ways to put a new spin on each Author Celebration!

The word essay means to wander, and many people define essays as trails of thought. So, it seems appropriate to celebrate, at this final moment, the new realizations children have come to about themselves as they've written throughout this unit. This celebration also gives parents a chance to notice and talk about the changes they have seen in their children as writers.

You'll notice that there is a lot of continuity between this Author Celebration and the others, and there is also some novelty. The mix is deliberate. I think people welcome a sense of continuity in the rituals of our lives. It means a lot to me that every single Christmas since I was a baby, my whole family spends Christmas Eve caroling through our neighborhood. I don't want to come up with a totally new way to spend Christmas Eves. In the same way, your children will welcome the way in which Author Celebrations are traditional events, proceeding in ways that people come to anticipate. Also, of course, there are practical advantages to Author Celebrations having a predictable structure. Parents come to understand how these events go, and then all of us can spend much less time and thought on the logistical details of the occasion (which will never be small when such a large group of people gather), and we can give more of our time and attention to the writers—to their writing and to our efforts to help them feel deeply and truly heard.

Signal for the symphony at the front of the class to begin. When they have finished, help everyone move to their small groups for the rest of the symphonies.

Three writers took their places in a line of chairs, and with a pencil/baton Mary signaled to the third child in the line. LaKeya picked up her essay and read: *[Figs. XVII-1, XVII-2, XVII-3, and XVII-4]*

We often talk about how these celebrations offer a time for offering support and affirmation for our children's writing lives. Truthfully, these celebrations can be times for support and affirmation for our teaching lives as well! Welcome these moments. We all need them in our lives.

It's Hard Being a Girl
LaKeya
It's hard being a girl. Being a girl is hard because we have mixed and sensitive feelings, we go through a lot of changes, and we worry how we look.

It's hard being a girl because we have mixed and sensitive feelings. I can be happy then in a minute I am mad. We have mood swings. For example, one time I told my sister to sing and then I told her to stop because she was making me mad. I get angry very easily. If someone hits me I will get mad and cry at the same time. One more example, I could seem very sweet but inside I hold a lot of anger from my mother's evil boyfriend. If I get what I want, I am sweet. When I am in mixed company, I am lala. Being a girl sometimes we also have surprising feelings. For example, when some one hits me I am supposed to be mad but instead I am a pool of sadness. But when I am supposed to be sad, I am happy instead. One day I will never forget is

Fig. XVII-1 LaKeya's final draft

December 16, 2003. I was getting ready to go to after school when my Uncle Duncan said we had to leave. I didn't want to leave. I felt irritated that my Uncle Duncan wanted to take me away. But when we got in front of our house, Daddy came out of his car crying. Then I wasn't irritated. I was puzzled. I stared crying because he was crying. He usually was strong about everything, Daddy sat us down and said, "Keya, Cha-cha, Grandma—our beloved grandma—is gone. She popped the daisies. She's dead." I regretted whatever I ever said to her. I wanted to have her come back to life and see me grow up, be a writer, go to college, and be there for my sweet sixteen. I would give my lungs and die than live and never see her again. That day, I had mixed feelings.

It's also hard being a girl because we go through changes. For example, our rear ends get bigger. I woke up one morning and saw that I was falling backwards. Another change is our thighs get fatter. That's hard because we get teased about them. One time at school the

Fig. XVII-2 LaKeya's final draft, page 2

class was at recess and then they were all around me. They said, "Hey, fatty pants, watch you doing ham legs?" and some kids said "turkey legs." We also crave foods. One time I was not hungry but then I wanted a hamburger. We also get cramps. One time I had really really bad cramps and then I could not move. And I can smell good one moment and then the next moment my armpits stink. Another change is we act grown. One time I had a grown face on and I did not realize that. I had a grown face on and my mother said "Wipe that grown smile off your face, La'Keya!"

It's also hard being a girl because we worry how we look. I can not care how I look and then in a moment I can look in the mirror every minute. One reason is that we have to use so many face and hair products. For example, we use creams, facials, and face soaps to help our face be very radiant. One morning I just woke up and my stepfather said, "Holy moly, your face is ashy!" I raced to

Fig. XVII-3 LaKeya's final draft, page 3

the bathroom and looked at the mirror and saw that my face was cracked all over my forehead, cheeks, and chin. By the time it was getting dark, he came home with sample moisturizers. Once he showed me that I realized I needed to put it on. It's hard because we don't care, but once we get an opinion, we worry. We also worry about how our hair looks. One time I woke up in my father's house and I saw my hair and screamed. I looked so awful. I went into the bathroom and didn't come out for half of an hour. Another example is we are always into how we look when we were close. For example, we say this, "is this too big? This is too loose. Help me out."

Being a girl is hard. It's hard to have all these sensitive and mixed feelings, and to go through so many changes, and to worry about how you look. It's confusing and sometimes it doesn't feel good. I know this because I'm a girl.

Fig. XVII-4 LaKeya's final draft, page 4

Then William picked up his essay and read: *[Figs. XVII-5, XVII-6, XVII-7, and XVII-8]*

Love Can Build a House That Stands Forever

My mom is the best mom a kid could ever have. Believe it or not, she cleans after she comes from work. She wakes up early every day and she also goes to work even when she is sick. She does all of these things because she loves the whole family.

The first way my mom works hard for the family is by cleaning after work.

One day when my mom came from work she couldn't believe it. The house was so dirty. There was dust all over the place! "What happened?!" she asked. Nobody answered. I couldn't believe it. After she came from work tired, she took the mop and broom and started cleaning. First she cleaned the kitchen. There were stains on the oven. The dishes were all dirty too. When she finished she was exhausted. I always thank her for what she does for the family.

She cleans the kitchen. She wants everything to be in order for dinner.

She cleans the bedroom. She knows I could do it but she does it anyway.

She cleans the bathroom. She knows it's nasty but she does it without complaints.

Not only does my mom work hard for the family by cleaning after work, but by waking up early every day. When I'm sleeping I can hear the creaking sound of the door of my bedroom. I could tell that she was getting my clothes. When I wake up she always has my clothes hanging from the chairs. When I put them on they fit just right and they look pretty too. If my mom wasn't beside me I wouldn't know what to do and I would be so disappointed.

She wakes up early every day to put my clothes in order. Depending on what activity I have.

She wakes up early every day to check my book bag in case I forgot a book or a sheet.

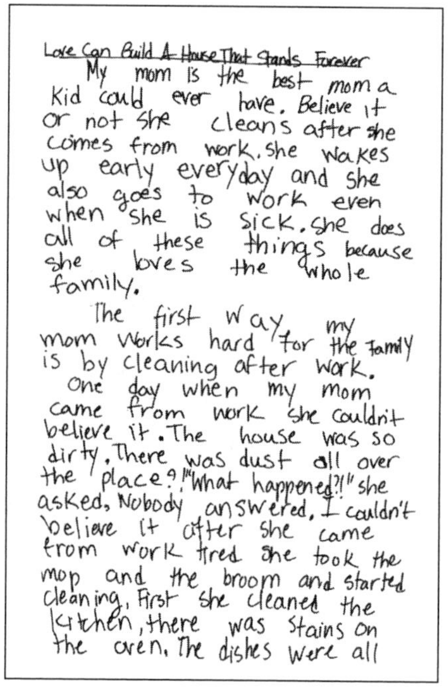
Love Can Build A House That Stands Forever
My mom is the best mom a kid could ever have. Believe it or not she cleans after she comes from work. She wakes up early everyday and she also goes to work even when she is sick. She does all of these things because she loves the whole family.
The first way my mom works hard for the family is by cleaning after work.
One day when my mom came from work she couldn't believe it. The house was so dirty. There was dust all over the place?! "What happened?!" she asked. Nobody answered. I couldn't believe it after she came from work tired she took the mop and the broom and started cleaning. First she cleaned the kitchen, there was stains on the oven. The dishes were all

Fig. XVII-5 William's final draft

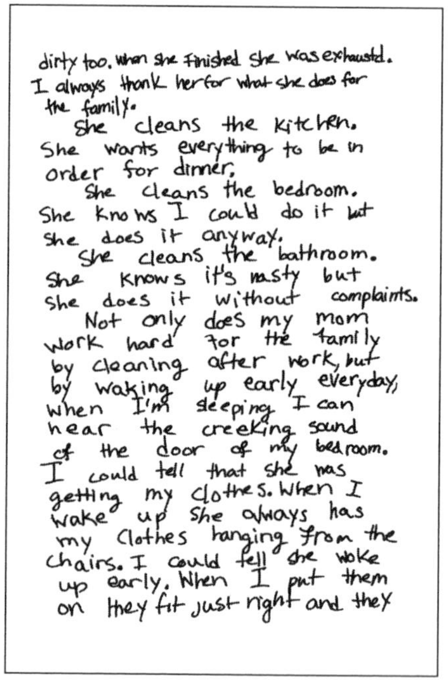
dirty too. When she finished she was exhausted. I always thank her for what she does for the family.
She cleans the kitchen. She wants everything to be in order for dinner.
She cleans the bedroom. She knows I could do it but she does it anyway.
She cleans the bathroom. She knows it's nasty but she does it without complaints.
Not only does my mom work hard for the family by cleaning after work, but by waking up early everyday. When I'm sleeping I can hear the creeking sound of the door of my bedroom. I could tell that she was getting my clothes. When I wake up she always has my clothes hanging from the chairs. I could tell she woke up early. When I put them on they fit just right and they

Fig. XVII-6 William's final draft, page 2

She wakes up early every day to see what is the temperature to see if I need a coat.

Perhaps the most important way why my mom works hard for the family is by never missing a day of work even when she is sick.

One morning my mom told me that she was sick. She sneezed. She coughed. She even wasted a pack of tissues. When she went to her job, that exact moment I felt that my mom could do anything. When she left I was worried. She left in an awful condition. When she got home she felt better.

"Hey, Mom, are you OK?" I said.

"I've never felt better," she said.

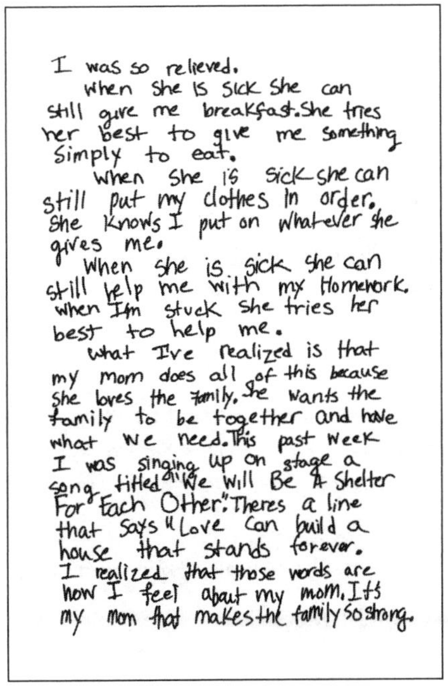

I was so relieved.

When she is sick she can still give me breakfast. She tries her best to give me something simply to eat.

When she is sick she can still put my clothes in order. She knows I put on whatever she gives me.

When she is sick she can still help me with my homework. When I'm stuck she tries her best to help me.

What I've realized is that my mom does all of this because she loves the family. She wants the family to be together and have what we need. This past week I was singing up on stage a song titled "We Will Be a Shelter For Each Other." There's a line that says "Love can build a house that stands forever." I realized that those words are how I feel about my mom. It's my mom that makes the family so strong.

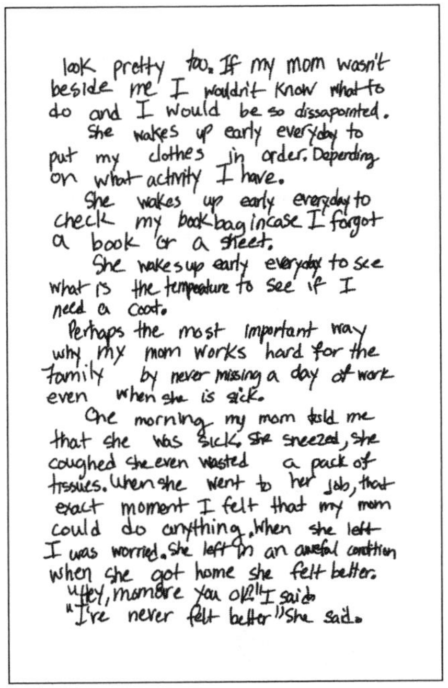

Fig. XVII-7 William's final draft, page 3

Fig. XVII-8 William's final draft, page 4

And finally, Fatmire read a portion of her final draft: [Figs. XVII-9–XVII-13]

Love Is Missing Someone When He's Away.

Everyone has someone who is special to them. Maybe it's their best friends, their sisters or brothers. But to me that someone is my dad because he is so close to me. My dad goes on trips a lot. I miss my dad when he is away because we have so much fun together. He takes care of me when I am sick and because when I am afraid he makes me safe.

One reason why I miss my dad is because we had so much fun together.

During the weekend we enjoy jogging together. We run around lakes.

After school we enjoy sitting at the computer. We play all these different kind of games.

At midnight we enjoy sitting on the sofa. We tell stories and jokes.

But when he's not around I don't jog with anyone, I don't sit down with anybody, and I don't stay at midnight and talk with anyone.

An example of this is when my dad went on a trip. I was lonely sitting by myself. My sister was doing homework and my mom was busy doing work. I was waiting to play with somebody.

"Lena, could you play with me?" I asked her.

"I can't," she said.

But all of a sudden the doorbell ring-ring-ring-ring. "Hello?" I asked.

"Hello," a guy said back.

"Daddy's coming," I yelled so that my family could hear me.

I buzzed him in. I heard footsteps.

"Daddy!" I yell.

"I love you" I said to him. " Me too" he said back.

My dad and I share good times together, but when he is away, I feel lonely and have no one to play with.

Fig. XVII-9 Fatmire's final draft

Fig. XVII-10 Fatmire's final draft, page 2

Fig. XVII-11 Fatmire's final draft, page 3

Fig. XVII-12 Fatmire's final draft, page 4

Fig. XVII-13 Fatmire's final draft, page 5

After the three readers had produced their symphony, writers dispersed to smaller circles of sharing, and the original readers acted as conductors while each group produced another symphony of their own. Some of the readers read only one selected passage from their essays, leaving lots of time for a museum of sharing afterwards.

When the symphonies are finished, help children take their places in the museum display of their writing work. Coach the visitors in listening to the children.

As half the children—two of the circles—assumed their places in museum booths, with each child pulling out the stack containing the child's notebook, files, drafts, and final draft, each with a few sticky notes places here or there saying, "Ask me," I asked the grown-up visitors to cluster around me for a moment. "Parents," I said. "Last time, you will remember that we wrote notes to the writers, giving them some feedback on their writing. Today, I am going to suggest that we don't write notes, but that we do give ourselves what the children and I call a 'self-assignment' to make a real connection with the writers. Would you try to speak to each of these writers in a way that help him or her feel as if someone has really truly listened? Every one of us knows that in life, there are not many people who really listen, and who really help us feel listened to. Let's be those people to this group of youngsters."

Then parents, along with the half the class not in stations, functioned as viewers at the museum. Drawing a chair alongside one writer, the parent would look over the child's work, dipping in to read parts of it. "Can you tell me what you did right here?" the parent would ask, gesturing to a sticky note. At some point, I reminded parents to limit their visits to any one station to just a few minutes so they could reach several children, and then, of course, we switched so that the children who had not yet had a chance to showcase their work were able to do so. [*Figs. XVII-14, XVII-15, and XVII-16*]

My Father is My Worst Enemy

Everyone deserves a good father. Everywhere I go I see kids spending time with their fathers, but not me. My father is my worst enemy. For example, he picks his wife over me, he makes me feel like a small kid next to Bigfoot, and he made me into a person I don't want to be.

My father is my worst enemy because he picks my stepmother over me. He lets his wife dominate him like a toy. For example, one day I was supposed to go to their house to sleep over. I was ready to go when I get a call from my father. He said " Sorry, but I can't pick you up because my wife is in the hospital." "I hope she feels better," that's what I said. Then a short while later my mom calls me and says my father was lying. My stepmother wasn't in the hospital. My stepmother just didn't want me to come. It wasn't a

We often think about celebrations as a time for affirming children and their writing, but the truth is that these are also times for affirming ourselves and our teaching.

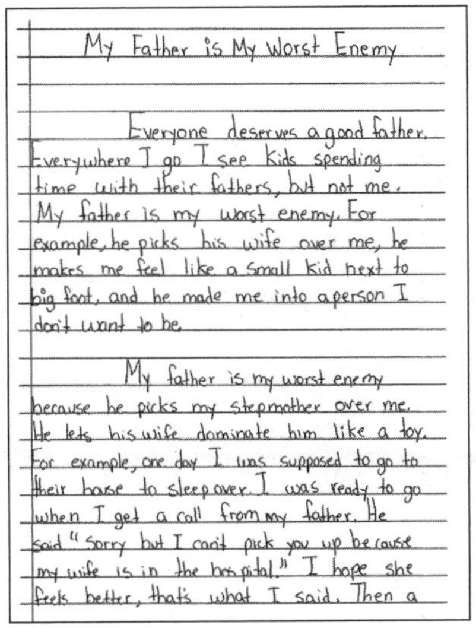

Fig. XVII-14 Tanya's final draft, page 1

real shock because my father has stood me up several times. I was so angry, but the worst part is he couldn't tell me the truth. Another time is when I was play fighting with my step-brother because he wanted me to. Then I scratched him by mistake on his neck. He told his mom that I scratched him on purpose. My stepmother came into the room and started yelling at me. My dad was right beside me and didn't even try to defend me. I got so mad I responded and said, "He hit me too."

My father is my worst enemy. He makes me feel like a small kid next to Bigfoot. I feel useless like when I was small or a younger child. I used to wait for my father to call me. Wishing the phone would ring, for him to take me to the movies or the park. He always told me lies and excuses. I can't believe he never ran out of what to say. Every time he let me down I'd get very upset. Even though I knew he would do it again it still would always hurt.

My father is my worst enemy. He made me into a person that I don't want to be. He made me angry and mean. I remember I used to be happy, friendly, and my friends used to call me "peppy." I wish I could tell him how much he hurt me and that he made me into a person I don't want to be. Like I used to be confident, now I'm insecure and can't make decisions on my own.

My father can be the worst father in the world, but I bet there are worse. There's nothing I can do to change it, what's done is done. He will always be my dad even if I don't want him to. I guess I'll have to deal with it.

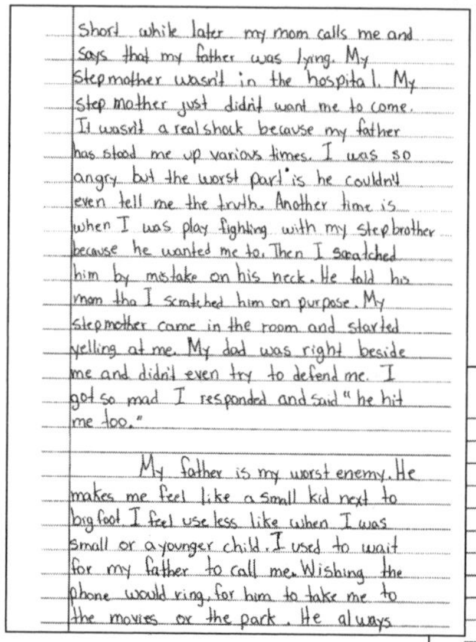

Fig. XVII-15 Tanya's final draft, page 2

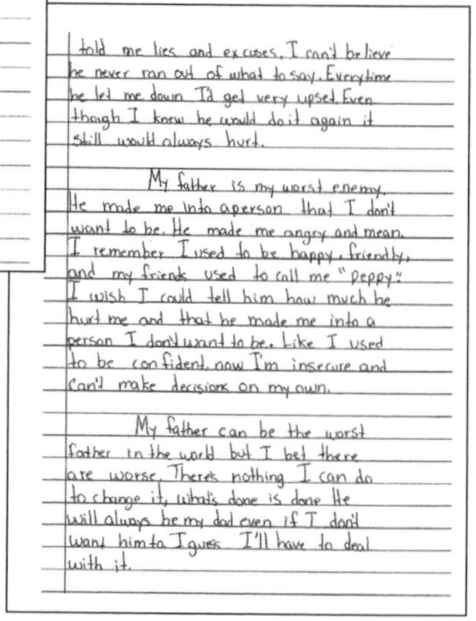

Fig. XVII-16 Tanya's final draft, page 3

At one point, Mary watched as James' father read his son's essay about how his play with his dad has changed over the years. "When I was little, I played in the park without my dad. I played on the jungle gym while my dad sat reading a book. But now when I go to the park with my dad, we have baseball catches together. We do funny catches and laugh together. I look back at the jungle gym and I think how things have changed."

James' father put the essay down and said to his son, "I'm proud you wrote about our relationship changing. It has gotten stronger. I think it is because you are growing up and changing—that's making the bond stronger."

Just before the celebration ended, William's mom—the mother whose love was celebrated in the opening reading about "Love Can Build a House"—whispered, "My son is becoming more compassionate. He thanks me and helps me more than he's ever done. I think writing has changed him!"

I think so too.

You'll need to circle among the groups unless you have other adults with you who can help. Folks will need just a bit of shepherding at the start of each circle of sharing. Then, once the readings have begun, you will want to model what it means to listen raptly, intensely.